STAR WARS
THE EMPIRE STRIKES BACK
UNAUTHORIZED TIMELINE

by

Justin Berger

Published in the United States by Anchorhead Publishing
Cover design and book layout: HKL Designs
Assistant Editor: Dan Johnson

First Edition

This book is dedicated to Irvin Kershner and Gary Kurtz.

Acknowledgements

A project like this is never the result of one person's endeavor. Over the making of this book I have received guidance and assistance from a number of people. At the top of that list is my childhood friend, Dan Johnson. He has been invaluable as an assistant editor, sounding board, fellow Star Wars fan, and creative cohort. A huge thank you to Kim D. M. Simmons who offered to take brand new photos of the original action figures for this book. I have come to know Kim over the past few years and he is not only a part of Star Wars history (as one of the original Kenner photographers), but he is a kind man with a big heart. His contributions to this book are very much appreciated. Nathan P. Butler's knowledge of Star Wars home video releases is nothing short of legendary and the information collected in his own book (*A Saga on Home Video*) has been indispensable as a resource for this book. Michael Coate has provided me with accurate box office numbers and specific events and dates that not only enriched the book, but also expanded my own personal knowledge of Star Wars history. Thanks to Jim Swearingen, Jeff Loeb, and Gary Gerani for pointing me in proper directions. A big thank you to Craig Miller for his *Empire* knowledge. Thanks to Jason White, Eddy Berst, Robert Williams, Scott Kirkwood, David Deans, and Paul Hayden for providing me with dates and information from pieces in their own private collections and/or their Star Wars knowledge. Thanks to Irvin Kershner and Gary Kurtz who made the greatest film of all time. I have dedicated this book to you both because of your drive and determination to make the best damn movie you could - RIP. Thanks to my parents for loving me and giving me the best childhood a kid could ask for. Last, but certainly not least, all of my love to my wife, Michelle, whose support, creative input, and guidance has helped make this book the best it can be and who continues to put up with my Star Wars collecting. I'd also like to give a special thank you to the maker, Mr. George Lucas. Your childhood inspired you to make Star Wars which inspired me in my childhood to always dream big and never stop believing in myself. Thank you.

Author's Note:

The information contained herein is derived from a myriad of resources including books, magazines, interviews, promotional materials, people associated with the production of the film and/or its promotional offshoots, and various websites.

The dates listed are as accurate as possible with the information currently available to the general public. Through extensive research I have done my best to identify and verify said dates and a general list of resources used for research and verification can be found in the bibliography section located at the end of the book.

I have recreated production-used call sheets which have been transcribed verbatim from the source documents and do contain spelling and spacing errors which are a result of the information being copied directly from the source in an effort to preserve the integrity of the documents. In some instances I have omitted duplicate information from some call sheets due to space constraints.

While I have done my best to include as many specific dates as possible, there is much information either unavailable to the public or lost to the passage of time. In some instances dates have been derived based on known information surrounding specific items and/or events. As such, some events are listed as having taken place either within a range of months, or at some point during an entire year. This is due to a lack of available information providing specificity as to the date of any such event.

The book begins in the year 1975 as these are the first dates with connections to *The Empire Strikes Back*. I have also included dates relating to the novel *Splinter of the Mind's Eye* as it was originally planned as the sequel to *Star Wars* and I feel that it deserves a place in this book.

Events taking place beyond the book's initial release date of 11/11/19 - while accurate at the time of printing - may be revised in future editions to reflect any changes to said events' dates.

TABLE OF CONTENTS

A long time ago, in a galaxy far, far away....

Preface

I'm a Star Wars fan. One of my very first memories is sitting in my living room on green shag carpet (it *was* the 70s) and seeing a commercial for *Star Wars* on TV. What sticks out most vividly is Luke Skywalker walking into Princess Leia's cell on the Death Star, removing his Stormtrooper helmet and proclaiming, "I'm Luke Skywalker, I'm here to rescue you!" My love affair with Star Wars began then and has endured over the past 40 plus years.

Having been born in 1975 I wasn't old enough to see *Star Wars* in theaters when it was released in 1977, nor was I old enough to have seen the sequel *The Empire Strikes Back* when it came out in 1980. It wasn't until 1983, at the age of nine, that I was finally able to experience my first Star Wars film in a proper setting when my parents took me to see *Return of the Jedi* at the Liberty Theater in my home town of Ellensburg, Washington. It was a watershed moment of my childhood that would shape the rest of my life to come.

Even though I remember playing with Star Wars toys as a kid, looking through the storybooks, and listening to the read-a-long records and cassette tapes, it wasn't until seeing *Jedi* that I was able to fully realize what Star Wars was all about. And while I may not have seen the first two movies in the theater, I did see *Star Wars* and *Empire* hundreds of times over thanks to my father who gave my family and I the gift of VHS in 1984.

Mind you I grew up in a very small town so the theatrical re-releases of both films weren't something I was aware of until much later in life. While I might not have experienced the full brunt of Star Wars fever, it was so popular that even my tiny redneck town felt an impact.

Of the three original films my favorite was (and always will be) *The Empire Strikes Back*. Even as a young child there was something magical about *Empire* that eclipsed the other two. From the battle of Hoth, through the swamps of Dagobah, to the dangers of Cloud City, I was completely enthralled by the beauty, the drama, the special effects, the sophistication, and the wisdom of what many consider to be the best Star Wars movie ever made and the greatest film sequel of all time.

The Eastern philosophies of Yoda's teachings of the Force shaped my own personal spiritual beliefs at a very young age. To this day I still feel the power of the words, "Luminous beings are we, not this crude matter."

But even more powerful than Yoda's wisdom was the weight of the film's climax. The ultimate battle between good and evil as Luke Skywalker and Darth Vader dueled in the bowels of Bespin. All seemed lost, and then came one of the biggest reveals in the history of film: Darth Vader telling Luke that he didn't kill his father, but that he *is* his father still blows kids' minds even to this day. It's such a powerful revelation that a figure so dark and so evil could actually be human and so deeply connected to our hero. The ramifications of that to my young mind were astounding. It blurred the lines between good and evil as I began to see humanity in Vader I never saw prior. Suddenly he was no longer this hulking black mass of evil, but something more. He was a father. Within his actions, underneath the megalomaniacal exterior, I sensed that he still loved his son - and that was a powerful and profound concept that was rarely seen at the time in something aimed at kids.

But even though Star Wars as a whole had made the biggest impact on my childhood, I was not immune to the powers of television marketing. By 1986 I had started to grow out of Star Wars and began obsessing over He-Man, G. I. Joe, and Transformers. Gone were the days of playing with Han Solo, R2-D2, Darth Vader, and the Millennium Falcon in my friends' back yards, it was a new era when after school cartoons dominated our attention. With no new Star Wars content (other than some made-for-television Ewok movies and Saturday morning cartoons) my friends and I had essentially moved on.

Still, Star Wars would always hold a very special place in my heart that nothing else could replace. It had been such a strong influence on my childhood that even as I grew older it still resonated with me long after I had abandoned my action figures, trading cards, and comic books.

It was roughly ten years later that I really focused on Star Wars again when the Special Editions were released in 1997. Like everyone else I was anxious to see the Original Trilogy on the big screen, especially since it would be my first time seeing *Star Wars* and *Empire* in the theater. Even though I hadn't really given much thought to Star Wars for many years the excitement had definitely returned and everyone, myself included, was eager for the Special Editions - at least until we saw them.

Like a lot of fans I wasn't keen on the changes George Lucas had made to the original films. While they were his movies to do with as he pleased, I still felt a bit of a sting when all was said and done. I had grown up with these movies, but they had been gratuitously changed – and in my opinion not for the better.

Two years later my interest in the prequel films was mild as the Special Editions had left a bad taste in my mouth. But, like a lot of people at the time, I went to the theater to see if the new Star Wars movie, *The Phantom Menace*, was any good. It wasn't – at least not to me. I still went and watched *Attack of the Clones* and *Revenge of the Sith* in the theater as well because it was Star Wars. Even though those films weren't the greatest, they were still a part of that world that I grew up with and still loved in my heart. So after seeing *Revenge of the Sith* in 2005 I felt like Star Wars was over and done with for me. It would just be something from my childhood I had fond memories of, but would never feel as strongly about as an adult.

Little did I know at the time how wrong I was.

It would be nearly another ten years before Star Wars would once again catch my attention - about a year prior to the release of *The Force Awakens.* Disney® had bought Lucasfilm and the excitement of a new sequel trilogy was on the horizon. Talk of Director J. J. Abrams using less CGI in favor of more practical sets and effects (not to mention the return of the Original Trilogy cast) had me growing a bit nostalgic.

Having lost, demolished, or sold off my original Star Wars toys from childhood, I decided to start re-collecting them. I began buying the original Kenner® Star Wars toys I had as a kid (including some I never had, but always wanted) and my passion for Star Wars became reignited in a big way.

I was living in the San Francisco Bay Area around this time and was approached to work on an independent Star Wars web series project. I took on the role of producer and used my experience in film and music video production to help the show's creator shoot a promotional teaser to garner interest in the project and give us something to push at Star Wars Celebration the following year.

As producer on the web series I reached out to the 501ˢᵗ Legion's Golden Gate Garrison - the same people Lucasfilm utilizes for their public events - and was fortunate to have them be a part of the production. It was honestly quite surreal having Darth Vader, Imperial Officers, and a group of Stormtroopers on set. My wife and I even included two of those same Stormtroopers as part of our wedding ceremony.

The following year the web series creator and I drove down from the Bay Area to Star Wars Celebration in Anaheim, California. It was the first Star Wars convention I had ever attended and it was a rebirth of sorts as the nine year old kid in me was overjoyed to be surrounded by not just the sights and sounds of my favorite franchise, but also all of the other fans there who shared in my rekindled passion for Star Wars.

Over the next four years the love of Star Wars that I had as a kid continued to grow and grow. Through social media I met others who shared my enthusiasm and connected with fellow fans who, like me, had just rediscovered the joy of it more recently as well as those who had been hardcore about it since the 70s, 80s, and 90s. Part of that rediscovery process included revisiting *The Empire Strikes Back* as an adult and learning more about it than I ever knew previously.

After joining Star Wars social media groups I began to see a lot of dates attached to documents and events related not just to *Empire*'s production and release, but also to extensions of the film - toys, books, promotions, and other derivatives.

Specific dates emerged throughout articles, interviews, production paperwork, and in books about the film. It was fascinating to me having such specific information about something created so many years ago. The more I read and the more dates I saw it occurred to me that no one had really put together a comprehensive timeline of these dates and the events tied to them. It was that lightbulb moment that gave me pause and was the genesis for my idea to compile them all into a single book - the book you now hold in your hands.

I began scouring the internet for dates, reading and re-reading books such as Alan Arnold's *A Journal of the Making of The Empire Strikes Back*, Michael Kaminski's *The Secret History of Star Wars*, and J. W. Rinzler's *The Making of The Empire Strikes Back*, reaching out to former Kenner and Lucasfilm employees, and even asking fellow fans and collectors for anything in their collections that had a date stamped on it. It was my intention to compile the most complete timeline of *The Empire Strikes Back* that had ever been assembled.

With the 40th Anniversary of *The Empire Strikes Back* right around the corner, it was a bit of kismet that the idea to put something like this together came when it did. It's taken me just over a year to finish and I'm really happy with the end result. I'd like to think that I've contributed in some small way to the Star Wars Universe and have been able to offer something both useful and entertaining to the Star Wars fan community.

Overall this book is a celebration of *The Empire Strikes Back* and a reflection of my love for the film and everything related to it. In the end I hope that you, the reader, get as much enjoyment from reading the information in this book as I did researching and putting it all together.

It's been a true labor of love and I'm overjoyed to be sharing it with my fellow Star Wars fans.

May the Force be with you, always....

- Justin Berger

™

Introduction

As temporal beings history plays an important and sometimes vital role in our lives. Living in a linear existence we are always referring to our past, not only to predict our future, but to also understand our present. It's this reconnoitering of the past that teaches us, informs us, and adds meaning to our lives. Writing a book such as this that focuses on the history of something experienced by so many can feel daunting. The need for accuracy is imperative, but can, at times, be elusive – as history itself often is.

Drawing from a myriad of resources I have compiled what I hope is an all-encompassing timeline of the film, *The Empire Strikes Back.* While this book focuses primarily on the history of *Empire,* I feel that to truly understand that film's history one must first appreciate the history of its cinematic predecessor, *Star Wars.*

The story of how *Star Wars* came to rule the world in the late 70s is one that has been told many times and many ways. The gist of course is the tale of a young George Lucas wanting to make a Western in space with a Flash Gordon serial feel to it and is turned down by every studio in Hollywood except one: Twentieth Century Fox. As the story goes, the film is shot on a shoe-string budget and then goes on to become the biggest movie of all time. We've all heard it – or at least bits and pieces of it - but the full story of how *Star Wars* came to be is as interesting as it is compelling.

In 1971 George Lucas and United Artists signed a development deal for two pictures, *American Graffiti*, and what Lucas at the time had called, *The Star Wars.* The studio ultimately passed on both films as they deemed *Graffiti* as "too experimental" and

Star Wars as "too risky." Universal Pictures picked up *American Graffiti* around the same time that Lucas had met Producer Gary Kurtz and the two ended up working together on what was Lucas' second film (the first being the experimental, *THX-1138*).

After United Artists had passed on *Star Wars* in 1973, Universal had the next first right of refusal on the project due to Lucas' contract with them for *Graffiti*. Universal had yet to release *Graffiti* at the time and due to issues he was having with them Lucas was relieved when the studio essentially passed on *Star Wars*. Lucas then shopped his "space western" idea to other studios including Twentieth Century Fox where Alan Ladd, Jr., (who had seen an early cut of *Graffiti*) met with Lucas to discuss the project. Ladd felt the young filmmaker had the talent to make something truly special and convinced then Fox President Gordon Stulberg to green light the film.

Just a few weeks after signing with Twentieth Century Fox *American Graffiti* was released to theaters and became a huge hit, turning Lucas into a millionaire overnight. With an influx of money from the film's success, Lucas and his wife, Marcia, moved up to the San Francisco Bay Area where they purchased a large house that they began renting out to other filmmakers. It was here that Lucas' production company, Lucasfilm, was truly born.

(Marcia and George Lucas editing STAR WARS ©1976 Julian Wasser/The LIFE Images Collection)

Over the next two years George Lucas would spend his time writing the script to *Star Wars*. It was an arduous task for the filmmaker and even though he ultimately succeeded in completing multiple drafts, the process left him never wanting to write again.

Lucas finished the script just as filming on *Star Wars* began in March of 1976.

(George Lucas (l) on the set of STAR WARS ©1976 LFL)

The production of *Star Wars* was riddled with a myriad of issues including location troubles, story problems, and budget disagreements (just to name a few). The stresses of directing ultimately sent Lucas to the hospital for what he thought was a heart attack, but ended up being a result of hypertension and exhaustion.

As the film neared completion Lucas required a last minute reshoot for the cantina scene costing upwards of one million dollars. The reshoot put the film over its initial 10 million dollar budget and strained relations between Lucas and the studio.

Adding insult to injury, the Marketing Department at Twentieth Century Fox had decided that the film's title was "box office poison" and chose to dump the movie's release to Memorial Day weekend – what most in the movie industry considered as a "dead week." To make matters worse, *Smokey and the Bandit* was slated for release that same week and featured the biggest movie star at the time, Burt Reynolds.

Alan Ladd, Jr., who by this time had become President of the studio, still believed in Lucas, and in the film, and did his best to offset this seeming disaster by making theater owners screen *Star Wars* if they wanted to show what most thought was going to be Fox's big hit that year, *The Other Side of Midnight*. [1]

Adding to this less than perfect timing of release, George Lucas had utilized Dolby® to create a 6-track audio experience for the film. Most theaters at the time didn't even bother using stereo, so when Twentieth Century Fox told theater owners that in order to screen the 70mm prints of *Star Wars* they had to upgrade to a Dolby system, not many were able to (or wanted to) make the changes necessary. [2]

On top of everything else Twentieth Century Fox lacked the awareness to properly market a film like *Star Wars*. It was Lucasfilm Marketing Manager Charles Lippincott who utilized his industry connections to facilitate deals with companies like Marvel Comics®, Kenner, and Ballantine Books® to push the movie to what he knew was going to be its core audience: sci-fi and fantasy fans. Lippincott was also instrumental in *Star Wars'* appearance at San Diego Comic-Con® in 1976 where he and *Star Wars* Producer Gary Kurtz brought costumes, props, a highlight reel, Mark Hamill (Luke Skywalker himself), and even C-3PO and R2-D2. The panel was a very low-key event by today's standards, but it did create a buzz throughout the science fiction community.

Finally, on May 25th, 1977, *Star Wars* was released to just 32 theaters in the United States. What happened next was something no one could have predicted.

Most fans and critics cite the opening scene of the Star Destroyer flying overhead, with the booming music of John Williams and rumbling sound effects created by sound designer Ben Burtt, as the pivotal moment when they knew *Star Wars* was unique and something special. This was due, in part, to the Dolby sound mix Lucas had created for the film, giving it a deeper and fuller sound. While it may have initially hindered the release of the movie, it was the sound that really helped make *Star Wars* an experience like no other.

No one had expected *Star Wars* to become as big as it did. Well, no one except maybe Steven Spielberg who, after seeing an early screening, proclaimed that it was going to be a huge hit. Even though the film's release started off strong, George Lucas still wasn't convinced the movie would be a success and chalked up the first week buzz to hardcore sci-fi fans who, as Lucas stated at one time, "will go see anything!"

(STAR WARS opening weekend ©1977 Gary Fong / San Francisco Chronicle)

It wasn't until Lucas and his wife, Marcia, were on vacation in Hawaii (with Steven Spielberg no less) that they received the news that *Star Wars* was exploding at the box office and had become a major event. Even Walter Cronkite was talking about *Star Wars* and that's when Lucas knew that the film he had wanted a break from was turning into something unexpected.

It didn't take long for the movie to become a hit and expand to over 1,000 theaters by August of that same year, at which point *Time* magazine reported Twentieth Century Fox's plans for a sequel. By this time Fox even began asking theater owners to screen *The Other Side of Midnight* if they wanted *Star Wars*.

Eventually it surpassed Steven Spielberg's *Jaws* as the highest grossing film of all time and became a worldwide phenomenon. After *Star Wars* Memorial Day weekend was no longer considered a "dead week" and ultimately became one of the highest grossing release periods for the movie industry.

Prior to the release of *Star Wars* George Lucas had planned on creating a trilogy under the banner, *The Adventures of Luke Skywalker*. In fact the Star Wars novel *Splinter of the Mind's Eye* was originally thought of by Lucas as a low budget sequel, but this idea was quickly abandoned once *Star Wars* became a blockbuster.

Lucas immediately began boasting about plans for 11 more Star Wars films (12 in all). Avoiding calling them sequels (due in part to Hollywood's negative stigma towards them at the time), Gary Kurtz and Lucas expressed the idea that the Star Wars movies would fall within the vein of *James Bond* films where each movie would connect to the larger universe, but be self-contained stories. They also talked about the films not being chronological and each one having a different director.

The two began putting together ideas for what they dubbed as simply, *Star Wars II*. The idea of a *James Bond* type of series was quickly scrapped as *Star Wars II*'s storyline would pick up a just few years after the events of *Star Wars* and continue the story of everyone's favorite Rebel heroes, Luke Skywalker, Han Solo, and Princess Leia as they continued to fight against the evil Lord Darth Vader and the Galactic Empire.

With another hit movie on his hands and millions of dollars coming in from both the film and its merchandising, George Lucas' motivation for *Star Wars II* soon became more than just a desire to make a sequel. He realized he could use the money from the second film to fund his dream project, Skywalker Ranch - a filmmaker's utopia that he would build in the picturesque hills of Marin County, just north of San Francisco.

George Lucas had wanted to distance himself from Hollywood very early on, but knew that he needed the studios' money in order to make his movies. His contempt for them had reached a boiling point when his previous film, *American Graffiti*, ended up with a few minutes cut out by Universal Pictures. This was the second time Lucas dealt with studios editing his movies as Warner Bros had cut scenes from his debut film, *THX-1138*. This meddling and control over his films infuriated Lucas who wanted to figure out a way to make movies without relying on the Hollywood system.

With the success of both *American Graffiti* and *Star Wars* Lucas was in a position to leave Hollywood altogether. Inspired by his friend Francis Ford Coppola's American Zoetrope Studios, Lucas decided to start his own filmmaking community 400 miles to the north. But to get there he first had to make another Star Wars picture that would generate enough money to both fund his dream project and render Lucasfilm independent from the corporate executives in Hollywood.

Preproduction on *Star Wars II* began in late 1977 as Lucas and Kurtz began the challenge of finding a director for the next installment as Lucas swore he would never direct again due to all of the troubles he experienced on *Star Wars*. Gary Kurtz pushed for veteran filmmaker Irvin Kershner who knew both Lucas and Kurtz through his time at USC as a professor, and was eventually chosen by Lucas because he knew "everything a Hollywood director should know without being Hollywood."[3]

(Irvin Kershner (l) and George Lucas (r) on the set of EMPIRE ©1979 LFL)

The following year was spent on preproduction of the sequel which included the reformation of Industrial Light and Magic to handle the special effects, and the expansion of Lucasfilm to cope with the larger production.

Lucas had no interest in writing the script so he hired science fiction author, Leigh Brackett. The two began story conferences in late 1977, and a first draft was completed in early 1978. After reading it, Lucas and Kurtz realized that Brackett might not be the right choice for *Empire*. Before Lucas could discuss this with her, Brackett unexpectedly died of cancer.

With nowhere to turn Lucas was forced to once again take on the role of writer. This time, however, the experience was more enjoyable for the filmmaker who finished two drafts of the screenplay within a couple of months. Still, Lucas eventually turned to screenwriter Lawrence Kasdan to take over the task of completing the final script.

Empire began filming in Norway on March 5th, 1979 and finished in England on September 24th of that same year. The following eight months were spent on special effects, miniatures, models, and general post production at ILM in California.

(Richard Edlund slates a post-production fx shot at Industrial Light and Magic ©1980 LFL)

The film ended up being over budget and behind schedule, but Lucas pushed his team, as well as himself, to finish the picture on time. Lucas had funded the movie out of his own pocket, so everything rode on the success of *Empire*. If the movie had failed not only would he have been in debt for millions of dollars, but his dream of Skywalker Ranch would have been destroyed and his career as a filmmaker would have imploded.

Then, on May 21st, 1980, *The Empire Strikes Back* was released to theaters.

The movie was another hit for Lucas and during its initial run grossed over 180 million dollars. Between the box office and the merchandising (which was bigger than ever), Lucas easily paid back his loans for the film's production and moved forward with Skywalker Ranch - solidifying his dream of leaving the Hollywood system for good. The film's success launched Lucasfilm to the next level as a preeminent production company and made ILM one of the go-to effects companies in the film industry.

Lucas quickly began preproduction on what he ultimately decided was the last chapter in the Star Wars saga, *Revenge of the Jedi*. The film's title was changed to *Return of the Jedi* just before release and it certified the Star Wars Trilogy as a cultural touchstone in cinematic history.

The Empire Strikes Back went on to become one of the most highly regarded films ever made and the favorite of many fans of the franchise. The film celebrates its 40th Anniversary in 2020 and will continue to live on as one of the greatest cinematic tales of all time.

(George Lucas (l) and Irvin Kershner (r) pose with Darth Vader ©1979 LFL)

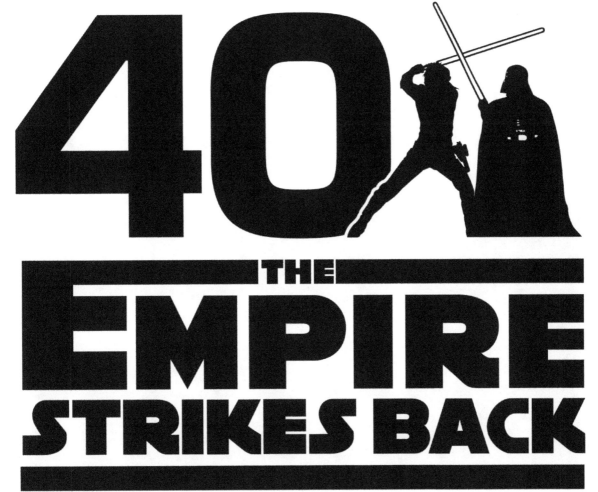

(Roger Castel's 'Gone with the Wind' style painting as the movie poster for EMPIRE ©1980 LFL)

GEORGE LUCAS
Executive Producer

MARK HAMILL
as Luke Skywalker

ANTHONY DANIELS
as C-3PO

DENNIS MUREN
Effects Director
of Photography

GARY KURTZ
Producer

HARRISON FORD
as Han Solo

DAVID PROWSE
as Darth Vader

BRIAN JOHNSON
Special Visual Effects

IRVIN KERSHNER
Director

CARRIE FISHER
as Princess Leia

PETER MAYHEW
as Chewbacca

RALPH McQUARRIE
Design Consultant &
Conceptual Artist

KENNY BAKER
as R2-D2

LAWRENCE KASDAN
Writer

BILLY DEE WILLIAMS
as Lando Calrissian

FRANK OZ
performing Yoda

JOE JOHNSTON
Art Director -
Visual Effects

1975

The earliest inception of ideas that eventually made their way into *The Empire Strikes Back* occurred this year. Multiple unused concept designs created for *Star Wars* were held over and ultimately used for the production of the sequel.

From Ralph McQuarrie's early Darth Vader concepts (the genesis of Boba Fett's final design by Joe Johnston) to the original idea of Alderaan as a floating Imperial prison (eventually becoming Cloud City); George Lucas consistently used old and unused material and incorporated it into something new. This recycling of ideas was reflected throughout the Star Wars Saga including *The Empire Strikes Back*.

February 20th, 1975

• Artist Ralph McQuarrie finishes a concept painting of a floating Imperial prison derived from an early draft of the original *Star Wars* script.

The prison idea was discarded in later drafts of the script and replaced with the Death Star. The floating prison design was later modified as the basis for Cloud City in *Empire*.

(Ralph McQuarrie early concept painting of the Imperial prison in STAR WARS ©1975 LFL)

1976

This was the first year that material was developed specifically for a *Star Wars* sequel.

Before *Star Wars* became a huge success, Lucas' plans for more Star Wars content focused on novels more than films. At best Lucas had hoped he would make enough money to produce a low budget sequel utilizing the same props and characters from *Star Wars*. In the worst case he would have continued the *Adventures of Luke Skywalker* in a series of books.

George Lucas and science fiction author Alan Dean Foster met late in the year to discuss ideas for a sequel to *Star Wars*. Foster had been a ghost writer for the *Star Wars* novelization and was the obvious choice to pen a follow-up. Out of that meeting emerged the foundation to what became the novel, *Splinter of the Mind's Eye*.

Splinter's story was to have served as the basis for a sequel film if all had gone as planned, but once *Star Wars* took off Lucas seized the opportunity to make a sequel that was bigger and more extravagant than the first film and *Splinter* just didn't cut it. Thus the book ended up being nothing more than filler content to tide fans over until *Empire*.

Foster continued to write Star Wars books throughout the franchise's existence and most recently novelized the sequel film, *The Force Awakens*.

October 13th & 20th, 1976
• George Lucas meets with author Alan Dean Foster to discuss a sequel story to *Star Wars* which would become the novel, *Splinter of the Mind's Eye*.

1977

One of the most notable years in Star Wars history, 1977 is the year of release for the film which launched the biggest movie franchise in the world, making George Lucas a household name and *Star Wars* a worldwide phenomenon.

The success of the film was a surprise to everyone involved including Lucas and Producer Gary Kurtz who had hoped at best for a modest return so they could make a low budget sequel. Instead the filmmakers started planning a big budget follow up which they had hoped would equal or surpass the success of the first film.

Preproduction and planning for the sequel movie began this year as *Star Wars* broke box office records, raked in tons of money, and created a demand for merchandise unlike any movie before it.

Lucas brought back artists Ralph McQuarrie and Joe Johnston to work on concept art for the sequel in an effort to retain the same design aesthetic as the first film (and in some instances utilized unused concepts and designs).

Story meetings were held towards the end of the year between Lucas and writer Leigh Brackett to flesh out the story elements that made up the first draft of the script while Lucas decided he didn't want to direct again, which left he and Kurtz to find a replacement.

January 11th, 1977
• Mark Hamill is injured in a car accident requiring reconstructive facial surgery. This was rumored to have been the reason for Luke's mauling by the Wampa in the opening scenes of *Empire*, but has been denied by both George Lucas and Mark Hamill. According to Lucas the scene was written to create tension and was not used to explain any changes to Hamill's face between films. Hamill stated that the make-up team only built upon his scars from the accident as the base for the make-up effects for Luke's damaged face.

A scene was shot for *Empire* which showed a medical droid removing a type of facial mask/bandage from Luke's face, but the scene was never used. Whether this scene had anything to do with Hamill's car accident is hard to say, but it's possible Lucas had it shot for contingency sake. This scene does, however, appear in the Marvel Comics adaption of *Empire*.

May 25th, 1977

• *Star Wars* is released in US theaters.
It became the highest grossing movie of all time, until Spielberg's *E.T.* surpassed it in 1982.

(STAR WARS theatrical release in 1977 ©1977 Paul Slade/Paris Match)

August 22nd, 1977

• *Time* magazine reports that Twentieth Century Fox is planning a *Star Wars* sequel.

September 14th & September 21st, 1977

• George Lucas meets with Ralph McQuarrie on both dates.
Out of these meetings a contract for McQuarrie to work on *Empire* was agreed upon and was dated, October 1st, 1977.

McQuarrie was integral to the original concepts for *Star Wars* as his artwork on the first film guided the direction of the overall aesthetic of the universe and helped create the look of characters, creatures, ships, and planets. Lucas wanted him back to retain that same look and feel of the original.

McQuarrie left the *Battlestar Galactica* movie project and passed up the opportunity to work on Ralph Bakshi's *Lord of the Rings* animated feature in order to begin preproduction concept art for *Empire*.

September 21ˢᵗ, 1977

• George Lucas finalizes a deal with Twentieth Century Fox for the *Star Wars* sequel. The contract stipulated that Lucas had final cut of the film and a larger percentage of merchandising rights. This was due, in large part, to Lucas funding the sequel himself through a deal with Bank of America which lowered the financial risk for the studio.

September 25ᵗʰ, 1977

• Ralph McQuarrie begins concept sketches for the Wookiee home planet, snow armor, snow vehicles, as well as a castle for Darth Vader.

October, 1977

• Ralph McQuarrie sketches out a helmet design that is an early concept for the character, Boba Fett.
Joe Johnston finalized the design of the character as a Super Stormtrooper. Eventually it was changed to the bounty hunter design seen in the final film.

October 1ˢᵗ, 1977

• Date of Ralph McQuarrie's contract with Lucasfilm for his work on *Empire*.

October 12ᵗʰ, 1977

• *Variety* magazine reports that the sequel to *Star Wars* begins shooting in January of 1979.

October 19ᵗʰ, 1977

• Ralph McQuarrie completes early concept sketches for the Wookiee home planet. George Lucas had wanted to utilize Wookiees in early drafts of the *Star Wars* script and have them be the ones to attack the Death Star at the end of the film. This idea was abandoned in *Star Wars*, but Lucas revisited it later in *Return of the Jedi* (only changing the Wookiees to Ewoks) and once again in *Revenge of the Sith* where we finally saw Chewbacca's home world of Kashyyyk* for the first time where the Wookiees battled the Separatist Droid Army.

For *Empire* the Wookiees' home planet was to be a part of Han Solo's storyline, but through later drafts of the script it was eventually written out altogether.

*Although Kashyyyk first appeared in the *Star Wars Holiday Special*, it was comprised only of production art and studio sets while the storyline itself was never considered canon.

October 26ᵗʰ-November 17ᵗʰ, 1977

• Ralph McQuarrie begins concept art for Armored Tank Walkers.

(Ralph McQuarrie's cover artwork for the SPLINTER OF THE MIND'S EYE novel ©1977 LFL)

October 31st, November 4th, November 7th & November 14th, 1977

• Ralph McQuarrie works on, and completes, the cover art for the novel, *Splinter of the Mind's Eye*.

November, 1977

• Ralph McQuarrie creates early concept sketches of "swamp monsters," creatures that would inhabit Dagobah.

• George Lucas rehires Joe Johnston as concept artist for *Empire*.
Like Ralph McQuarrie, Joe Johnston worked on *Star Wars* as a conceptual artist. He was also tapped to portray the Stormtroopers seen standing outside of the Death Star when the Millennium Falcon is hauled into the landing bay via tractor beam in the first film. Both of the "spacetroopers" were Johnston shot at different times and later merged in post-production. He also made a cameo appearance in *Empire* as a Rebel soldier on Hoth along with Ralph McQuarrie who appeared in the same scene.

• After signing on to work on *Empire*, Johnston begins sketching out Imperial vehicles including tanks which eventually become AT-AT walkers.
Johnston also began designs for Rebel Soldier outfits, Imperial Snow Trooper outfits, snow lizards, and starships including what eventually became the Cloud Car on Bespin.

(Joe Johnston's sketches of Imperial Snowtrooper outfit designs ©1978 LFL)

November 24th, 1977

• The first Lucasfilm Thanksgiving for employees, friends, and family takes place at the Park House offices (the home purchased by George and Marcia Lucas upon moving to the Bay Area which served as the headquarters of Lucasfilm prior to Skywalker Ranch). Lucas eventually started giving whole turkeys to all Lucasfilm employees each Thanksgiving.

November 28th, 1977

• Date of the *Star Wars* sequel treatment titled *The Empire Strikes Back Story Treatment by George Lucas.*

While the treatment bears the same date as the first day of conference meetings with writer Leigh Brackett the treatment itself was most likely written after this date once the meetings were over and story notes were compiled.

November 28th-December 2nd, 1977

• Story conferences between Leigh Brackett and George Lucas occur.

These meetings were tape recorded and transcribed to total 51 typed pages. The first mention of Yoda appeared during this time by the name, "Minch Yoda." This was also the first official mention of the film's final title, *The Empire Strikes Back*, as this title appeared both on the initial treatment and on the transcript of the meetings as *CHAPTER II – THE EMPIRE STRIKES BACK STORY CONFERENCE*. However, Brackett's first draft of the script simply read: *Star Wars Sequel.*

During this time Hoth was referred to as the "Ice Planet" since "Hoth" was originally the name given to the gas planet, Bespin - but that would obviously change in later drafts.

December, 1977

• Ralph McQuarrie completes multiple concept paintings of Darth Vader's castle to be shown in *Empire*.

The idea of Vader's castle was eventually scrapped for *Empire*, however, the concept would be revisited in the 2016 Star Wars film, *Rogue One*.

• McQuarrie completes *Noble Aliens* artwork which includes the note, "more otherworldly – Close Encounters", as well as concept art for Snow Lizards and Snow Monsters.

December 7th – 9th, 1977

• Ralph McQuarrie completes the first official production painting for *Empire* titled: *Metal (Vader's) Castle.*

December 9th, 1977

• Ralph McQuarrie and George Lucas meet to go over his concept art for the film.

Lucas told McQuarrie that he wanted to see Vader's castle in a lava environment. The two also went over McQuarrie's 29 sketches of tanks and snow lizards.

(Ralph McQuarrie's early concept painting of Darth Vader's castle ©1977 LFL)

1978

1978 was the year of preproduction for *Empire*. With the success of *Star Wars* the sequel allowed for a bigger and bolder story than was originally planned which in turn required a bigger cast, bigger crew, and a bigger budget.

Ralph McQuarrie and Joe Johnston were rehired for *Empire* the previous year and continued creating sketches of creatures, ships, vehicles, and characters. George Lucas worked on further development of the story while he simultaneously dealt with expanding his existing companies, Lucasfilm and Industrial Light and Magic.

January, 1978

• Joe Johnston finishes sketches of AT-AT walkers.
The design for the Walkers was inspired by the giant walking ships from H. G. Wells' *War of the Worlds*, a U.S. Steel® advertisement for "future vehicles" drawn by artist Syd Mead, and the General Electric® Walking Truck by R. Mosher.

An urban legend that circulates to this day claims George Lucas was inspired for the AT-AT design by the shipping cranes along the San Francisco Bay in Oakland, CA (which do somewhat resemble the final AT-AT design), however, Lucas, Joe Johnston, and others involved with *Empire*'s production have consistently denied this.

• Johnston sketches out a storyboard sequence in which Rebel tanks use tow cables to trip up the four-legged AT-AT walkers and topple them to the ground.
The tanks in these storyboards resembled the Rebel gun turrets that ended up on screen. They ultimately lost their tank treads and the tow cables were used by the Snowspeeders in the final film.

• Johnston also sketches ideas for native aliens on Cloud City, some of whom have four arms.
These aliens were later changed to the small, pig-like creatures called Ugnaughts.

January 4th, 1978

• George Lucas purchases property on Lankershim Blvd in Los Angeles, CA.
Previously a storage warehouse for eggs owned by Olson Bros. Egg Company, Lucas renovated the space into offices.

Lucasfilm employees dubbed it "The Egg Company" (for obvious reasons) to keep people from realizing its true function. The property sat directly across from Universal Studios and was purchased for $1,050,000. [4]

January 16th-18th, 1978

• Ralph McQuarrie finishes sketches of Cloud City.

January 25th, 1978

• *The Hollywood Reporter* leaks the title of the Star Wars sequel: *The Empire Strikes Back.*
The leak was hardly noticed by anyone at the time.

February, 1978

• Joe Johnston creates the first concept sketches of "Minch Yoda."

• Ralph McQuarrie and Joe Johnston sketch out concepts for the Rebel Snowspeeders.

(Ralph McQuarrie concept painting 'Rodent Mount' ©1978 LFL)

February 9th-10th & February 13th-14th, 1978

• Ralph McQuarrie creates the painting *Rodent Mount* which depicts a Rebel rider atop a furry, two-legged lizard-like creature (an early Tauntaun concept) fleeing from two Imperial Walkers.

February 12th, 1978

• The novel *Splinter of the Mind's Eye* is published in hardback.

Splinter of the Mind's Eye introduced fans to the Kiber crystal. Originally a plot point in *Star Wars*, the Kiber (also spelled Kyber or Kaiburr) crystal was eventually removed from the script and saved for later use. Lucas' concept for the Kiber Crystal was that it was used to harness the Force and make anyone who wielded it vastly more powerful.

The idea was picked up later on in the Star Wars Expanded Universe, *The Clone Wars* animated series, as well as in new canon stories including the film, *Rogue One*. The original concept would change, however, as Kiber crystals would become the power source for lightsabers. This idea was explored more fully in *The Clone Wars* animated series and expanded upon in *Rogue One* as they were used as the power source for the Death Star's giant laser cannon that could destroy entire planets by focusing the crystal's power.

(SPLINTER final cover art by Ralph McQuarrie ©1978 LFL)

The planet Mimban also originated in this novel and was later used in the 2018 film, *Solo: A Star Wars Story*, as the name of the planet where Han Solo meets Chewbacca.

Splinter* also emphasized a romantic relationship between Luke Skywalker and Princess Leia (more intimate than what appears in *Empire*) that eventually became irrelevant and slightly awkward once it was revealed that they were in fact siblings in *Return of the Jedi.*

*The novel's story did not play into canon and was completely disregarded by the films.

February 13th, 1978

• An official offer is made to Director Irvin Kershner from Lucasfilm's production lawyer, Tom Pollock, to helm the *Star Wars* sequel.
Kershner requested the film to read, "A Film by Irvin Kershner" at the beginning, however, Pollock made it clear that the sequel would have the same opening as the original film with only company logos.

Kershner made sure he had the freedom to make the movie he wanted, which Lucas acquiesced as he felt the veteran director would make a good film while respecting the budget.

February 15th, 1978

• Lucasfilm sends Irvin Kershner a deal memo as attorneys on both sides begin hashing out the details for the director's final contract.

February 16th, 1978

• ILM artist Reg Bream finishes the blueprint drawings for Darth Vader's meditation chamber.

February 17th, 1978

• George Lucas sends a memo to Gary Kurtz outlining the parameters of his position. This included being unable to offer percentage points on the film to anyone without Lucas' approval and also demanded that Kurtz keep in close contact with Lucasfilm CEO Charlie Weber. The memo also stated that anything more than 10 percent over budget during production had to be approved by either Lucas or Weber.

February 20th-22nd, 1978

• Ralph McQuarrie finishes the concept painting, *Armored Landspeeders Bring Down Walker.*
The painting depicted early concept Snowspeeders flying away from a downed walker, similar to the final scene in the movie where an AT-AT falls "face first" to the ground.

February 21st, 1978

• The first draft of the *Empire* script is completed by Leigh Brackett and sent to Lucasfilm.

This draft was not officially titled as Brackett simply wrote "Star Wars Sequel" at the top of the first page. This first draft included the ghost of Luke's father appearing on Dagobah to reveal that Luke had a sister and also had Han Solo leaving Hoth to search for his long-lost father-figure per George Lucas' story notes.

The Han plot did not appear in any subsequent drafts and instead Han's storyline was changed to resemble more of what appears in the final film. Even though Brackett's script included Lucas' ideas and concepts, the dialogue and execution of the script was far from what Lucas or Kurtz envisioned. Lucas redlined the script and decided that Brackett might not be the right choice as writer.

February 25th, 1978

• George Lucas, Irvin Kershner, and Ralph McQuarrie meet at the Beverly Hills Hotel to go over the film's concept art.

February 27th, 1978

• Black Falcon, Ltd., a subsidiary of Lucasfilm, is incorporated.

All licensing, marketing, and merchandise management was put under its care just over four months later on July 1st.

(Black Falcon emblem ©1978 Black Falcon, Ltd)

Feb-March, 1978

• Joe Johnston completes sketches of Boba Fett.

At the time he was described as a "Super Stormtrooper" and clad in all white armor.

March, 1978

• The title *Star Wars Episode II: The Empire Strikes Back* is registered with the Motion Picture Association of America.

March, 1978 (cont.)

• Mark Hamill, Harrison Ford, and Carrie Fisher have their first script conferences with George Lucas and Irvin Kershner at this time, confirming Ford's return for the sequel. Hamill and Fisher had already signed on for sequels while Ford had originally only committed to one film.

• Joe Johnston completes an intricate sketch of Boba Fett's armor and weapons.

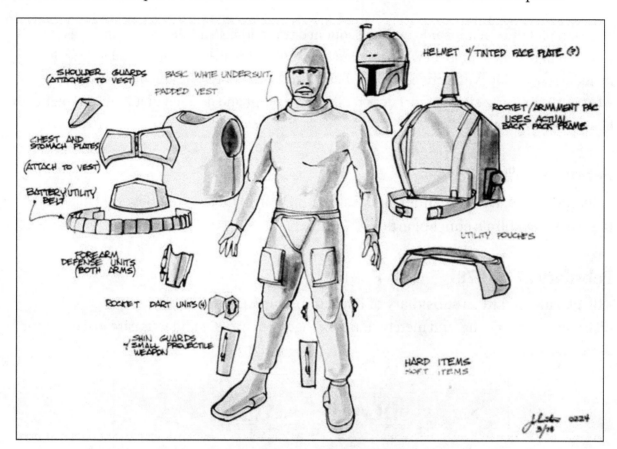

(sketch of Boba Fett's armor by Joe Johnston ©1978 LFL)

March 13th, 1978

• Special Effects Supervisor Brian Johnson arrives at ILM to start setting up effects for *Empire*.

Twentieth Century Fox wanted Johnson to work on Ridley Scott's *Alien*, but being already tied to *Empire*, and not wanting to work on two films simultaneously, he declined. Fox contacted George Lucas and Gary Kurtz about their request and both agreed that since they weren't ready for effects at the time due to the script not being finished Johnson was free to work on *Alien*, which he did.

March 14th, 1978

• Legal paperwork begins on the Kerner building – the new home for Industrial Light and Magic in San Rafael, CA.

The building's name was derived from the street it sits on: 3210 Kerner Blvd.

March 15th, 1978

• ILM draftsman Richard Dawking completes blueprint drawings of the Millennium Falcon's undercarriage assembly modifications.

March 18th, 1978

• *Empire* script writer Leigh Brackett dies at the age of 60.

March 22nd, 1978

• A press release is sent out regarding Leigh Brackett's death.

The press release stated the cause of death as "a long bout with cancer."

March 26th, 1978

• George Lucas and his wife, Marcia, vacation in Mexico with friends.

Lucas spent the entire time in the hotel room rewriting the script to *Empire* due to Brackett's sudden passing.

April, 1978

• George Lucas finishes the second draft of the *Empire* script.

This draft included the first iteration of Darth Vader revealing he is Luke Skywalker's father. Other additions included Han Solo being frozen and Luke getting his arm (not hand) cut off. This second draft was also the first appearance of the opening crawl text which was ultimately revised and shortened for the final film.

• During this time Lucas revises the second draft and soon after completes a third draft.

The scene in which Boba Fett's ship follows the Millennium Falcon was first introduced in this third draft.

• It is likely that *Empire* was changed from Episode II to Episode V during this time as well.

April, 1978 (cont.)

• In Issue #4 of *Little Shoppe of Horrors* magazine (published in the UK), David Prowse is interviewed and says that Darth Vader is Luke's father.
Prowse claimed he merely guessed at this and had no idea it was actually true.

• During this time Effects Director of Photography Dennis Muren is first contacted by Lucasfilm to come back to work on the second Star Wars film.

April 4th, 1978

• Producer Robert Watts and Production Designer John Barry meet with George Lucas, Gary Kurtz, and Irvin Kershner in Los Angeles, CA to go over location ideas for the film.
This was Kershner's first time meeting with Watts and Barry who presented photos of locations in Finse, Norway for Hoth as well as Scandinavia and Kenya for Dagobah.

• Ralph McQuarrie reads the second draft of the film's script.

April 5th, 1978

• Ralph McQuarrie creates sketches of the Imperial Probe Droid.

April 6th, 1978

• Ralph McQuarrie's preparatory sketch for *Med Center* art bears this date.

• McQuarrie creates more sketches of the Imperial Probe Droid.

April 11th-13th & April 17th, 1978

• Ralph McQuarrie completes *Cityscape*, a concept painting which features Lando Calrissian and Princess Leia on Cloud City.

April 12th, 1978

• The first paperback edition and the Book Club Edition hardcover of *Splinter of the Mind's Eye* are published by Del Rey/Ballantine Books.

April 19th-20th, 1978

• Ralph McQuarrie completes the *Med Center* painting which features Luke Skywalker in the bacta tank as we see in the final film with the 2-1B Medical Droid standing next to it as Han Solo and Princess Leia look on from an observation room.

April 20th-22nd, 1978

• Ralph McQuarrie completes a number of additional sketches of the Imperial Probe Droid.

April 24th-26th, 1978

• Ralph McQuarrie completes the *Ice Cave* concept painting which showcases the interior of the Rebel hangar on Hoth featuring the Millennium Falcon, X-wings, early concept designs of the Snowspeeders, and an early concept design of the Tauntaun. Ralph McQuarrie and Joe Johnston had conflicting ideas on the design of the Snowspeeder, but Johnston eventually took McQuarrie's design and developed it into the final design as seen in the film.

(Ralph McQuarrie's "Ice Cave" painting ©1978 LFL)

April 26th, 1978

• Irvin Kershner signs his contract with Lucasfilm to direct *Empire*.

April 27th, 1978

• Date of the first Lucasfilm internal budget for *Empire* created by ILM General Manager Jim Bloom.
The budget totaled $15,494,475.00. [4]

• *Splinter of the Mind's Eye* novel is published in paperback by Sphere Books.

April 28th, 1978

• Lucasfilm internal memo bearing this date which shows a chart of all departments involved in *Empire* as well as guidelines for computer access created by Jim Bloom.

May, 1978

• Executive Producer Gary Kurtz, Producer Robert Watts, and Art Director Norman Reynolds travel to Finse, Norway to confirm locations for shooting the Hoth scenes.

May 10th-11th, 1978

• Ralph McQuarrie completes the second *Ice Cave* concept painting which is a reverse view of the Hoth hangar from his original painting of the same name.

May 12th, 1978

• Diagram of interior Ice Cave and Corridors elevations drawn by Ted Ambrose.

May 18th-19th & May 22nd, 1978

• Ralph McQuarrie completes the painting, *Communications Center.*

May 26th & May 29th-30th, 1978

• Ralph McQuarrie completes the painting, *Ice Cave Exterior*, which features an early Tauntaun design.

June, 1978

• Joe Johnston completes more sketches of Boba Fett.

• George Lucas takes a large group of people to the property that will be the future location of Skywalker Ranch for a picnic lunch where he explains his vision of the facility.

June 8th, 1978

• Deals are confirmed with Mark Hamill, Carrie Fisher, and Harrison Ford to return for the sequel.

• Joe Johnston completes a concept sketch of an early Tauntaun and rider design in which the Tauntaun would be operated by a man in a suit.

June 12th-15th, 1978
• Ralph McQuarrie finishes a painting of *Cloud Cars over Cloud City with Flying Beasties*.

June 15th, 1978
• Contracts for Mark Hamill, Carrie Fisher, and Harrison Ford to return for *Empire* are signed.

• Screenwriter Lawrence Kasdan turns in his first draft of the *Raiders of the Lost Ark* script to George Lucas who immediately asks him to rewrite *Empire*.
Kasdan mentioned to Lucas that he should really read the *Raiders* script first. Lucas agreed to read it that night and that if he didn't like it he would retract his offer.

Lucas loved the script and Kasdan was brought on board immediately to start work on *Empire*.

June 20th-22nd, 1978
• Ralph McQuarrie begins the concept painting, *X-wing in Bog*.
This painting took him eight hours, but wasn't finished until the following month.

June 23rd-24th & June 26th, 1978
• Ralph McQuarrie finishes the painting *Attack on Generator* which takes him 14 hours to complete.

June 27th, 1978
• Sound Designer Ben Burtt sends a memo to George Lucas outlining projected expenses for sound equipment as well as travel costs for sound recording.

(Ben Burtt (l) showcases the prototype Boba Fett armor ©1978 LFL)

June 28th, 1978
• A 20 minute in-person test of Boba Fett is shown to George Lucas at the Park House offices and is recorded on video.
The demonstration featured an all-white Boba Fett costume worn by Assistant Film Editor

Duwayne Dunham. The demo was moderated by sound designer Ben Burtt and showcased a variety of Boba Fett's armor features including his rocket pack, grappling hook, darts, braided hair trophies, and working flamethrower.

Due to a propane leak, Duwayne Dunham's arm caught fire while testing the flamethrower. Because of this the flamethrower idea was immediately scrapped.

June 28th-June 30th, 1978
• Chapter II production and design meetings take place.

July 1st, 1978
• Management of licensing, marketing, and merchandise is taken over by Black Falcon, Ltd., the Lucasfilm subsidiary.

• As of this date the profit split between Lucasfilm and Twentieth Century Fox for *Empire* is 80/20 in favor of Lucasfilm.

• A loan-out contract is signed on this day between Lucasfilm and Chapter II Company that allows George Lucas to pay himself.
The contract made it so Lucas received a $10,000 payment as writer for the story treatment as well as an additional $10,000 as executive producer, but most importantly it gave him five gross points from the film's profits. [4]

July 3rd, 1978
• Artist Ivor Beddoes begins work on *Empire*.

• Make-Up and Special Creature Designer Stuart Freeborn is contracted to work on *Empire*.

July 5th, 1978
• ILM draftsman Ted Ambrose completes blueprint drawings of the Millennium Falcon.

July 11th, 1978
• First annual Lucasfilm 4th of July company picnic.
About 25 people attended this inaugural event. Moving forward Lucasfilm company picnics continued to grow every year in both attendance and prestige.

July 12th, 1978
• Ralph McQuarrie finishes the painting, *Falcon into Crater*.

July 13th, 1978
• Ralph McQuarrie finishes a painting of a large Rebel Ion Cannon on the planet Hoth firing into space titled, *Big Gun*.

July 15th-17th, 1978
• Ralph McQuarrie finishes a concept painting of the exterior of Yoda's dwelling. The painting was titled, *Minch House [exterior]*.

July 18th, 1978
• Building improvements are approved for the Kerner facility.

(Ralph McQuarrie's painting of Darth Vader aboard his Star Destroyer ©1978 LFL)

July 18th-20th, 1978
• Ralph McQuarrie finishes a concept painting of Darth Vader on the bridge of his Star Destroyer.

July 19th, 1978
• A deal memo is sent from Norman Kurland to Lucasfilm attorney Tom Pollock on this day that retroactively solidifies the contract between scriptwriter Lawrence Kasdan and the Chapter II Company.
Kasdan was paid $40,000 for rewriting the *Empire* script and an additional $20,000 for the final polish. [4]

July 20th, 1978
• Ralph McQuarrie retouches and finishes his concept painting, *X-wing in Bog*.

• Metal armature diagram of an early Tauntaun concept is drawn by Steve Cooper.

July 20th-21st, 1978
• Ralph McQuarrie finishes the concept painting for the giant Space Slug titled, *Giant Worm*.

July 22nd, 1978
• Stage plan drawing of the Rebel hangar on Hoth completed by Michael Lamont.

July 23rd, 1978
• David Prowse appears at UC Berkeley in the Bay Area, CA where he signs autographs, answers questions, and talks to a crowd of over 1,000 fans.
Once again Prowse said that Darth Vader was Luke Skywalker's father - the same story he told to *Little Shoppe of Horrors* Magazine in April of that same year.

This supports the claim from Prowse that he only made a guess and had no prior knowledge of the reveal since George Lucas had only seemingly come up with the idea while writing the second draft of the *Empire* script in March. Prowse could never have known anything about the plot line at this time (much less in April) and most likely it was simply a funny anecdote Prowse used in interviews as no one at the time would have ever considered that Darth Vader could actually be Luke Skywalker's father.

Lucasfilm eventually began keeping tabs on interviews with the stars of the films and who was leaking what and Prowse was always at the top of the list as having spoiled the most information about the movies. This resulted in George Lucas banning Prowse from attending all official Star Wars events such as Star Wars Celebration. At the time of printing this ban is still in effect.

July 24th-25th, 1978
• Ralph McQuarrie finishes the concept art for *Dusk Battle on Cloud City*.

July 26th-27th, 1978
• Ralph McQuarrie finishes the concept art for *Rebel Big Gun, Control Booth*.

July 28th, 1978
• Preliminary Probot Design plans are drawn up by Alan Tomkins.

July 31st-August 1st, 1978
• Ralph McQuarrie finishes the concept art for *Dawn Greeting*– a depiction of Lando Calrissian greeting Han Solo, Chewbacca, Princess Leia, and C-3PO on the Cloud City Docking Bay.

August, 1978
• Joe Johnston creates a number of sketches, further developing Ralph McQuarrie's earlier sketches from April, of the Imperial Probe Droid.

August 3rd-4th, 1978
• Ralph McQuarrie completes the concept painting, *Second View, Imperial Star Destroyer.*

August 4th, 1978
• Lucasfilm publicly announces the title of the *Star Wars* sequel as *The Empire Strikes Back.*
The name for the sequel was coined by Gary Kurtz during *Star Wars* promotional tours in foreign markets. After being hounded repeatedly by the press about the name of the sequel Kurtz made up the title, *The Empire Strikes Back,* just to get them to stop asking.

The name stuck and was used as the official title of the film.

• Internal Lucasfilm *Star Wars Sequel Fact Sheet* bears this date.

August 4th-11th, 1978
• The Hoth battlefield scenes are revised and storyboarded.

August 7th, 1978
• Assistant Art Director of Visual Effects Nilo Rodis-Jamero begins work at ILM.

August 8th, 1978
• Stop-motion animator Phil Tippett is rehired for *Empire* and begins work at ILM.
Tippett had headed the team who created the stop-motion alien chess scene in the first Star Wars film.

August 10th, 1978
• Ralph McQuarrie reads Lawrence Kasdan's third draft script of *Empire.*

• Internal Lucasfilm *Star Wars Sequel Fact Sheet* is distributed on this date from Unit Publicist Joan Eisenberg to Assistant Production Manager Pat Carr and other Lucasfilm personnel including Gary Kurtz, Robert Watts, Norman Reynolds, Brian Johnson, Stuart Freeborn, and others.
The fact sheet specified not to share it with members of the press or the public.

(Phil Tippett works on an early concept of the Tauntaun for stop-motion animation ©1978 LFL)

August 14th, 1978

• Date of Preliminary Unit List No: 1 sheet for *Empire* listing each Department Head and their assistants.

August 16th, 1978

• Effects Director of Photography Dennis Muren and Special Visual Effects wizard Richard Edlund begin working at ILM on *Empire*.

• Optical Photography Supervisor Bruce Nicholson also begins work at ILM on this day.

August 17th, 1978

• Preliminary elevations and proportions drawing of Snow Walker, Snowspeeder, and soldier completed by Alan Tomkins.

• Chief Model Maker Lorne Peterson is rehired and begins work on *Empire* at ILM.

August 17th-19th, 1978

• Ralph McQuarrie finishes the concept painting, *Sword Fight, Interior Work Room*.

August 18th, 1978

• Director Irvin Kershner travels from Los Angeles, CA to San Anselmo, CA for a script meeting with George Lucas and Lawrence Kasdan.

Kershner was reimbursed $123.08 for his travel expenses. [4]

August 21st-22nd, 1978

• Ralph McQuarrie finishes the concept painting, *Sword Fight on Antenna*.

(Lorne Peterson works on the Millennium Falcon model at ILM ©1979 LFL)

August 22nd, 1978

• Elstree Studios memo from Elstree Managing Director Andrew Mitchell to Producer Robert Watts confirming the booking of stages for the production of *Empire*.

The memo also stated which stages were not available at the time due to Stanley Kubrick shooting his film, *The Shining*.

August 23rd, 1978

• Set Designer Steve Cooper completes blueprint drawings for the Millennium Falcon's interior cockpit and elevations.

August 25th, 1978
• Lucasfilm and the Estate of Leigh Brackett draw up a contract to confirm her contribution and compensation beyond that of her original agreement with Lucasfilm. Out of respect George Lucas left Brackett's name on the picture as writer alongside Kasdan although little (if any) of her original script remained intact in subsequent drafts.

September 4th, 1978
• ILM artist D. Shields completes blueprint drawings for the Millennium Falcon's turret guns and passageway.

September 5th, 1978
• Model makers, Paul Huston and Steve Gawley (previously part of the *Star Wars* team), return to ILM to begin work on *Empire*.

September 14th, 1978
• Elstree Studios memo from Managing Director Andrew Mitchell to Producer Robert Watts regarding the stages in use by Stanley Kubrick for *The Shining* and the dates and rates for said stages.
The total cost amounted to £309,700 including a 20% discount on tariff rates.

September 24th, 1978
• Darth Vader and Boba Fett both appear in the San Anselmo County Fair Parade in California and later sign autographs for fans.
This was the very first public appearance of Boba Fett. By this time the all-white armor was changed to the multi-colored armor similar to what appears in the final film.

Fett was performed by Duwayne Dunham.

September 25th-28th, 1978
• Ralph McQuarrie completes the concept painting for the *East Landing Platform* on Cloud City.

October, 1978
• The Fourth Draft of the script is written by Lawrence Kasdan.
At this point very little (if any) of Leigh Brackett's original script remained.

• *Empire* story conferences between Lawrence Kasdan, Irvin Kershner, Gary Kurtz, and George Lucas take place.
These conferences were recorded and are thought to have taken place towards the end of October due to Kasdan's completion of a draft around this time and Kershner's trip to

England where he began to draw storyboards. During these conferences the film became more focused on character development. Kershner has stated that during this time he and Gary Kurtz were focused on character, Kasdan on dialogue, and Lucas on plot and action.

• Costume designer John Mollo begins work on *Empire* towards the end of the month drawing sketches of assorted costumes for Field Commander Veers, Rebel Snowtroopers, Princess Leia's snow outfit, Rebel Starfighter pilots, and Star Destroyer crew members.

October 2nd, 1978
• Model maker Tom Budduck is hired at ILM to work on *Empire*.

October 4th, 1978
• Art Director Alan Tomkins completes blueprint drawings of the Rebel Command Center.

October 16th, 1978
• Construction drawing for Snowspeeder gun muzzle is completed by Assistant Art Director Fred Hole.

• Machine Shop Supervisor at ILM Gene Whiteman is hired.

October 17th, 1978
• A contract is signed between the American production arm of Chapter II Corporation and the just formed English counterpart, Chapter II Productions Limited.
This contract allowed the company to begin work in England.

October 24th, 1978
• Fourth Draft revisions of the script are completed.
These were most likely the result of the story conferences between Kurtz, Kasdan, Kershner, and Lucas.

October 28th, 1978
• Irvin Kershner arrives in London to oversee the building of sets.

October 29th-30th, 1978
• Ralph McQuarrie arrives in London to help Director Irvin Kershner visualize and storyboard complicated action scenes.

October 29th-30th, 1978 (cont.)

• McQuarrie reads the fourth draft of the script and meets the production team at EMI Studios.

• During this time Irvin Kershner storyboards the entire film.
Kershner compiled his drawings into a book and sent a copy to George Lucas.
The book made it easier for the two to stay on the same page (literally) as they were both able to use it as a reference during production since Lucas spent most of his time in America while Kershner was filming in Norway and England.

November, 1978

• Nilo Rodis-Jamero finishes sketches of the AT-AT cockpit interior.

• Ralph McQuarrie and Ivor Beddoes begin reworking some of the storyboards for the film.

• Development begins on the Yoda puppet by the Jim Henson Company.

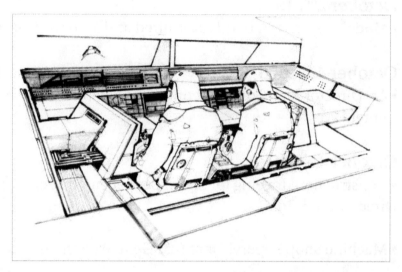

(sketch of AT-AT cockpit interior by Nilo Rodis-Jamero ©1978 LFL)

November 2nd, 1978

• Set Designer Steve Cooper completes blueprint drawings of the Millennium Falcon's hold set.

November 6th, 1978

• Visual Effects Editorial Supervisor Conrad Buff begins work on *Empire*.

November 9th, 1978

• Contracts are finalized for Peter Mayhew and David Prowse.

November 14th, 1978

• Gary Kurtz sends a letter to John Breglio regarding Editor Paul Hirsch, who would be editing the film during production to speed up the post-production process.

(Peter Mayhew (r) with Stuart Freeborn on the set of STAR WARS ©1976 LFL)

November 15ᵗʰ, 1978
• ILM production administrator Dick Gallegly writes a letter to Brian Johnson to let him know that things are "beginning to hum" at ILM.

November 16ᵗʰ, 1978
• Joe Johnston sketches an early concept head of the AT-AT walker.

November 17ᵗʰ, 1978
• *The Star Wars Holiday Special* airs on the CBS® Network to 13 million viewers.
Bewildered fans were shown a series of comedy sketches and musical numbers cut between a storyline of Chewbacca and Han trying to get back to Chewie's family on his home world to celebrate the Wookiee Life Day holiday while being pursued by the Empire.

The special was conceived of by George Lucas who wanted to keep *Star Wars* fresh in the public's minds until *Empire* would be released in 1980. Lucas wanted a holiday special, but it had to be non-denominational due to the fact that it was part of the Star Wars universe which did not contain Earthly religious beliefs. Thus he created the Wookiee Life Day, a celebration of family, joy, and harmony.

The live-action special featured a nine minute cartoon around

(Chewbacca's father, "Itchy", from the Star Wars Holiday Special ©1978 CBS / LFL)

the half-way point which first introduced the character of Boba Fett as a good guy, but later revealed him to be an agent of Darth Vader. Most cite the animated portion as the only good thing to come out of the special. The cartoon was animated by a Canadian animation company called Nelvana who were later used to animate the *Droids* and *Ewoks* cartoons.

The original *Star Wars* cast was opposed to a TV special, but reluctantly reprised their roles as a seeming obligation to Lucas. Harrison Ford, Mark Hamill, Carrie Fisher, Anthony Daniels, and Peter Mayhew were part of the cast which also included Bea Arthur, Art Carney, Harvey Korman, and a musical number by the band Jefferson Starship.
The special was an embarrassment to all involved and never aired again. Lucas distanced himself from it as did the cast. A small segment of fans have continued to appreciate the special for its slice of 70s nostalgia and Star Wars absurdity.

(Boba Fett (r) from the STAR WARS HOLIDAY SPECIAL ©1978 LFL)

November 19th, 1978
• Joe Johnston sketches a variation of the AT-AT walker's head.

November 27th, 1978
• Model maker Mike Fulmer is hired at ILM to work on *Empire*.

• ILM draftsman Richard Dawking completes a blueprint drawing of the Millennium Falcon's radar dish.

December, 1978
• Construction of the full-size Millennium Falcon begins in Pembroke Dock in Pembrokeshire, South West Wales.

December 5th, 1978
• Lawrence Kasdan, Irvin Kershner, and George Lucas make minor revisions to the Fourth Draft script.

(Ralph McQuarrie sketch of downed Imperial AT-AT walker ©1978 LFL)

December 12th, 1978
• Ralph McQuarrie sketches a downed Imperial Walker.

• Early construction drawing of a Rebel laser cannon is completed by Michael Lamont.

December 13th, 1978
• ILM draftsman Richard Dawking completes blueprint drawings of the Millennium Falcon's ramp and docking bay details.

December 14th, 1978
• New sketches are made for Boba Fett's ship, Slave 1.

• Joe Johnston completes the final concept sketch for Darth Vader's Super Star Destroyer.

December 15th, 1978
• Billy Dee Williams' contract with Lucasfilm is signed.

December 18th, 1978
• Model maker Sam Zolltheis is hired at ILM to work on *Empire*.

• ILM draftsman Richard Dawking completes blueprint drawings for the Millennium Falcon's external plan of paneling and dressing to the underside.

December 22nd, 1978
• Updated Lucasfilm internal budget report for *Empire* puts total US and UK direct costs at $21,473,328. [4]

December 27th, 1978
• Sketches of the 2-1B Medical Droid are completed by draftsman Michael Boone.

(Billy Dee Williams as Lando Calrissian ©1979 LFL)

1979

January, 1979
• The contractual start date of principal photography as outlined in the Lucasfilm/Twentieth Century Fox deal for the *Star Wars* sequel film.

• Location Manager Phil Kohler is assigned to prepare the Finse base camp and the two camps on the Hardangerjøkulen glacier.

• Writer Alan Arnold visits Pembroke Dock to see the construction of the full-size Millennium Falcon.

January 1st, 1979
• The "roto shop" at ILM opens its doors on this day, supervised by Peter Kuran. This refers to rotoscoping, a process in which an artist paints over frames of film or parts of an image are removed and placed over a different image or images. The most common elements in the Star Wars Trilogy that used this process were the lightsaber blades, laser bolts, and the use of matte paintings to superimpose live elements over painted backgrounds.

January 1st & 4th, 1979
• Lawrence Kasdan makes minor revisions to the Fourth Draft script.

January 3rd, 1979
• Sid Ganis is hired as Head of Marketing at Lucasfilm per a suggestion to George Lucas from Francis Ford Coppola.

January 8th, 1979
• Patricia Blau is hired to run the front office at Lucasfilm.

• James Earl Jones is confirmed to return as the voice of Darth Vader. Jones stipulated that he did not want to be billed in the film's credits.

• Director of Photography Peter Suschitzky signs his contract to work on *Empire*.

January 12th, 1979

Phil Tippett makes notes for adjustments to the Tauntaun opening scene.

January 15th, 1979

• Model maker Charles Bailey is hired by ILM to work on *Empire*.

January 16th, 1979

• A production office is established in Oslo, Norway.

January 22nd, 1979

• Interior Ice Cave/Corridors blueprint drawing completed by Michael Boone.

January 24th, 1979

• Stage 3 at Elstree Studios catches fire on the set of Stanley Kubrick's *The Shining*. This event set back production on *Empire* as Kubrick was moved to another stage, thus denying Lucasfilm access to two stages they had originally planned on using.

January 25th, 1979

• The recce (location survey) team leaves London for Finse, Norway.

• Alan Arnold interviews Kenny Baker for the book, *A Journal of the Making of The Empire Strikes Back*.

January 26th, 1979

• Production notes specify that parts of the ILM building in San Rafael, CA still need heat at this time.

January 27th, 1979

• Set Designer Steve Cooper completes blueprints of Luke's X-wing being lifted out of the swamp on Dagobah.

January 28th, 1979

• Joe Johnston redesigns the AT-ST "Chicken Walker" from his original 1977 design.

February 5th, 1979

• Dennis Muren films an elephant named Mardji at Marine World to establish the characteristics of the AT-AT's walk.
She was the same elephant used as the Bantha in *Star Wars*.

February 11th, 1979
• The opening scenes with the Probe Droid are storyboarded.

February 12th, 1979
• Start date of ILM's visual effects photography.

• Art Director Alan Tomkins and Brian Johnson arrive in Norway.

February 13th, 1979
• Phil Tippett begins shooting a "blur test" with the stop-motion Tauntaun.

February 15th, 1979
• Elstree Studios breakdown sheet of refurbishing costs for *Empire* is written up on this date.
Included in the breakdown were costs for offices, labor, materials, and more totaling £26,140.86.

February 17th, 1979
• Mark Hamill, Harrison Ford, and Carrie Fisher arrive in London.

February 18th, 1979
• Set Designer Steve Cooper completes blueprints of the hologram chamber Darth Vader uses to speak with the Emperor.

February 19th, 1979
• Correspondence from Irvin Kershner to George Lucas regarding revisions to script pages 143-160.

February 20th, 1979
• The Fifth Draft of the *Empire* script is completed.
This shooting script is credited to Lawrence Kasdan and Leigh Brackett, although none of Brackett's script contributions survived. The front page of the script reads: STAR WARS, EPISODE FIVE, THE EMPIRE STRIKES BACK, BY LEIGH BRACKETT AND LARRY KASDAN, FROM THE NOVEL BY GEORGE LUCAS.

This draft contains the first appearance of the giant Space Slug.

• The production team in Norway receives written permission to shoot aerial footage with a helicopter.

It was the first aerial filming permission granted by Norway to a foreign registered aircraft.

February 22nd, 1979
• The ILM building passes inspection.

February 23rd, 1979
• Phil Tippett casts the Tauntaun model in rubber.

February 25th, 1979
• Construction crew arrives in Norway.

(Carrie Fisher in Norway ©1979 LFL)

February 28th, 1979
• Producer Gary Kurtz, Mark Hamill, Carrie Fisher, and writer/publicist Alan Arnold arrive in Oslo, Norway.

Although none of her scenes were filmed during this time, Carrie Fisher stated that she joined the others in Norway because she enjoyed traveling and being on set. Accompanying Mark Hamill was his then-pregnant wife, Marilou.

• The construction crew begins digging trenches in the freezing snow that would be used by the Rebel Soldiers during the Hoth battle.

March 1ˢᵗ, 1979
• A press conference is held in Oslo, Norway where Producer Gary Kurtz reveals that the next Star Wars film is to begin filming the following Monday.
In attendance were Kurtz, Mark Hamill, and Carrie Fisher.

March 2ⁿᵈ, 1979
• Director Irvin Kershner, Peter Mayhew, and First Assistant Director David Tomblin arrive in Finse, Norway.

March 3ʳᵈ, 1979
• Irvin Kershner, Mark Hamill, Carrie Fisher, Alan Arnold, and others begin their journey to the Hardangerjøkulen glacier.

March 5ᵗʰ, 1979
• PRODUCTION CALL SHEET ON PAGE 70.

• *Empire* filming begins in Norway at the Hardangerjøkulen glacier near the town of Finse.
The production's timing coincided with the worst winter storm the area had seen in 50 years which caused many hardships during filming.

March 6ᵗʰ, 1979
• Writer and Unit Publicist Alan Arnold, documenting the production for the book *A Journal of the Making of The Empire Strikes Back*, sends a worldwide news dispatch to wire services discussing the blizzard that has made shooting difficult as well as the intricacies of shooting a film of this scale in such a remote location.

• Harrison Ford arrives in Finse, Norway.
A last minute decision to bring Harrison Ford to Finse was made and the actor flew out of London to Norway. Due to avalanches blocking the train route, Ford had to ride in a snowplow for 25 miles to reach the shooting location. The trip was long and arduous and the actor ended up arriving around midnight with his scenes to begin filming the next morning.

Ford had not expected to be shooting in Norway as it was planned that his scenes would be filmed on a soundstage. When called in at the last minute to Norway he realized his costume was designed for a soundstage shoot and not an actual cold environment which made the experience that much more difficult for the actor.

"THE EMPIRE STRIKES BACK"

CALL SHEET No. 1

PLAN A:

If the weather is good, please turn to
PLAN B over page. Weather decision will
be made at Breakfast.

DATE: MONDAY 5th March 1979

UNIT CALL: 07:30 leave
07.00 Call for Camera Department and
Construction to prepare tracking area.

SETS: EXT. SNOWDRIFT
         EXT. PLAIN OF HOTH
         EXT. SNOWDRIFT BY TAUNTAUN

SC. NOS: 31. 32. DUSK
            29. 30. DUSK
            33. DUSK

DIRECTOR: IRVIN KERSHNER

ARTISTE	CHARACTER	TRANSPORT	MAKE UP	SET
MARK HAMILL	LUKE	Cat 4	07.00	06.30

Double:

A.N. OTHER	for HAN	Cat 5		

Props: Luke's belt, goggles, laser sword, binoculars, Han's belt and
          all accessories, Han's riding Tauntaun, Han's dead Tauntaun, and all
          accessories for Tauntauns.

SFX: 2 Wind Machines

Construction Dressing: Flame for Wampa.
                         Wind Breakers to be carried at all locations.
                         Track sub frames required at Location: 07.00

2nd UNIT:

To stand by Main Unit with possibility of shooting Scenes 23, 28.

SETS:

EXT. ENTRANCE TO ICE GORGE.   Scene 23 DUSK
INT. TRENCH   Scene 26 DUSK
EXT. PLAIN OF H OTH (Matte Shot) Scene 28 DUSK

Doubles:
A. N. Other   for LUKE

Crowd:
1 TROOPER) To be taken from crew
1 OFFICER) Wardrobe to be notified of personnel

Props: Hand gun for Officer, gun on Tripod, small Binoculars

Art. Dept: INT. TRENCH set to be dressed

Electricians: yellow light source to come from Trench

(Harrison Ford films his scenes as Han Solo searching for Luke Skywalker on Hoth ©1979 LFL)

March 7ᵗʰ, 1979

• Harrison Ford begins filming his scenes for *Empire* ahead of schedule.
On this day scenes of Han Solo on his Tauntaun, searching for Luke Skywalker, were shot.

• The scene of the Wampa dragging Luke through the snow is shot on this day.
The Wampa was performed by Des Webb who had to wear stilts to achieve the height of the creature. This proved extremely difficult in the snow and resulted in Webb toppling over several times during filming.

March 8ᵗʰ-9ᵗʰ, 1979

• The film crew shoots scenes of Mark Hamill as Luke Skywalker sitting on his Tauntaun when he takes off his goggles to get a better look at the nearby meteor impact and informs Han Solo.
Also shot on this day was the scene of Han finding Luke lying in the snow. Due to the weather conditions both scenes were filmed just outside the hotel at which the crew was staying.

March 9ᵗʰ, 1979

• A contingent of Norwegian mountain-rescue skiers are brought in to act as Hoth soldiers.
For their service Lucasfilm donated money to the Norwegian Red Cross.

March 9th, 1979 (cont.)

• The scene in which Han Solo stuffs Luke Skywalker into the belly of his Tauntaun is shot on this day.

(Harrison Ford (l) and crew film outside the hotel in Norway ©1979 LFL)

March 10th, 1979

• The crew moves location to Camp Sharman, an ice slope that serves as the backdrop for the scene in which Luke turns to see the Millennium Falcon flee the ice planet. This location was also used for the encounter between Han Solo, Chewbacca, and the Imperial Probe Droid.

March 11th, 1979

• The final day of 1st Unit photography in Norway.
The cast and crew left for London the next day except for Mark Hamill, Wampa performer, Des Webb, and the 2nd Unit crew who hoped for the weather to clear so they could capture the last shots needed on location.

• The scenes of Luke turning to see the Falcon fleeing Hoth and escaping his crashed Snowspeeder are shot.

March 12th, 1979

• George Lucas arrives in London for the start of production at Elstree Studios.

• Gary Kurtz returns to London and sees his family before returning to the studio to meet with the department heads and catch up on correspondence.

• *The Sun* newspaper in the UK runs a featured article titled "Star Wars On Ice."
The article mentioned that writer Joe Steeples and photographer Steve Markeson had flown by helicopter to the location in Norway where *Empire* was being filmed and had taken photos.

• ILM ships the brand new Empireflex camera to Norway for 2nd Unit shots.

• Interior Star Destroyer Flooring Layout blueprints completed by draftsman "B D".

March 13th, 1979

• The production's 1st Unit moves to Elstree Studios in London.
    Irvin Kershner: *"Let's see, the first scene we shot in London after we returned from Norway, was the hold of Han Solo's Millennium Falcon. That's a new set—something you didn't see in* Star Wars. *We see the hold and the engine room."*
Kershner arrived at the Studio at 7:30am.

• Harrison Ford and Carrie Fisher shoot the kiss between Han Solo and Princess Leia aboard the Millennium Falcon, although by day's end the scene remains unfinished.

• The 2nd Unit film crew shoots Mark Hamill on the glacier in Norway after weather conditions improve.

• George Lucas, Gary Kurtz, and Irvin Kershner watch footage from Norway in the evening.
The reaction was overall a positive one.

• Set Designer Steve Cooper completes blueprint drawings of the Millennium Falcon's interior layout and the "greebly" dressing of the front mandible.
"Greebly" (also called "greeble") is a term coined by George Lucas referring to fine details covering the surface of a larger object. The term has since become common nomenclature in model making circles.

March 14th, 1979

• PRODUCTION CALL SHEET ON PAGE 75.

March 14th, 1979 (cont.)

• Revisions are made to the shooting script including dialogue changes and the cutting of scenes.

• The Millennium Falcon's escape from Hoth and the Asteroid Field scenes are shot on this day on the Falcon's interior cockpit set.

March 15th, 1979

• PRODUCTION CALL SHEET ON PAGE 76.

• The scene in which the Millennium Falcon escapes through the teeth of the giant Space Slug is shot from the interior of the Falcon's cockpit against blue screen.

• Mark Hamill is fitted for wardrobe and begins fencing rehearsals with stunt coordinator Peter Diamond and sword master Bob Anderson.

• Rear undercarriage of the Millennium Falcon blueprint drawings completed at ILM.

• The studio shooting schedule is sent out to the cast and crew with the date range of March 16th – April 16th.

((l to r) Carrie Fisher, Harrison Ford, Peter Mayhew, and Anthony Daniels film inside the Millennium Falcon cockpit set ©1979 LFL)

CHAPTER II PRODUCTIONS LTD.
Call Sheet No. 2 (Studio)

PRODUCTION: "THE EMPIRE STRIKES BACK"   DATE: Wednesday, 14th March, 1979.
DIRECTOR: IRVIN KERSHNER   UNIT CALL: 08.30 hrs.

SETS: SC. NOS:
INT. MILLENNIUM FALCON (Stage 8)   289pt. (Space)
                                                  S/BY Sc. 297, 299.

ARTISTE :		ROLE:	D/R:	M/UP:	READY:
CARRIE FISHER		LEIA	76/78	07.00	08.30
HARRISON FORD		HAN	86/88	07.50	08.30
ANTHONY DANIELS		THREEPIO	129	08.00	08.30
PETER MAYHEW		CHEWBACCA	127	08.00	08.30

STAND-INS:
LIZ COKE	for	Miss Fisher	)		
JACK DEARLOVE	for	Mr. Ford	)		
ALAN HARRIS	for	Mr. Daniels	)	08.00	08.30
MARK PRESTON	for	Mr. Mayhew	)		

PROPS:
Dummy soft tools to fall on Han. Walding tool. Hydro spanners. Goggles for
welding. Breathing masks. Loose cases and boxes reqd. Chewbacca's crossbow &
bandolier.
CAMERA:
Double head fx. required.

ART DEPT:
1. Practical gauges/hyperdrive panel required.
2. Removable roof section piece.
3. Moveable section piece for reverses.

SPECIAL FX:
1. Welding tool fx. required.
2. Cabin lights dim then go out Sc. 297.
ELECTRICAL:
Flashing console light fx.

CATERING:
AM & PM Break on Stage 8 for approx.. 75 persons.

TRANSPORT:
Car 1:   Peter Lowsey to collect Miss Fisher at 6.20 from home. To arrive
              at EMI Studios by 7.00 a.m.
Car 2:   Peter Ferretti to collect Mr. Ford at 7.20 from hotel, to arrive
              at EMI Studios by 7.50 a.m.
Car 3:   T. Pritchard collect Mr. Daniels at 7.30 from home, to arrive at
              EMI Studios by 8 a.m.
Car 4:   Vic Minay to collect Mr. Mayhew at 6.45 a.m. to arrive at EMI Studios
              by 8 a.m.
Car 5:   Roy Najda to collect Mr. Hamill from h ome at 8.30 a.m. and
              work to instructions.
Car 6:   John Newsy - work to Irvin Kershner's instructions.

                                          DAVID TOMBLIN - Assistant Director

CHAPTER II PRODUCTIONS LTD.
Call Sheet No. 3 (Studio)

PRODUCTION: "THE EMPIRE STRIKES BACK"   DATE: Thursday, 15ᵗʰ March, 1979.
DIRECTOR: IRVIN KERSHNER   UNIT CALL: 08:30

SETS: SC. NOS:
INT. MILLENNIUM FALCON (Stage 8)   289pt. to complete
                                                 297, 299. S.409, 430, T431.
                                                              (T430)

ARTISTE :			ROLE:	D/R:	M/UP:	READY:
CARRIE FISHER			LEIA	76/78	07.00	08.30
HARRISON FORD			HAN	86/88	07.50	08.30
ANTHONY DANIELS			THREEPIO	129	08.00	08.30
PETER MAYHEW			CHEWBACCA	127	10.15	10.45
KENNY BAKER			ARTOO	121	S/BY AT HOME – T.B.A.	

STAND-INS:
LIZ COKE	FOR	Miss Fisher)				
J. DEARLOVE	FOR	Mr. Ford)				
ALAN HARRIS	FOR	Mr. Daniels)		08.00		08.30
STEPHEN MEEKS	"	Mr. Mayhew)				

PROPS:
Welding tool. Hydro spanner. Goggles for welding. Breathing masks.
Loose cases and boxes reqd. Chewbacca's crossbow & bandolier.
Circuit panel for Artoo Sc. T.431.

CAMERA:
Double head fx. required.

ART DEPT:
1. Panel for Chewie to hit (Sc. 430)
2. Falling Artoo unit required.

SPECIAL FX:
1. Welding tool fx. required.
2. Artoo mending arm fx.

ELECTRICAL:
1. Flashing console light fx.
2. Cabin lights dim then go out (Sc. 297)

CATERING:
AM & PM Break on Stage 8 for approx.. 75 persons.

DAVID TOMBLIN
Assistant Director

PROGRAMME FOR THURSDAY, 15/3/79
MARK HAMILL	Berman's fitting	10.30 a.m.
	Water/fencing rehearsals...	Afternoon
4 PIGMEN)......................................	Costume fittings @	All day
2 SMALL MEN)	Barman's	

March 16th, 1979

• PRODUCTION CALL SHEET ON PAGE 78.

• Stage Layout blueprint for "Bog Planet" (Dagobah set) is completed by Set Designer Steve Cooper.

• Two more scenes are shot on the Millennium Falcon set this day including the escape from Cloud City and R2's repairing of the hyperdrive.

• The 2nd Unit crew in Norway films the radar dish explosion for the Hoth battle.

(a Rebel Soldier (Carl Bang) operates the laser/radar dish on Hoth ©1979 LFL)

(R2-D2 repairs the hyperdrive on the Millennium Falcon ©1979 LFL)

CHAPTER II PRODUCTIONS LTD.

PRODUCTION:	"THE EMPIRE STRIKES BACK"		DATE:	Friday, 16th March, 1979.	
DIRECTOR:	IRVIN KERSHNER		UNIT CALL:	08:30 hrs.	

SET:
1. INT. MILLENNIUM FALCON   Stage 8
2. INT. MEDICAL CENTRE   Stage 1
3. TEST: 5.30 p.m.   WAMPA EXPLOSION TEST   T.B.A.

ARTISTE :	CHARACTER:	D/R:	M/UP:	READY:

1) <u>INT. FALCON HOLD:</u> Scs. 297pt.. 299pt.. S409, 430, T431.

CARRIE FISHER	LEIA	76/78	07.00	08.30
HARRISON FORD	HAN	86/88	07.50	08.30
ANTHONY DANIELS	THREEPIO	129	08.00	08.30
PETER MAYHEW	CHEWBACCA	127	08.00	08.30
KENNY BAKER	ARTOO	121	09.00	09.30

STAND-INS:

LIZ COKE	for	Miss Fisher)		
J. DEARLOVE	for	Mr. Ford)		
ALAN HARRIS	for	Mr. Daniels)	08.00	08.30
STEPHEN MEEKS	for	Mr. Mayhew)		

PROPS: Breathing masks. Loose cases and boxes reqd. Chewbacca's crossbow and bandolier. Circuit panel for Artoo Sc. T431.

CAMERA: Double head fx. required.

ART DEPT:
1. Panel for Chewie to hit (Sc. 430)
2. Falling Artoo unit required.

SPECIAL FX:
1. Welding tool fx. required.
2. Artoo mending arm fx.

ELECTRICAL:
1. Flashing console light fx.

---

1) <u>INT. MEDICAL CENTRE:</u> Scs. 42, 43, 57 (Rehearsal)

CARRIE FISHER	LEIA	76/78	From above	
HARRISON FORD	HAN	86/88	From above	
MARK HAMILL	LUKE	80/82	11.15	12.00
ANTHONY DANIELS	THREEPIO	129	From above	
PETER MAYHEW	CHEWBACCA	127	From above	
KENNY BAKER	ARTOO	121	From above	

STAND-INS:

From above				
JOHN GIBSON	for	Mr. Hamill	10.30	11.00

STUNT ARRANGEMENTS:

PETER DIAMOND	Co-ordinator)		9.30	10.00
REG HARDING	Stand-in/Double)			

PROPS: Breathing mask, nose clips. Medical dressing.

ART DEPT: 1. Harness fx.   2. Bubbling water fx.

SPECIAL FX:	2 x Medical droids required.
ELECTRICAL:	1. Flashing light/dimmer shutter fx.
M/UP:	1. Waterproof scar/damage fx. on Luke.
CAMERA:	3 cameras required.
WARDROBE:	Dressing gown for Luke sc. 57.
MEDICAL:	Nurse to S/BY from 9.00 a.m.

<u>DAVID TOMBLIN</u>
Assistant Director

March 17th, 1979

• Gary Kurtz and Irvin Kershner meet up to go over planning for the following week.

• Kurtz and Kershner meet up later that evening with George Lucas to look at costumes - specifically Carrie Fisher's various outfits.

• Plans are submitted to George Lucas to expand the Kerner facility for ILM.

• The scene in which the Rebel soldiers retreat from the trenches during the Hoth battle is shot by the 2nd Unit crew in Norway.

March 18th, 1979

• Gary Kurtz and Irvin Kershner meet with the actors to go over the entire script and make many dialogue changes.

• The 2nd Unit crew, still filming in Norway, shoots the location that will serve as the entrance to the Rebel base on Hoth.

March 19th, 1979

• Filming begins in the medical center set with Mark Hamill being submerged in a giant transparent tank filled with chlorinated water for the bacta tank scene.
In order to adequately light the water tank a giant mirror had to be suspended above it. On two separate occasions the overhead mirror shattered – one of which was right before Mark Hamill was supposed to be lowered into the tank. It's possible that Hamill may have been seriously injured or even killed if the glass had broken while he was inside the tank.

• More revisions are made to the shooting script by Director Irvin Kershner and the actors.

March 20th, 1979

• PRODUCTION CALL SHEET ON PAGE 81.

March 21st, 1979

• PRODUCTION CALL SHEET ON PAGE 82.

• Alan Arnold interviews Gary Kurtz's assistant Bunny Alsup and Associate Producer Robert Watts for the book, *A Journal of the Making of The Empire Strikes Back*.

March 22nd, 1979

• Billy Dee Williams arrives in London.

• Script revisions take place and elevator scenes in Cloud City are removed from the script.

• Weather conditions worsen in Norway for the 2nd Unit crew.

March 22nd-25th, 1979

• Scenes in the Rebel Command Center are shot including Han Solo's proclamation that he has to leave.
Scenes of Wampas being detected inside the Rebel base and a Rebel soldier who is killed after spotting the Imperial Probe Droid were also shot, but eventually cut from the final film.

• Jeremy Bulloch is fitted for his Boba Fett costume.
It took 20 minutes to put the costume on.

March 23rd, 1979

• Billy Dee Williams is fitted for his costume.

March 24th, 1979

• Irvin Kershner reviews the sets and the script as he prepares for the following week of shooting.

March 25th, 1979

• A drawing of the camera angle set-up for the interior cockpit of the Snowspeeder is completed by Assistant Art Director Michael Lamont.

March 26th, 1979

• George Lucas and Gary Kurtz meet with Robert Stigwood (RSO Records) to produce and distribute the film's soundtrack.

• ILM makes plans for a new optical printer – a device used to create special effects. With a $500,000 price tag, and dealing with composites on a white background, the justification for the prototype printer was heavily discussed and debated by ILM.

The optical printer allowed multiple layers of images to be projected simultaneously resulting in a single image. One of the most recognizable shots from *Empire* that features this process is the asteroid chase with the Millennium Falcon being pursued by TIE Fighters.

```
                                                                    Call Sheet
                    CHAPTER II PRODUCTIONS LTD.                      Studio No: 6

 PRODUCTION:    "THE EMPIRE STRIKES BACK"          DATE:     Tuesday, 20th March, 1979.
 DIRECTOR:      IRVIN KERSHNER                      UNIT CALL:       08:30 hrs.

 SET:                                              STAGE:
 1. INT. MEDICAL CENTRE                            Stage 1
 2. REHEARSAL: INT. ICE CORRIDOR                   Stage 1
 ------------------------------------------------------------------------------------
         ARTISTE :                  CHARACTER:     D/R:        M/UP:         READY:
 ------------------------------------------------------------------------------------
1)    INT. MEDICAL CENTRE: Sc. 57

      CARRIE FISHER                  LEIA          76/78       07.00         08.30
      HARRISON FORD                  HAN           86/88       07.50         08.30
      MARK HAMILL                    LUKE          80/82       07.50         08.30
      ANTHONY DANIELS                THREEPIO      129         08.00         08.30
      PETER MAYHEW                   CHEWBACCA     127         08.00         08.30
      KENNY BAKER                    ARTOO         121         08.15         08.30

      STAND-INS:
      LIZ COKE          for    Miss Fisher   )
      JACK DEARLOVE     for    Mr. Ford      )
      JOHN GIBSON       for    Mr. Hamill    )
      ALAN HARRIS       for    Mr. Daniels   )            08.00         08.30
      STEPHEN MEEKS     for    Mr. Mayhew    )

      PROPS:                   Breathing mask, nose clips.  Medical dressing.

      ART DEPT:                Harness fx.

      SPECIAL FX:              1. Medical droids required.
                               2. Bubbling water fx.
                               3. Droid to have patting fx.

      ELECTRICAL:              1. Flashing light/dimmer shutter fx.
      M/UP:                    Damage fx. on Luke (Sc.57)
      WARDROBE:                Dressing gown for Luke (Sc. 57)
      MEDICAL:                 Nurse to S/BY from 8.30 a.m.
      CATERING:                AM & PM breaks on Stage 1 for approx. 75 people.


      2) ARTISTES' REHEARSAL: Sc. 15

      CARRIE FISHER            LEIA          76/78       From above
      HARRISON FORD            HAN           86/88       From above


                                    TEST
      Steam atmosphere test fx. in Ice Corridor - Stage 1 ..... P.M.


                                            DAVID TOMBLIN
                                            Assistant Director


 Note:   Video taping of Norwegian rushes to be done in Cutting Rooms with
         Dick Hewitt in attendance, On Tuesday 20/3.
```

```
                        CHAPTER II PRODUCTIONS LTD.          Call Sheet
                                                             Studio No: 7

PRODUCTION:     "THE EMPIRE STRIKES BACK"        DATE:    Wednesday, 21tst March, 1979.
DIRECTOR:       IRVIN KERSHNER                    UNIT CALL:        08:30 hrs.

SET:                                             STAGE:
1. INT. MEDICAL CENTRE                           Stage 1
2. INT. ICE CORRIDOR                             Stage 1
-------------------------------------------------------------------------------------
ARTISTE  :                      CHARACTER:    D/R:      M/UP:         READY:
-------------------------------------------------------------------------------------
1) INT. MEDICAL CENTRE: Sc. 57 to complete, 43pt. (Chewie Close-up), 42pt. (inserts)

CARRIE FISHER              LEIA             76/78      7.00          8.30
HARRISON FORD              HAN              86/88      7.50          8.30
MARK HAMILL                LUKE             80/82      7.50          8.30
ANTHONY DANIELS            THREEPIO         129        8.00          8.30
PETER MAYHEW               CHEWBACCA        127        8.00          8.30
KENNY BAKER                ARTOO            121        TO BE ADVISED

STAND-INS:
LIZ COKE            for     Miss Fisher  )
JACK DEARLOVE       for     Mr. Ford     )
JOHN GIBSON         for     Mr. Hamill   )              8.00         8.30
ALAN HARRIS         for     Mr. Daniels  )
STEPHEN MEEKS       for     Mr. Mayhew   )

PROPS:                     Medical dressing

SPECIAL FX:                1.Medical droids required
                           2.Droid to have patting fx.

M/UP:                      Dame fx. on Luke (Sc. 57)

WARDROBE:                  Dressing gown for Luke (Sc. 57)


1) INT. ICE CORRIDOR: Sc. 15 (Day)

CARRIE FISHER              LEIA             76/78      From above
HARRISON FORD              HAN              86/88      From above

STAND-INS:
LIZ COKE            for     Miss Fisher  )            From above
JACK DEARLOVE       for     Mr. Ford     )

CROWD ARTISTES:
7 Rebel Men                )
3 Rebel Women              )                          10.00        10.30

PROPS:                     Weapons for Rebel Soldiers.

SPECIAL FX:                1.  To S/BY to operate Wampa arm through ice.
                           2.  General atmosphere fx.

ART DEPT:                  Crumbling ice fx.

WARDROBE:                  Pilot helmet dressing required for crowd.

M/UP:                      Articulated hand for Wampa (time permitted).


                        PROGRAMME: TEST REHEARSALS
M/UP:       EILEEN BAKER - face mould: Stuart Freeborn .......A.M.
FENCING:        MARK HAMILL      )        Fight rehearsal .....P.M.
                PETER DIAMOND    )


        PLEASE NOTE THAT THERE SHOULD BE NO SMOKING ON THE ICE CORRIDOR SET & PLEASE BE
        CAREFUL NOT TO THROW ANY RUBBISH ON THE FLOOR ON THIS SET.

                        D. Tomblin - Asst. Director
```

March 26th-28th, 1979
• The following scenes are shot and completed: Han reports that the Probe Droid has self-destructed, General Rieekan tells a Rebel officer that they will start the evacuation, Han returns to the Command Center to take Leia to safety, and they escape through the ice corridors as the base is attacked.

March 27th, 1979
• George Lucas flies home to California to continue working on the film's special effects at ILM.

• Actor Bruce Boa (General Rieekan) finishes his scenes and wraps on *Empire*.

March 28th, 1979
• PRODUCTION CALL SHEET ON PAGE 84.

• ILM films more AT-AT Walker tests.

March 29th, 1979
• PRODUCTION CALL SHEET ON PAGE 85.

(Han Solo (Harrison Ford) (l) speaks to General Rieekan (Bruce Boa) (c) as Leia (Carrie Fisher) (r) looks on ©1979 LFL)

CHAPTER II PRODUCTIONS LTD.   Call Sheet No: 12
                                                     (Studio)

PRODUCTION:	"THE EMPIRE STRIKES BACK"	DATE:	Wednesday, 28th March, 1979.
DIRECTOR:	IRVIN KERSHNER	UNIT CALL:	08:30 hrs.

SETS: STAGE 1:
1. INT. COMMAND CENTRE/ICE CORRIDOR
2. INT. MAIN ICE TUNNELS

ARTISTE :	CHARACTER:	D/R:	M/UP:	READY:
1) INT. COMMAND CENTRE/ICE CORRIDOR: Scs. 178pt., 180, T285, 15 to comp.				
CARRIE FISHER	LEIA	76/78	7.00	8.30
HARRISON FORD	HAN	86/88	8.00	8.30
ANTHONY DANIELS	THREEPIO	129	8.15	8.30
DAVE PROWSE	DARTH VADER	133	9.00	for Rehearsal
KENNY BAKER	ARTOO	121	S/BY at home	T.B.A.
JERRY HARTE	HEAD CONTROLLER	131	TO BE ADVISED	
STAND-INS:				
LIZ COKE	for Miss Fisher)			
JACK DEARLOVE	for Mr. Ford)		8.00	8.30
ALAN HARRIS	for Mr. Daniels)			
MORAY BUSH	for Mr. Prowse)			
CROWD:				
3 MEN) REBELS			8.00	8.30
2 WOMEN)			7.30	8.30
15 SNOW TROOPERS			8.30	9.00
CHRIS PARSONS	WHITE THREEPIO		8.30	9.00
STUNT ARTISTES:				
PETER DIAMOND	Stunt Co-ordinator		S/BY from 8.30	

PROPS: Com-link for Han. Weapons for rebels and snow troops.
ART DEPT: Falling ice - large section to fall Sc. T205.
SP. FX: Steam/Spark fx. Cave in/explosions fx.
MEDICAL: Nurse to S/BY on set from 8.30 a.m.

---

2) INT. MAIN ICE TUNNEL: Sc. 25				
HARRISON FORD	HAN	From above		
RAY HASSETT	DECK OFFICER	TO BE ADVISED		
NORWICH DUFF	2ND OFFICER	TO BE ADVISED		
STAND-IN:				
JACK DEARLOVE	for Mr. Ford	From above		
CROWD:				
10 REBEL SOLDIER			8.30	9.00
5 REBEL SOLDIERS			From above	

PROPS: All Tauntaun equipment, weapons for Rebel Soldiers,
             droid thermometer. Broken Hardware.
SP.FX: Medical droid.
ART DEPT: 1. Pool of water 2. Dead Tauntaun fx.
MAKE-UP: 1 Speical Tauntaun head reqd. 2. Tauntaun feet reqd.

                         TESTS/REHEARSALS
1. Mark Hamill - fencing from 10 a.m.
2. Billy Dee Williams - Wardrobe fitting at Berman's 10 a.m.
3. Blue Screen Test - Stage 8
4. Audition: Cloud city Men/Women - 10.30 a.m. (EMI - Stage 1 & 2)

CHAPTER II PRODUCTIONS LTD.   Call Sheet No: 13
                                                          (Studio)

PRODUCTION: "THE EMPIRE STRIKES BACK"   DATE: Thursday, 29th March, 1979.
DIRECTOR: IRVIN KERSHNER   UNIT CALL: 08:30 hrs.

SETS: STAGE 1:
INT. MAIN ICE TUNNEL   Sc. 25
INT. ICE CORRIDOR   Sc. S205

ARTISTE		CHARACTER:	D/R:	M/UP:	READY:
HARRISON FORD		HAN	86/88	8.30	9.00
RAY HASSETT		DECK OFFICER	131	8.15	8.30
NORWICH DUFF		2ND OFFICER	131	8.15	8.30
DAVE PROWSE		DARTH VADER	133	11.30	For Rehearsal
DES WEBB		WAMPA		8.30	9.00
STAND-IN:					
ALAN HARRIS	for	Mr. Ford		8.00	8.30
MURRAY BUSH	for	Mr. Prowse		10.30	11.00
CROWD ARTISTES:					
15 Rebel Soldiers			8.00	8.30	
7 SNOW TROOPERS			8.30		9.00

PROPS: All Tauntaun equipment, weapons for Rebel Soldiers & Snow troopers,
           droid thermometer. Broken hardware.

SP. FX: Medical droid.

ART DEPT: 1. Pool of water.   2. Dead Tauntaun fx.

M/UP: 1. Special Tauntaun head reqd.   2. Tauntaun feet reqd.

MEDICAL: Nurse to S/BY on set from 8.30 a.m.

                          TEST/REHEARSAL
MARK HAMILL ...... FENCING REHEARSAL   P/UP 9.15 a.m. to be at EMI by 10am.

ART DEPT. .... To S/BY to rig breakaway set piece on completion of Sc. 25

CATERING: AM & PM Breaks for 110 Persons on Stage 1.

TRANSPORT: 1. P. Ferretti to P/UP Harrison Ford at 7.50 - to arrive by 8.30
            2. R. Najda to P/UP M. Hamill at 9.15 to arrive by 10 a.m.

                                      DAVID TOMBLIN
                                      Asst. Director

March 29th, 1979 (cont.)

• A scene is shot that will later be cut from the final film: a Tauntaun is found dead in the Rebel Base - the victim of a Wampa attack.

This storyline would be removed from the film; however, a small portion of the scene remained. When Han Solo talks to one of the Rebel soldiers about going out to look for Luke on Tauntaun the 2-1B medical droid can be seen examining a dead Tauntaun although nothing about it is mentioned on camera.

(a dead Tauntaun is examined by a 2-1B Medical Droid ©1979 LFL)

March 30th, 1979

• Rehearsals for Bespin scenes are underway while a scene is shot where a Wampa breaks through one of the ice walls of the Rebel base.

The storyline regarding Wampas was completely dropped and there is neither footage nor mention in the final film of them invading the Rebel base.

• A general meeting is held at ILM to discuss building security and to introduce new employees.

April 1st, 1979

• Mark Hamill stand-in Colin Skeaping is filmed on location in Norway dressed as

Luke Skywalker falling into the snow after detaching from the belly of the AT-AT.

April 2nd, 1979

• Executives from General Mills visit the *Empire* set.
General Mills owned Palitoy at the time and were licensed by Lucasfilm to manufacture and distribute Star Wars toys in the 1970s and 1980s in the UK.

• 2nd Unit conducts lighting tests for Cloud City shots.

• Irvin Kershner, Gary Kurtz, Mark Hamill, Carrie Fisher, Harrison Ford, and Billy Dee Williams go out this evening for a Japanese dinner.

April 3rd, 1979

• The entire day is spent shooting more of the Wampa attack on the Rebel Base.

• The 2nd Unit crew finishes shooting in Norway.

April 4th, 1979

• The 2nd Unit crew returns to England.

• 1st Unit shoots interior Cloud City scenes with Harrison Ford, Carrie Fisher, Billy Dee Williams, Peter Mayhew, Anthony Daniels, and John Hollis.

• A memo from Andrew Mitchell at Elstree Studios is sent to John Shepherd requesting £10,000 to be 'charged against renovations and decoration to the Studio premises at present occupied by "Star Wars – The Empire Strikes Back".'

April 5th, 1979

• PRODUCTION CALL SHEET ON PAGE 89.

• An internal Elstree Studios memo is sent from D. J. Skinner to Andrew Mitchell regarding the building of another studio for the *Empire* production and the subsequent costs and fees of such.

April 6th, 1979
• PRODUCTION CALL SHEET ON PAGE 90.

April 9th-April 10th, 1979
• George Lucas reviews footage of dailies and has an assistant take notes regarding instructions relating to specific shots.

April 10th, 1979
• PRODUCTION CALL SHEET ON PAGE 91.

(Jeremy Bulloch as Boba Fett ©1979 LFL)

• Jeremy Bulloch's first day of filming as Boba Fett.
Scenes shot included Fett escorting Han Solo's body in carbonite and shooting at Luke Skywalker in the corridors of Cloud City.

April 12th, 1979
• 41 of Ralph McQuarrie's paintings are filmed for the *Empire* teaser trailer.

April 13th, 1979
• ILM General Manager Jim Bloom returns to the United States from Norway.

April 17th, 1979
• The patents for the R2-D2 and C-3PO characters are issued by the US Patent Office to George Lucas. The designers for R2-D2 were listed as Ralph McQuarrie and John Stears.

```
                        CHAPTER II PRODUCTIONS LTD.              Call Sheet No: 18
                                                                      (Studio)

PRODUCTION:     "THE EMPIRE STRIKES BACK"          DATE:   Thursday, 5th April, 1979.
DIRECTOR:       IRVIN KERSHNER                      UNIT CALL:     08:30 hrs.      Stage 2

SETS:                                              STAGE 1:
1.  INT. CORRIDORS CLOUD CITY                      Scs: 352, 354, 356 …. Day
2.  INT. ANTE ROOM                                 Sc:  355 …………………… Day
----------------------------------------------------------------------------------------
ARTISTE  :                      CHARACTER:     D/R:        M/UP:          READY:
----------------------------------------------------------------------------------------
1) INT. CORRIDORS CLOUD CITY:        Scs. 352, 354, 356 … Day

CARRIE FISHER                   LEIA           76/78       8.30           10.00
HARRISON FORD                   HAN            86/88       9.30           10.00
BILLY DEE WILLIAMS              LANDO          90          7.30           9.00
ANTHONY DANIELS                 THREEPIO       129         9.30           10.00
PETER MAYHEW                    CHEWBACCA      92          9.30           10.00
JOHN HOLLIS                     LANDO'S AIDE   131         8.00           9.00

STAND-INS:
LIZ COKE                for    Miss Fisher            )
JACK DEARLOVE           for    Mr. Ford               )    8.00           8.30
QUENTIN PIERRE          for    Mr. Billy Dee Williams )
ALAN HARRIS             for    Mr. Daniels            )
STEVEN MEEK             for    Mr. Mayhew             )

CROWD ARTISTES:
6 ASSTD.GUARDS - LANDO  )
3 MINERS - MEN          )                                  7.30           8.30
2 MAINTENANCE MEN       )
1 ROBOT - THREEPIO      )

PROPS:          Weapons for Cloud City Guards.  Tools for maintenance men.
                Brain augmentor for aide.
ART DEPT/        1 remote Artoo required
SPECIAL FX:
----------------------------------------------------------------------------------------
ART DEPT:       Test 3PO/Chewie back harness.  Cloud City Corridors.
----------------------------------------------------------------------------------------

2) INT. ANTE-ROOM:   Sc. 355 …. Day

ANTHONY DANIELS                 THREEPIO       From above

Stand-in:
ALAN HARRIS             for Mr. Daniels         From above

ART DEPT:       Threepio robot to explode.
SPECIAL FX:     Explosion/ray bolt fx. on Threepio.
----------------------------------------------------------------------------------------

NURSE:          From 2nd Camera Unit.

CATERING:       AM & PM breaks for approx.. 110 persons.
----------------------------------------------------------------------------------------

                                                   DAVID TOMBLIN
                                                   Assistant Director
```

CHAPTER II PRODUCTIONS LTD.

Call Sheet No: 19
(Studio)

PRODUCTION: "THE EMPIRE STRIKES BACK"   DATE: Friday, 6th April, 1979.
DIRECTOR: IRVIN KERSHNER   UNIT CALL: 08:30 hrs.
                                                 STAGE 2:

SETS: STAGE 1:
1. INT. ANTE ROOM (to complete)   Sc: 355 to complete .... Dawn
2. INT. LIVING QUARTERS   Sc: 360pt. .... Day

ARTISTE :	CHARACTER:	D/R:	M/UP:	READY:

1) INT. ANTE-ROOM: Sc. 355 ...... Dawn (to complete)

ARTISTE	CHARACTER	D/R	M/UP	READY
ANTHONY DANIELS	THREEPIO		TO BE ADVISED	
PETER MAYHEW	CHEWBACCA		8.00	8.30

STAND-INS:
ALAN HARRIS	for	Mr. Daniels	TO BE ADVISED	
STEVEN MEEK	for	Mr. Mayhew	8.00	8.

ART DEPT: Threepio robot to explode.
SPECIAL FX: Explosion/ray bolt fx. on Threepio.

ART DEPT: Test 3PO/Chewie back harness. Cloud City Corridors.

---

2) INT. LIVING QUARTERS: Sc. 360 pt. ..... Day

ARTISTE	CHARACTER	D/R	M/UP	READY
CARRIE FISHER	LEIA	76/78	7.45	9.15
HARRISON FORD	HAN	86/88	8.30	9.00
BILLY DEE WILLIAMS	LANDO	90	8.30	9.30
PETER MAYHEW	CHEWBACCA	92	From above	

Stand-in:
LIZ COKE	for	Miss Fisher	)	
JACK DEARLOVE	for	Mr. Ford	)	
QUENTIN PIERRE	for	Mr. Billy Dee Williams)	8.00	8.30
STEVEN MEEK	for	Mr. Mayhew	) From above	

PROPS: Box of 'Threepio' for Chewie.

ELECTRICAL: Sunlight fx. required.

TEST

ART DEPT: Mould: Cathy Munro .... 'Alien'

NURSE: From 2nd Camera Unit.

CATERING: AM & PM breaks for approx.. 110 persons.

DAVID TOMBLIN
Assistant Director

CHAPTER II PRODUCTIONS LTD.   Call Sheet No: 21
                                                          (Studio)

PRODUCTION: "THE EMPIRE STRIKES BACK"   DATE: Tuesday, 10th April, 1979.
DIRECTOR: IRVIN KERSHNER   UNIT CALL: 08:30 hrs.
SETS: STAGE 1:
1. INT. LIVING QUARTERS   Sc. 360 to complete
2. INT. CORRIDOR   Scs.   380, 381, 382, 383, R386,
                                                        S386, 386.

ARTISTE :	CHARACTER:	D/R:	M/UP:	READY:

1) INT. LIVING QUARTERS: Sc. 360 to complete ….Day

ARTISTE	CHARACTER	D/R	M/UP	READY
CARRIE FISHER	LEIA	76/78	7.15	8.45
HARRISON FORD	HAN	86/88	8.15	8.45
BILLY DEE WILLIAMS	LANDO		7.45	8.45
PETER MAYHEW	CHEWBACCA	127	8.15	8.45

STAND-INS:

			M/UP	READY
LIZ COKE	for	Ms. Fisher	8.00	8.30
JACK DEARLOVE	for	Mr. Ford	8.00	8.30
QUENTIN PIERRE	for	Mr. Billy Dee Williams	8.00	8.30
STEVEN MEEK	for	Mr. Mayhew	8.00	8.30

PROPS: Box of 'Threepio' for Chewie.
ELECTRICAL: Sunlights fx. required.

2) INT. CORRIDOR: Scs.   380, 381, 382, R386, S386, 386.

ARTISTE	CHARACTER	D/R	M/UP	READY
CARRIE FISHER	LEIA		From above	
HARRISON FORD	HAN		From above	
BILLY DEE WILLIAMS	LANDO		From above	
PETER MAYHEW	CHEWIE		From above	
MARK HAMILL	LUKE		9.15	10.00
ANTHONY DANIELS	THREEPIO	129	TO BE ADVISED	
KENNY BAKER	ARTOO	131	S/BY AT HOME T.B.A.	
JEREMY BULLOCH	BOBA FETT	133	9.15	10.00

STAND-INS:

			M/UP	READY
LIZ COKE	for	Ms. Fisher	From above	
JACK DEARLOVE	for	Mr. Ford	" "	
QUENTIN PIERRE	for	Mr. Billy Dee Williams	" "	
JOE GIBSON	for	Mr. Hamill	8.30	9.00
ALAN HARRIS	for	Mr. Daniels	8.30	9.00

STUNT ARTISTES:

			M/UP	READY
PETER DIAMOND		STORMTROOPER	S/BY FROM	8.30
COLIN SKEAPING		STORMTROOPER	S/BY FROM	8.30

CROWD ARTISTES:

2 LANDO GUARDS (Sc. 380)	)			
6 STORMTROOPERS	)		8.30	9.00

PROPS: Weapons for Lando Guards.   'Han' frozen dummy. Stormtrooper weapons for Leia and Han Sc. R386.

ARMOURER: To S/BY for practical firing weapons.
SP. FX: 1. S/BY with remote Artoo Unit.
              2. S/BY with laser hit fx. on panel and troopers (Sc. 380).

ART DEPT: 1. Floating Han dummy fx.
              2. Repeatable panel for exploding (Sc. 380)

M/UP   )
HAIR   )   Leia in semi-damage stage (Sc. 380)
W/ROBE)

MEDICAL: Nurse to S/BY from 2nd Unit.

CATERING: AM & PM breaks for 110 people.

                                                 DAVID TOMBLIN
                                                 Assistant Director

(Carrie Fisher (l) Peter Mayhew (c) and Harrison Ford (r) on the set of Cloud City ©1979 LFL)

(Luke Skywalker (Mark Hamill) stumbles upon Boba Fett on Cloud City ©1979 LFL)

April 18th, 1979
• PRODUCTION CALL SHEET ON PAGE 94.

April 19th, 1979
• PRODUCTION CALL SHEET ON PAGE 95.

• The scene where Lando is strangled by Chewbacca is shot on this day.

• The patent for the Millennium Falcon is issued by the US Patent Office to George Lucas.

April 20th, 1979
• PRODUCTION CALL SHEET ON PAGE 96.

• Harrison Ford flies to Morocco for a short holiday with permission from Gary Kurtz.

(Peter Mayhew and Billy Dee Williams on the Cloud City set ©1979 LFL)

• Rehearsal for the bounty hunters on Darth Vader's Star Destroyer.

• Joe Johnston and Phil Tippett complete a short animation of a Tauntaun's legs running.
The animation was created by tracing over footage of the back legs of a horse. The footage of the horse was shot by ILM at Stinson beach in Marin County, California.

• The full-size Millennium Falcon is assembled at Elstree Studios.
The full-size Falcon would be used for exterior shots of the ship in the Rebel Hangar on Hoth, inside the Space Slug, and on Cloud City's exterior landing platform.

April 23rd, 1979
• Mark Hamill shoots his scenes in the Wampa cave, hanging upside down.
Some of these 2nd Unit scenes were directed by Producer Gary Kurtz.

```
                    CHAPTER II PRODUCTIONS LTD.              Call Sheet No: 25
                                                                  (Studio)

PRODUCTION:     "THE EMPIRE STRIKES BACK"        DATE:    Wednesday, 18th April, 1979.
DIRECTOR:       IRVIN KERSHNER                    UNIT CALL:      08:30 hrs.
SETS:                                             STAGE 2:
1.  INT. CLOUD CITY CORRIDORS
2.  INT. LIVING QUARTERS CLOUD CITY (2nd cam.)
```

ARTISTE :		CHARACTER:	D/R:	M/UP:	READY:

---

1) INT. CLOUD CITY CORRIDORS: SCS. 381, 382pt. 383, 385pt. R386, S386, 386.

ARTISTE		CHARACTER	D/R	M/UP	READY
CARRIE FISHER		LEIA	76/78	7.45	9.15
MARK HAMILL		LUKE	80/82	7.45	8.45
BILLY DEE WILLIAMS		LANDO	90	8.15	9.15
PETER MAYHEW		CHEWBACCA	92	8.45	9.15
ANTHONY DANIELS		THREEPIO	129	S/BY TO BE ADVISED	
KENNY BAKER		ARTOO	131	S/BY FROM 9 a.m. at studio	
JEREMY BULLOCH		IMPERIAL OFFICER	133	8.00	8.45

STAND-INS:

LIZ COKE	for	Ms. Fisher		8.30	9.00
JOE GIBSON	for	Mr. Hamill		8.00	8.30
QUENTIN PIERRE	for	Mr. Billy Dee Williams		8.30	9.00
STEVEN MEEK	for	Mr. Mayhew		8.30	9.00

STUNT ARTISTES:

COLIN SKEAPING		STUNT STORMTROOPER (Sc. 381pt.)	S/BY from 8.30 a.m.	

CROWD ARTISTES:

4 STORMTROOPERS (Sc. 381)		8.00	8.30

PROPS: Weapons for Lando Guards. 'Han' frozen dummy. Threepio parts for Chewie's back.
            Bindings on Chewie. Wrist radio transmitter for Lando (Sc. 385pt.)

SP. FX: 1. S/BY with remote Artoo unit.
            2. S/BY with explosion/laser hit from Stormtrooper (Sc. 381).

WARDROBE: Change of costume for Leia Sc. 381.

---

2) INT. LIVING QUARTERS: Scs. 380pt. (Matte), 385pt. (2nd camera)

MARK HAMILL		LUKE	80/82	from Main Unit	
JOHN HILLIS		LANDO'S AIDE	Hammer Hse.	8.00	8.30

STAND-IN:

JOHN GIBSON	for Mr. Hamill		from above

PROPS: Luke's gun. Brain augmentor.

ART DEPT: Brain augmentor to flash on cue Sc. 385pt.

MEDICAL: Nurse to S/BY from 2nd Unit.

CATERING: AM & PM breaks for 95 persons on Stage 2.

```
                                                      DAVID TOMBLIN
                                                      Assistant Director
```

CHAPTER II PRODUCTIONS LTD.   Call Sheet No: 26
                                                    (Studio)

PRODUCTION: "THE EMPIRE STRIKES BACK"   DATE: Thursday, 19th April, 1979.
DIRECTOR: IRVIN KERSHNER   UNIT CALL: 08:30 hrs.
SETS: STAGE 2:
1. INT. CLOUD CITY CORRIDORS
2. INT. LIVING QUARTERS CLOUD CITY (2ⁿᵈ cam.)

ARTISTE :		CHARACTER:	D/R:	M/UP:	READY:

1) INT. CLOUD CITY CORRIDORS: SCS. ….. 365pt,382pt,381pt,R386, S386, 386.

CARRIE FISHER		LEIA	76/78	7.15	8.45
BILLY DEE WILLIAMS		LANDO	90	7.45	8.45
PETER MAYHEW		CHEWBACCA	92	8.15	8.45
ANTHONY DANIELS		THREEPIO	129	S/BY TO BE ADVISED	
KENNY BAKER		ARTOO	131	S/BY TO BE ADVISED	
JEREMY BULLOCH		IMPERIAL OFFICER	133	8.00	8.30
JOHN HOLLIS		LANDO'S AIDE	Hammer Hse		

STAND-INS:

LIZ COKE	for	Ms. Fisher		8.30	9.00
JOE GIBSON	for	Mr. Hamill		8.00	8.30
QUENTIN PIERRE	for	Mr. Billy Dee Williams		8.30	9.00
STEVEN MEEK	for	Mr. Mayhew		8.30	9.00
ALAN HARRIS	for	Mr. Daniels		TO BE ADVISED	

STUNT ARTISTES:
COLIN SKEAPING   STUNT STORMTROOPER (Sc. 381pt.)   S/BY from 8.30 a.m.

CROWD ARTISTES:

4 STORMTROOPERS (Sc. 381)		8.00	8.30
12 LANDO GUARDS		7.30	8.30

PROPS: Weapons for Lando Guards. 'Han' frozen dummy. Threepio parts for Chewie's back.
               Bindings on Chewie. Wrist radio transmitter for Lando (Sc. 385pt.)

SP. FX: 1. S/BY with remote Artoo unit.
               2. S/BY with explosion/laser hit from Stormtrooper (Sc. 381).

WARDROBE: Change of costume for Leia

---

2) INT. LIVING QUARTERS: Scs. 380pt. (Matte), 385pt. (2nd camera)

MARK HAMILL		LUKE	80/82	TO BE ADVISED
JOHN HILLIS		LANDO'S AIDE	Hammer Hse.	FROM MAIN UNIT

STAND-IN:
JOHN GIBSON   for Mr. Hamill   from above

PROPS: Luke's gun. Brain augmentor.

ART DEPT: Brain augmentor to flash on cue Sc. 385pt.

MEDICAL: Nurse to S/BY from 2ⁿᵈ Unit.

CATERING: AM & PM breaks for 95 persons on Stage 2.

                                              DAVID TOMBLIN
                                              Assistant Director

```
                    CHAPTER II PRODUCTIONS LTD.            Call Sheet No: 27
                                                              (Studio)

PRODUCTION:    "THE EMPIRE STRIKES BACK"        DATE:    Friday, 20th April, 1979.
DIRECTOR:      IRVIN KERSHNER                   UNIT CALL:         08:30 hrs.
SET:                                            STAGE 2:
INT. CLOUD CITY CORRIDORS
5 REHEARSALS (SEE BELOW)
```

ARTISTE :	CHARACTER:	D/R:	M/UP:	READY:

1) INT. CLOUD CITY CORRIDORS: SCS. ….. 305pt. to complete, R386,S386,386,301pt.,380,383pt.

ARTISTE	CHARACTER	D/R	M/UP	READY
CARRIE FISHER	LEIA	76/78	7.15	8.45
MARK HAMILL	LUKE	80/82	S/BY at home	
BILLY DEE WILLIAMS	LANDO	90	7.45	8.45
PETER MAYHEW	CHEWBACCA	92	8.15	8.45
ANTHONY DANIELS	THREEPIO	129	S/BY from	9.00
KENNY BAKER	ARTOO	131	S/BY TO BE ADVISED	
JEREMY BULLOCH	IMPERIAL OFFICER/		8.00	8.30
	BOBA FETT			

STAND-INS:

				M/UP	READY
LIZ COKE	for	Ms. Fisher		8.00	8.30
JOE GIBSON	for	Mr. Hamill		10.00	10.30
QUENTIN PIERRE	for	Mr. B. D. Williams		8.00	8.30
STEVEN MEEK	for	Mr. Mayhew		8.00	8.30
ALAN HARRIS	for	Mr. Daniels		TO BE ADVISED	

CROWD ARTISTES:

		READY
4 STORMTROOPERS (Sc. 381)	8.00	8.30

PROPS: Threepio parts for Chewie's back. Bindings on Chewie. Wrist radio transmitter for
              Lando (Sc. 385pt.)

SP. FX: 1. S/BY with remote Artoo unit.
              2. S/BY with explosion/laser hit from Stormtrooper (Sc. 381).

2. REHEARSAL BOUNTY HUNTERS FOR VADER'S SHIP: 2 p.m.

3. REHEARSAL DAVE PROWSE/DARTH VADER

MEDICAL: Nurse to S/BY on set from 8.30 a.m.

CATERING: AM & PM breaks for 95 persons on Stage 2.

                                                    DAVID TOMBLIN
                                                    Assistant Director

(Lando Calrissian (Billy Dee Williams) (l) and an Imperial Officer (Jeremy Bulloch) (r) escorts Leia and Chewbacca through Cloud City ©1979 LFL)

April 24ᵗʰ, 1979

• PRODUCTION CALL SHEET ON PAGE 98.

• Production wraps shooting on the Cloud City sets.

April 25ᵗʰ, 1979

• PRODUCTION CALL SHEETS ON PAGE 99-100.

April 26ᵗʰ, 1979

• The scene with the bounty hunters on Darth Vader's Star Destroyer is completed.

April 27ᵗʰ, 1979

• Footage from Norway is ready for George Lucas to screen.
The footage was disappointing to those who saw it as it was shaky and uneven.

• Producer Robert Watts sends out a memo to production stating that the Main Hangar shooting will begin on Friday, May 18ᵗʰ, 1979 as planned regardless of the production's schedule status at the time.

```
                        CHAPTER II PRODUCTIONS LTD.        Call Sheet No: 29
                                                              (Studio)

    PRODUCTION:    "THE EMPIRE STRIKES BACK"      DATE:   Tuesday, 24th April, 1979.
    DIRECTOR:      IRVIN KERSHNER                  UNIT CALL:          08:30 hrs.

    SET:                                           STAGE 5
    INT. VADER'S STARDESTROYER
```

ARTISTE :		CHARACTER:	D/R:	M/UP:	READY:

INT. VADER'S STARDESTROYER: Scs. 55pt., 59pt., 280pt.

ARTISTE		CHARACTER	D/R	M/UP	READY
DAVE PROWSE		VADER	133	8.00	8.30
JULIAN GLOVER		VEERS	Stage 4:37B	7.45	8.30
KENNETH COLLEY		PIETT	379	7.45	8.30
MICHAEL SHEARD		OZZEL	380	7.45	8.30

STAND-INS:

MORAY BUSH	for	Mr. Prowse)			
ALAN MEACHAM	for	Mr. Colley)		8.00	8.30
ALAN HARRIS	for	Mr. Glover)			
A.N. OTHER	for	Mr. Sheard)			

CROWD ARTISTES:

4 OFFICERS	)		
8 CONTROLLERS	)	7.30	8.30

WARDROBE: Change of insignia for Piett Sc. 280 pt.

ELECTRICAL: Possible light fx. from asteroid collision Sc. 280.

BLUE SCREEN: Stan Sayer to S/BY on set from 8.30

CATERING: AM & PM for 100 persons on Stage 5.

MEDICAL: Nurse to S/BY on Stage 5 from 8.30 a.m.

DAVID TOMBLIN
Assistant Director

CHAPTER II PRODUCTIONS LTD.   Call Sheet No: 30
                                                    (Studio)

PRODUCTION: "THE EMPIRE STRIKES BACK"   DATE: Wednesday, 25th April, 1979.
DIRECTOR: IRVIN KERSHNER   UNIT CALL: 08:30 hrs.

SET: STAGE 5
INT. VADER'S STARDESTROYER   Scs. 55 to complete, 59pt., 280pt.,
                                             316, 334, T429, T430, S432

ARTISTE :		CHARACTER:	D/R:	M/UP:	READY:
DAVE PROWSE		VADER	133	8.00	8.30
JULIAN GLOVER		VEERS	378	8.00	8.30
KENNETH COLLEY		PIETT	379	8.00	8.30
MICHAEL SHEARD		OZZEL	380	8.00	8.30
MICHAEL CULVER		NEEDA	432	7.45	8.30
JEREMY BULLOCH		BOBA FETT	131	S/BY TO BE ADVISED	
ROBIN SCOBEY		CONTROLLER	433	S/BY TO BE ADVISED	

STAND-INS:
ROY EVERSON	for	Dave Prowse	)		
ALAN HARRIS	for	Julian Glover	)		
ALAN MEACHAM	for	Kenneth Colley	)	8.00	8.30
A.N. OTHER	for	Michael Sheard	)		

CROWD ARTISTES:
3 OFFICERS	)				
8 CONTROLLERS	)			8.00	8.30
CATHY MUNRO		BOUNTY HUNTER (1) (Lobster Head)		8.30	10.30
A.N. OTHER		BOUNTY HUNTER (2) (Lizard Head)		8.30	10.30
MORAY BUSH		BOUNTY HUNTER (3) (Human)		8.30	10.30
CHRIS PARSONS		BOUNTY HUNTER (4) (Insect Head)		8.30	10.30

PROPS: Weapons for Boba Fett and other Bounty Hunters. Respirators for Lobster Head.

ELECTRICAL: Light fx. Sc. 280 required for Asteroid Collision.

WARDROBE: Change of Insignia for Piett Sc. 280 pt.

BLUE SCREEN: Stan Sayer to S/BY on set from 8.30

CATERING: AM & PM for 100 persons on Stage 5.

ART DEPT./SFX: 1. Space probe … Bounty Hunter (5) required.
                  2. War droid ….. Bounty Hunter (6) required.

STILLS SESSION

BILLY DEE WILLIAMS ………. 11.30 a.m. Makeup/Hair …….. 2.30 Ready

---

DAVID TOMBLIN
Assistant Director

CHAPTER II PRODUCTIONS LTD.   Call Sheet No: 30A
                                          (Studio)

PRODUCTION: "THE EMPIRE STRIKES BACK"   DATE: Wednesday, 25th April, 1979.
DIRECTOR: IRVIN KERSHNER   UNIT CALL: 08:30 hrs.

SET: STAGE 1
INT./EXT. ICE GORGE   Scs. 21-22k to complete

ARTISTE :		CHARACTER:	D/R:	M/UP:	READY:
MARK HAMILL		LUKE	80/82	8.00	8.45
DES WEBB		WAMPA		S/BY FROM 8.30	
STAND-INS:					
JOE GIBSON	for	Mr. Hamill		8.00	8.30
STUNT ARTISTES:					
PETER DIAMOND		Co-ordinator	)		
COLIN SKEAPING		Double Luke	)	S/BY FROM 8.30	

PROPS: Laser sword. Luke's equipment. Mattresses for fall pad.

MAKEUP: 1. Frozen blood fx. on Luke.
             2. S/BY with articulated Wampa arm.

SPECIAL FX: To S/BY with wind/snow fx.

ART DEPT: 1. Hanging harness fx. (D. Botell) required.
             2. Frozen boots required (SC. 22k).

MEDICAL: Nurse to S/BY from 08.30 a.m.

CATERING: AM & PM breaks on Stage 1 for approximately 45 persons.

TRANSPORT:

Roy Najda to collect Mr. Hamill at 7.15 a.m. to arrive at tsutiod by 8 a.m.

DAVID TOMBLIN
Assistant Director

(the Millennium Falcon is assembled at Elstree Studios on the Hoth hangar set ©1979 LFL)

(Darth Vader (David Prowse) (l) instructs Boba Fett (Jeremy Bulloch) (r) "No disintegrations!"
©1979 LFL)

(Gary Kurz (l) directs Mark Hamill (r) in the Wampa cave ©1979 LFL)

May, 1979
• ILM conducts an AT-AT Walker screen test.
It was decided that shooting the AT-ATs against blue screen didn't look right so they decided to shoot them against matte paintings.

May 1st, 1979
• PRODUCTION CALL SHEET ON PAGE 103.

May 2nd, 1979
• PRODUCTION CALL SHEET ON PAGE 104.

• Filming of Darth Vader in his meditation sphere begins.

May 4th, 1979
• PRODUCTION CALL SHEET ON PAGE 105.

• Harrison Ford returns from vacation with a gastric infection.

CHAPTER II PRODUCTIONS LTD.   Call Sheet No: 34
                                         (Studio)

PRODUCTION: "THE EMPIRE STRIKES BACK"   DATE: Tuesday, 1st May, 1979.
DIRECTOR: IRVIN KERSHNER   UNIT CALL: 08:30 hrs.

1. INT. VADER'S STARDESTROYER . . . . STAGE 5:
                                         Scs. 280pt. (Piett), T430,S432,T429.55pt

2.   2nd Camera: ICE CORRIDOR Sc.44pt. . . . . STAGE 1

ARTISTE :		CHARACTER:	D/R:	M/UP:	READY:
DAVE PROWSE		VADER	133	8.00	8.30
KENNETH COLLEY		PIETT	379	8.00	8.30
STAND-INS:					
ROY EVERSON	for	Dave Prowse		8.00	8.30
ALAN MEACHAM	for	Kenneth Colley		8.00	8.30
CROWD ARTISTES:					
2 OFFICERS			)		
10 CONTROLLERS			)	8.00	8.30
MIKE REYNELL		Deck Officer	)		

BLUE SCREEN: Stan Sayer to S/BY on set from 8.30 a.m.

CATERING: AM & PM for 110 persons on Stage 5.

MEDICAL: Nurse to S/BY on Stage 5 from 8.30 a.m.

                                         DAVID TOMBLIN
                                         Assistant Director

REHEARSAL/FENCING: MARK HAMILL . . . . 10.30 a.m.

2ND CAMERA UNIT: INT. ICE CORRIDOR (Sc. 44pt.)

1. Remote Artoo Unit required.
2. Atmosphere fx.

TRANSPORT: Roy Najda to collect Mr. Hamill at 9.45 a.m. to arrive by 10.30 a.m.

CHAPTER II PRODUCTIONS LTD.   Call Sheet No: 35
                                          (Studio)

PRODUCTION: "THE EMPIRE STRIKES BACK"   DATE: Wednesday, 2nd May, 1979.
DIRECTOR: IRVIN KERSHNER   UNIT CALL: 08:30 hrs.
SETS:
1. INT. VADER'S STARDESTROYER . . . .   STAGE 5: Scs. 219, T430 to comp.
                                                                  T429 to comp, 280 pt.
                                                        (2nd camera): Scs. 55pt. 280pt.
2. INT. VADER'S CHAMBER . . . .   Rehearsal/Lineup Sc. 244. (Stage 5)   3. 2nd
Camera: ICE CORRIDOE . . . .   Stage 1: Sc.44pt.

ARTISTE :		CHARACTER:	D/R:	M/UP:	READY:
1. INT. VADER'S STARDESTROYER: Scs. 219, T430to comp.,T429 to comp., 280pt. & (2nd cam as above)					
DAVE PROWSE		VADER	133	8.00	8.30
KENNETH COLLEY		PIETT	379	8.00	8.30
MICHAEL CULVER		NEEDA	433	8.00	8.30
STAND-INS:					
ROY EVERSON	for	Dave Prowse		8.00	8.30
ALAN MEACHAM	for	Kenneth Colley		8.00	8.30
ALAN HARRIS	for	Michael Culver		8.00	8.30
CROWD ARTISTES:					
2 OFFICERS			)		
10 CONTROLLERS			)	8.00	8.30
MIKE REYNELL		Deck Officer	)		

BLUE SCREEN: Stan Sayer to S/BY on set from 8.30 a.m.

MEDICAL: Nurse to S/BY on Stage 5 from 8.30 a.m.

CATERING: AM & PM for 110 persons on Stage 5.
                   AM Break for 40 persons on Stage 1

---

2. INT. VADER'S CHAMBER: REHEARSAL/LINEUP: Sc. 244   (STAGE 5)

DAVE PROWSE   Vader)   Rehearsal From above
KENNETH COLLEY   Piett)

---

3. INT.ICE CORRIDOE (Sc. 44pt.) – 2nd camera unit   (STAGE 1)

1. Remote Artoo Unite required.
2. Atmosphere fx.

                                                  DAVID TOMBLIN
                                                  Assistant Director

CHAPTER II PRODUCTIONS LTD.   <u>Call Sheet No: 37</u>
(Studio)

PRODUCTION:	"THE EMPIRE STRIKES BACK"	<u>DATE</u>:	Friday, 4th May, 1979.	
DIRECTOR:	IRVIN KERSHNER	<u>UNIT CALL</u>:	08:30 hrs.	

SETS:
1. INT. VADER'S CHAMBER . . . . (STAGE 5) . . . . . .   Scs. 59pt., 244 to comp., 294pt.
2. INT. LUKE'S SNOWSPEEDER. . . . (STAGE 8) . . . .   Prelight/Rehearsal

ARTISTE :		CHARACTER:	D/R:	M/UP:	READY:
1. INT. VADER'S CHAMBER: Scs. 59pt., 244 to comp., 294pt.				(Stage 5)	
DAVE PROWSE		VADER	133	8.00	8.30
JULIAN GLOVER		VEERS	378	8.00	8.30
KENNETH COLLEY		PIETT	379	8.30	9.00
STAND-INS:					
ROY EVERSON	for	Mr. Prowse	)		
ALAN HARRIS	for	Mr. Glover	)	8.00	8.30
ALAN MEACHAM	for	Mr. Colley	)		
CROWD ARTISTES:					
2 VADER GUARDS			)		
2 CONTROLLERS			)	7.45	8.30

EDITORIAL:	Moviola with Plate Sc. 59 required on set.
SFX:	S/BY with retractable "chamber" fx.
ELECTRICAL:	1. Flashing red light fx. (Sc. 294pt.)
	2. Meditation light fx. (Sc. 59)
	3. Hologram light fx. on Vader (Sc. 294pt.)
CAMERA DEPT:	Camera crane required with driver.

2. INT. LUKE'S SNOWSPEEDER: Rehearsal/Prelight.   (STAGE 8)

MARK HAMILL		LUKE	Fencing rehearsal	10.30	
STAND-IN:					
JOE GIBSON	for	Mr. Hamill		10.30	11.00

BLUE BACKING: Stan Sayer to S/BY from 8.30 a.m.

CATERING:	AM & PM breaks for 110 persons on Stage 5 please.
TRANSPORT:	Roy Nadja to collect Mr. Hamill at 9.45 a.m. to arrive by 10.30 a.m.

DAVID TOMBLIN
Assistant Director

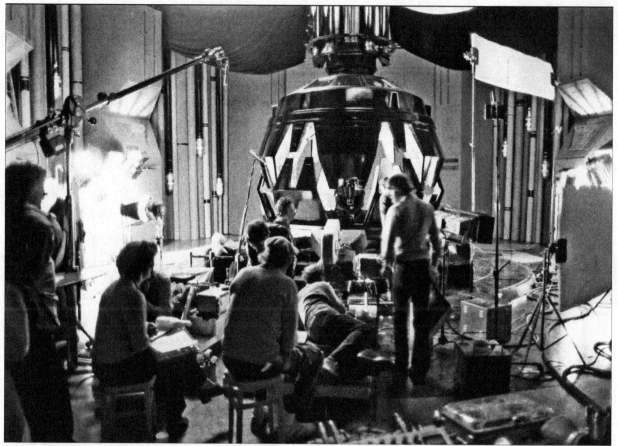

(The EMPIRE crew shoot Darth Vader (David Prowse) in his meditation chamber ©1979 LFL)

May 6th, 1979

• George Lucas flies to London to help get production back on schedule.

May 7th, 1979

• Gary Kurtz gives Mark and Marilou Hamill a baby shower as they expect their first born, Nathan Hamill.

• Carrie Fisher returns to London after a short vacation in the United States.

May 8th-10th, 1979

• Interior Millennium Falcon cockpit scenes are filmed during this time.

(Mark and Marilou Hamill ©1979 LFL)

May 9th, 1979

• PRODUCTION CALL SHEET ON PAGE 108.

May 9th-10th, 1979

• The Snowspeeder cockpit scenes are shot against blue screen.

May 10th, 1979

• A small fire breaks out on the Millennium Falcon set.

• 2nd Unit shoots the AT-AT cockpit scenes.

May 12th, 1979

• George Lucas takes Sir Alec Guinness to lunch at Guinness' favorite restaurant – Neal's in Covent Garden.

May 13th, 1979

• Alan Arnold interviews Editor Paul Hirsch, and Director Irvin Kershner for the book, *A Journal of the Making of the Empire Strikes Back.*

• George Lucas flies back to the United States.

May 14th, 1979

• PRODUCTION CALL SHEET ON PAGE 109.

May 16th, 1979

• PRODUCTION CALL SHEET ON PAGE 110.

May 17th, 1979

• PRODUCTION CALL SHEET ON PAGE 111.

May 17th-18th, 1979

• 1st Unit moves to the Prison Cell set to shoot the scenes of Han, Leia, and Chewie.

CHAPTER II PRODUCTIONS LTD.   Call Sheet No: 39
                                                    (Studio)

PRODUCTION: "THE EMPIRE STRIKES BACK"   DATE: Wednesday, 9th May, 1979.
DIRECTOR: IRVIN KERSHNER   UNIT CALL: 08:30 hrs.
SETS: STAGE 8:
1. INT. LUKE'S SNOWSPEEDER   Scs: 88,91,92,98,100,103,104,105,
                                               107,108,140,147,149,152,155pt.,
                                               156pt.,163pt.

2. INT. ZEV'S SNOWSPEEDER   Scs: 38, R40.
3. INT. ZEV'S SNOWSPEEDER   Scs: 148, 150, 151
4. INT. WEDGE'S SNOWSPEEDER   Scs: 119,12,122,124,125,127,131,
                                               132,134.
5. INT. HOBBIE'S SNOWSPEEDER   Scs: 101, U194.

ARTISTE :	CHARACTER:	D/R:	M/UP:	READY:
MARK HAMILL	LUKE	80/82	8.00	8.45
JOHN MORTON	DACK	131	8.00	8.45
DENIS LAWSON	WEDGE	Stage 4	8.30	9.00
RICHARD OLDFIELD	HOBBIE	Stage 4	8.30	9.00
EUGENE LIPINKSI	WEDGE'S GUNNER	Stage 4	8.30	9.00
CHRISTOPHER MALCOLM	ZEV	Stage 4	8.30	9.00

STAND-INS:
JOE GIBSON   for   Mr. Hamill   )
JACK DEARLOVE   for   Mr. Morton   )
ALAN MEACHAM   for   Mr. Lawson   )   8.00   8.30
ALAN HARRIS   for   Mr. Oldfield   )

CROWD ARTISTES:
2 CROWD GUNNERS   8.00   8.30

BLUE BACKING: Stan Sayer to S/BY from 8.30 am.

MAKEUP: Blood fx. on Dack; Face wound Zev required (Sc. 148);
                     Wound fx. Hobbie (Sc. U194).

ELECTRICAL: Moving light fx. required.

EDITORIAL: Moviola with related clips required.

SP.FX: 1. Smouldering panel fx.
                     2. Flash bar fx. required.

CAMERA: Crane required.

CATERING: AM & PM breaks for 110 persons on Stage 8
────
TRANSPORT:
Roy Nadja to collect Mr. Hamill at 7.15 a.m. to arrive by 8 a.m.

DAVID TOMBLIN
Assistant Director

```
                    CHAPTER II PRODUCTIONS LTD.              Call Sheet No: 42
                                                                  (Studio)

PRODUCTION:     "THE EMPIRE STRIKES BACK"        DATE:   Monday, 14th May, 1979.
DIRECTOR:       IRVIN KERSHNER                   UNIT CALL:      08:30 hrs.
SETS:
1.  INT. CORRIDOE/DINING ROOM        (Stage 2)   Scs. 364pt. sequence to complete.
2.  S/BY EXT. FALCON HATCH           (Stage 9)   Sc.  423

_____

ARTISTE  :                       CHARACTER:      D/R:      M/UP:          READY:
_____

1) INT. CORRIDOR/DINING ROOM:  Scs. 364pt. sequence to complete

CARRIE FISHER                    LEIA           76/78     7.15           8.45
HARRISON FORD                    HAN            86/88     8.15           8.45
BILLY DEE WILLIAMS               LANDO          90        7.15           8.45
PETER MAYHEW                     CHEWBACCA      92        8.00           8.45
DAVE PROWSE                      DARTH VADER    133       8.15           8.45
JEREMY BULLOCH                   BOBA FETT      131       8.15           8.45
JOHN HOLLIS                      LANDO'S AIDE   Hammer Hse 8.15          8.45

STAND-INS:
CAROLINE CLARKSON                for    Ms. Fisher          )
JACK DEARLOVE                    for    Mr. Ford            )
QUENTIN PIERRE                   for    Mr. B. D. Williams  )   8.00     8.30
STEVEN MEEK                      for    Mr. Mayhew          )
ROY EVERSON                      for    Mr. Prowse          )

CROWD ARTISTES:
6 STORMTROOPERS                                            7.45         8.30
1 WOMAN (CLOUD CITY)                                       7.45         8.30
2 MALE CIVILIANS                                           8.00         8.30

STUNT ARTISTES:
PETER DIAMOND                                    TO S/BY FROM          8.30
COLIN SKEAPING                                       "        "         "
BOB ANDERSON                                         "        "         "

PROPS:              Banquet dressing. Weapons for Stormtroopers/Boba Fett.
                    S/BY with mattresses for short fight sequence.
SFX.ART DEPT:       1)  Lando's aide brain agumentor to turn on when cued.
                    2)  Laser hit explosion fx.
                    3)  Gun on jerk wire for reverse action fx.

_____

2) S/BY EXT. FALCON HATCH:  Sc. 423

MARK HAMILL                      LUKE              From 2nd Unit
BILLY DEE WILLIAMS               LANDO             From above

STAND-INS: . . . . . . . . . . . . . . . . . . . . . . . From above
Plus: JOE GIBSON          for     Mr. Hamill              From 2nd Unit

STUNT:
PETER DIAMOND/COLIN SKEAPING                       To S/BY from above

PROPS:       Luke's gun. Belt harness for Lando.

M/UP:        Luke wounded aftermath of Vader fight.

WARDROBE:    Luke wounded/damaged aftermath of Vader fight.

SFX:         Explosion fx. on hull.

_____

CATERING:    AM Break for 120 persons (2 trolleys) on Stage 2.
             PM Break - TO BE ADVISED.

                                              DAVID TOMBLIN
                                              Assistant Director
```

CHAPTER II PRODUCTIONS LTD.   Call Sheet No: 44
                                                    (Studio)

PRODUCTION: "THE EMPIRE STRIKES BACK"   DATE: Monday, 16th May, 1979.
DIRECTOR: IRVIN KERSHNER   UNIT CALL: 08:30 hrs.
SETS: STAGE 5:
1. INT. MILLENNIUM FALCON COCKPIT
        a) Cavern . . . .   Scs. 282, 296, 300, 301, 302.
        b) Space . . . .   Scs. 337, 214, 215, 216, 221, 222,
                                                            223, 235, 260, 261.

ARTISTE :	CHARACTER:	D/R:	M/UP:	READY:

1.   INT. MILLENNIUM FALCON:

ARTISTE	CHARACTER	D/R	M/UP	READY
CARRIE FISHER	LEIA	76/78	7.30	9.00
HARRISON FORD	HAN	86/88	8.30	9.00
ANTHONY DANIELS	THREEPIO	129	8.30	9.00
PETER MAYHEW	CHEWBACCA	92	8.30	9.00

STAND-INS:
CAROLINE CLARKSON	for	Ms. Fisher	)	
JACK DEARLOVE	for	Mr. Ford	)	
ALAN HARRIS	for	Mr. Daniels	) 8.00	8.30
STEVEN MEEK	for	Mr. Mayhew	)	

PROPS: Loose dressing in Cabin Sc. 282pt. Ship's log Sc. 337.

CAMERA: Sea head fx. required.

ART DEPT: Computer map/flashing console fx.

MAKEUP: Mynock bird reqd. for Sc. 296.

ELECTRICAL: Systems and engine lights to dim out Sc. 282.

SFX: Laser/flak hit fx. required.

CATERING: AM & PM breaks for 100 people on Stage 5 please.

                                                    DAVID TOMBLIN
                                                    Assistant Director

EDITOR'S NOTE: Did you know that it was Carrie Fisher's companion's
                    birthday on May 16th?

```
                          CHAPTER II PRODUCTIONS LTD.              Call Sheet No: 42
                                                                        (Studio)

    PRODUCTION:    "THE EMPIRE STRIKES BACK"       DATE:   Thursday, 17th May, 1979.
    DIRECTOR:      IRVIN KERSHNER                   UNIT CALL:       08.30 hrs.
    SET:                                            STAGE 2:
    INT. LARGE CELL                                 Scs. 370, 372

    ---------------------------------------------------------------------------------

    ARTISTE  :                       CHARACTER:       D/R:        M/UP:         READY:

    ---------------------------------------------------------------------------------

    1) INT. CORRIDOR/DINING ROOM:  Scs. 364pt. sequence to complete

    CARRIE FISHER                    LEIA            76/78    8.00   8.30 reh.    9.30
    HARRISON FORD                    HAN             86/88           8.30 reh.    9.30
    BILLY DEE WILLIAMS               LANDO           90       8.00   8.30 reh.    Then 2nd
                                                                                  Unit
    ANTHONY DANIELS                  THREEPIO        129             8.00         8.30
    PETER MAYHEW                     CHEWBACCA       92              8.00         8.30


    STAND-INS:
    CAROLINE CLARKSON                for    Ms. Fisher            )
    JACK DEARLOVE                    for    Mr. Ford              )
    QUENTIN PIERRE                   for    Mr. Dee Williams      )    8.00        8.30
    ALAN HARRIS                      for    Mr. Daniels           )
    STEVEN MEEK                      for    Mr. Mayhew            )


    STUNT ARTISTES:
    PETER DIAMOND                    ARRANGER               TO S/BY FROM         8.00
    A.N. OTHER                       LANDO GUARD            Rehearsal            8.30
    A.N. OTHER                       LANDO GUARD            Rehearsal            8.30


    PROPS:              Dummy weapons for Lando Guards.  Tools for mending Threepio.
                        Weapons for Stormtroopers.  Mattresses


    CROWD ARTISTES:
    4 STORMTROOPERS                                         8.00                 9.00

    ART DEPT/            1.  Screeching noise fx. reqd.
    SPECIAL FX:          2.  Cut down remote 3PO with practical light fx.



    MAKEUP:              1.  Han after effects of torture.
                         2.  Leia after effects of torture.
                         3.  S/BY with blood fx. on Han and Lando.


    WARDROBE:            1.  Leia without jacket for Sc. 372.
                         2.  S/BY with arm and knee pads for principals.

    ELECTRICAL:          Pulsating light fx. Sc. 370.

    CATERING:            AM & PM breaks for 110 persons on Stage 2 please.


                                                      DAVID TOMBLIN
                                                      Assistant Director


    NOTE:    Protective overshoes are available in the Production Office
             for any crew members requiring same.
```

May 17th-18th, 1979 (cont.)

• 2nd Unit shoots Mark Hamill and Billy Dee Williams in a scene ultimately cut from the final film: Lando rescues Luke from beneath Cloud City atop the Millennium Falcon.

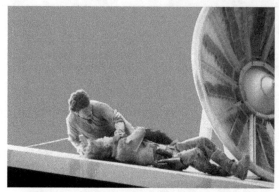

May 18th, 1979

• Scheduled start date of shooting on the main Rebel Hangar set.

This was pushed back to May 22nd.

(Billy Dee Williams and Mark Hamill in the deleted rescue scene ©1979 LFL)

May 20th, 1979

• The scene in which C-3PO tells R2-D2 to come inside as the small astromech scans for signs of life in the approaching blizzard on Hoth is shot.

• Leia's speech to the pilots about getting the transports to safety is shot as well.

(Anthony Daniels as C-3PO telling R2-D2 to come back inside the Rebel base ©1979 LFL)

May 22nd, 1979

• The *Empire* set at Elstree that houses the Rebel Hangar (which includes the full-size Millennium Falcon, X-wing fighters, Snowspeeders, and various droids and humans) begins shooting on this day.

(Elstree Studios dressed as the Rebel Hangar on Hoth ©1979 LFL)

• May 30th–31st, 1979

Scenes are shot of Luke and Dack taking off in their Snowspeeder, Han is told that Luke is missing, and cracks start to open above the Millennium Falcon in the hangar.

May 31st, 1979

• Production Designer John Barry collapses on set while directing 2nd Unit on *Empire*.

• Original expiration date of Kenner's Boba Fett mail-away offer.
Kenner offered a free Boba Fett figure if you mailed in four proofs of purchase.

The offer was extended through March 31st, 1980 and again until December 31st, 1980. Both times stickers were applied to the cardbacks over the original expiration date to avoid printing new cardbacks. The offer appeared on Kenner's *Star Wars* 20-back action figure packaging.

• ILM conducts screen tests of the AT-AT Walker's walking motion.

May 31st, 1979 (cont.)

• Unit Production Note stating that the studio is having the roads resurfaced on 2/6/79, 3/6/79, and 6/4/79 and that the main gate will be closed on June 2nd & 3rd.

Summer 1979

• *Bantha Tracks*, issue 5: First reveal about Boba Fett's history connected to the Clone Wars.

George Lucas: *"Not much is known about Boba Fett. He wears part of the uniform of the Imperial Shocktroopers, warriors from the olden time. Shocktroopers came from the far side of the galaxy and there aren't many of them left. They were wiped out by the Jedi Knights during the Clone Wars."*

June 1st, 1979

• Kenner includes the Boba Fett action figure in the case assortment of figures shipped to retailers.

• The cast and crew move back to the cockpit of the Millennium Falcon set.

• Production Designer John Barry dies unexpectedly from meningitis while in the hospital.

June 2nd-3rd, 1979

• Filming begins on the Darth Vader/Luke Skywalker duel.
Vader's role in the duel was primarily performed by sword master Bob Anderson.

June 4th, 1979

• PRODUCTION CALL SHEETS ON PAGES 115-116.

• Internal ILM typed memo listing all models and sets as well as the date they were started and the date they are needed.
Also included a list of completed sets and models at the time; the Millennium Falcon (Full Size), Millennium Falcon (Baby), Stardestroyer (Small), Tie Ship (Full Size), Tie Ship (Baby), X-wing, Asteroid Crater, Asteroid Chasm, Asteroid Surface, Asteroids, Junk, and Imperial Fleet (Tie and Stardestroyers)[sic].

• Health Notice issued to all crew members due to John Barry's sudden death caused by meningitis.

• Listed on internal ILM memo as date "8ft. Stardestroyer" model needed.

```
                    CHAPTER II PRODUCTIONS LTD.              Call Sheet No: 56
                                                                  (Studio)

PRODUCTION:     "THE EMPIRE STRIKES BACK"          DATE:   Monday, 4th June, 1979.
DIRECTOR:       IRVIN KERSHNER                      UNIT CALL:      08:30 hrs.
SETS:                                              STAGE 8:
INT. MILLENNIUM FALCON COCKPIT
     a)  Cavern . . . . . . . . . . . . . . . . . .   Scs. 302.
     b)  Space . . . . . . . . . . . . . . . . .      Scs. 337, 214, 215, 216, 221, 222,
                                                           223, 235, 260, 321, 323, 324,
                                                           325.
_____

ARTISTE  :                         CHARACTER:     D/R:       M/UP:        READY:
_____

INT. MILLENNIUM FALCON:

CARRIE FISHER                      LEIA           76/78      7.30         9.00
HARRISON FORD                      HAN            86/88      8.30         9.00
ANTHONY DANIELS                    THREEPIO       129        8.30         9.00
PETER MAYHEW                       CHEWBACCA      92         8.30         9.00

STAND-INS:
JANE HENLEY         for    Ms. Fisher   )
JACK DEARLOVE       for    Mr. Ford     )
ALAN HARRIS         for    Mr. Daniels  )            8.00         8.30
STEVEN MEEK         for    Mr. Mayhew   )


PROPS:          Loose dressing in Cabin.  Ship's log Sc. 337.

CAMERA:         Sea head fx. required.

ART DEPT:       Computer map/flashing console fx.


ELECTRICAL:     Systems and engine lights to dim out.

SPECIAL FX:     Laser/flak hit fx. required.

CATERING:       AM & PM breaks for 100 people on Stage 8 please.



                                             DAVID TOMBLIN
                                             Assistant Director
```

<u>CHAPTER II PRODUCTIONS LTD.</u>   <u>Call Sheet No: 56A</u>
                                                           (Studio)

PRODUCTION: "THE EMPIRE STRIKES BACK"   <u>DATE</u>:   Monday, 4th June, 1979.
<u>DIRECTOR</u>:   IRVIN KERSHNER   <u>UNIT CALL</u>:   08:30 hrs.
<u>SETS</u>:   <u>"STAR WARS" STAGE</u>
INT. MAIN HANGAR DECK   Scs. S208, 202pt., T207.
                                                     C/Up Han (Sc. 114)
                                                     C/Up Chewie (Sc. 24pt.)
                                                     C/Up Chewie (Sc. 61pt.)

ARTISTE :		CHARACTER:	D/R:	M/UP:	READY:
CARRIE FISHER		LEIA	76/78	FROM MAIN UNIT	
HARRISON FORD		HAN	86/88	FROM MAIN UNIT	
PETER MAYHEW		CHEWBACCA	92	FROM MAIN UNIT	
ANTHONY DANIELS		THREEPIO	129	FROM MAIN UNIT	
DAVE PROWSE		VADER	133	8.00	8.30
STUNT ARTISTE:					
COLIN SKEAPING		REBEL DRIVER		8.30	9.00
STAND-IN:					
STEVE CALCUTT	for	Mr. Mayhew		8.30	9.00
ROY EVERSON	for	Mr. Prowse		8.00	8.30
CROWD ARTISTES:					
10 MEN		IMPERIAL SNOWTROOPERS		8.00	8.30

PROPS: Supplies for unloading, goggles for Han, weapons for crowd.
                    'Tools' for workers. Welding unit for Chewie. Face shield
                    for Chewie. Weapons for Snowtroopers.

SPECIAL FX: 1. To S/BY with atmosphere fx.
                    2. To S/BY with falling ice fx. (Sc. 202).

WARDROBE/
PRODUCTION: 2 mobile caravans to be ready from 7.30 a.m.

CATERING: 2 trolleys for crowd artistes (60 people) on STAR WARS Stage.

                                                    <u>DAVID TOMBLIN</u>
                                                    Assistant Director

June 4th, 1979 (cont.)
• Listed on internal ILM memo as build start date of "Vader's Stardestroyer" model.

June 5th, 1979
• PRODUCTION CALL SHEET ON PAGE 118.

June 6th, 1979
• Carrie Fisher, Harrison Ford, and Mark Hamill join Eric Idle and Michael Palin (Monty Python) and the Rolling Stones for a party at Eric Idle's flat where Carrie Fisher is staying while filming *Empire*.
Everyone stayed up all night drinking and didn't get any sleep. Harrison and Carrie went to work the next day to film their characters' arrival on Bespin where they meet Lando Calrissian.
      Carrie Fisher: *"That morning we shot our arrival at Cloud City, where we meet Billy Dee Williams. And it's one of the very few times in the series both Harrison and I smile."*

• Imperial Probe Droid storyboard revised.

June 8th, 1979
• PRODUCTION CALL SHEET ON PAGE 119.

• Filming begins on the Carbon Freezing Chamber set.
Cited by many on the crew (including Irvin Kershner) as the most difficult shoot of the entire production (excluding Norway).
It was dark, hot, and dangerous as all sides of the set had a sheer drop of several feet. In fact one of the extras dressed as a Stormtrooper fell off one of the sides during filming.

June 11th, 1979
• Cast and crew attend memorial services for John Barry.
      Gary Kurtz: *"We all mourn John Barry. Apart from his exceptional talent, to which the success of Star Wars owes much, he was the most lovable of men who carried very lightly and disarmingly his great wealth of experience and creativity."*

• Listed on internal ILM memo as date "Snowspeeder #1" model needed.

June 12th, 1979
• PRODUCTION CALL SHEET ON PAGE 120.

• Joe Johnston finishes sketch of Darth Vader's Super Star Destroyer.

CHAPTER II PRODUCTIONS LTD.   Call Sheet No: 57
                                                    (Studio)

PRODUCTION: "THE EMPIRE STRIKES BACK"   DATE: Tuesday, 5th June, 1979.
DIRECTOR: IRVIN KERSHNER   UNIT CALL: 08:30 hrs.
SETS: STAGE 8:
INT. MILLENNIUM FALCON COCKPIT
    a) Space . . . .   Scs. 221, 222, 223, 321, 323, 324, 325,
                                                          429, V429, U430, S431, 431pt.
    b) Cloud City . . . .   Scs. 348, V407, 413.

ARTISTE :   CHARACTER: D/R: M/UP: READY:

INT. MILLENNIUM FALCON:

CARRIE FISHER   LEIA   76/78   7.30   9.00
HARRISON FORD   HAN   86/88   8.30   9.00
ANTHONY DANIELS   THREEPIO   129   8.30   9.00
PETER MAYHEW   CHEWBACCA   92   8.30   9.00
BILLY DEE WILLIAMS   LANDO   90   9.00   10.30
STAND-INS:
JANE HENLEY   for   Ms. Fisher   )
JACK DEARLOVE   for   Mr. Ford   )
ALAN HARRIS   for   Mr. Daniels   )   8.00   8.30
STEVEN MEEK   for   Mr. Mayhew   )
LEROY GOLDING   for   Mr. Williams)

PROPS: Loose dressing in Cabin. Ship's log Sc. 337.

CAMERA: Sea head fx. required.

ART DEPT: Computer map/flashing console fx.

ELECTRICAL: Systems and engine lights to dim out.

SPECIAL FX: 1) Laser/flak hit fx. required.   2)Spark fx. required.

CATERING: AM & PM breaks for 100 people on Stage 8 please.

                                                 DAVID TOMBLIN
                                                 Assistant Director

IMPORTANT NOTE TO ALL CREW MEMBERS:

If you have not yet received the special Health Notice that was issued today (Monday, 4th, June, 1979)
would you please collect a copy from the Production Office. The Medical Officer for Environmental Health
(Hartfordshire Area Health Authority) - Dr. Maurice D. Susman - will be available for consultation from
9.30 a.m. tomorrow Tuesday, 5th June, 1979 in the Studio Medical Centre. If you wish to see him would you
please inform one of the Assistant Directors who will in turn inform Pat Carr.

```
MAIN & 2ND UNITS COMBINED          CHAPTER II PRODUCTIONS LTD.          Call Sheet No: 60
                                                                              (Studio)

     PRODUCTION:    "THE EMPIRE STRIKES BACK"          DATE:    Friday, 8th June, 1979.
     DIRECTOR:      IRVIN KERSHNER                      UNIT CALL:        08:30 hrs.
     SETS:                                              STAGE 8:
     1.  INT. MILLENNIUM FALCON COCKPIT
           a)  Cloud City . . . . . . . . . . . . . . . . . .   Scs. 426D.
           b)  Space . . . . . . . . . . . . . . . . . . .      Scs. 429,V429,U430,S431,431.
           c)  Sunset . . . . . . . . . . . . . . . . . . .     Scs. 434.
           d)  Hangar . . . . . . . . . . . . . . . . . . .     Scs. 61pt.
           e)  Cockpit/Hold . . . . . . . . . . . . . . .       Sc:  406pt. (Artoo/3PO).

     2.  CARBON FREEZING                                STAGE 4:  Sc. 376
```

ARTISTE :		CHARACTER:	D/R:	M/UP:	READY:

1. INT. MILLENNIUM FALCON COCKPIT:

ARTISTE		CHARACTER	D/R	M/UP	READY
CARRIE FISHER		LEIA	76/78	7.30	9.00
MARK HAMILL		LUKE	80/82	8.00	9.00
PETER MAYHEW		CHEWBACCA	92	8.30	9.00
BILLY DEE WILLIAMS		LANDO	90	7.30	9.00

STAND-INS:
JANE HENLY	for	Ms. Fisher	)
JOE GIBSON	for	Mr. Hamill	)
STEVEN MEEK	for	Mr. Mayhew	)
A.N. OTHER	for	Mr. Williams	)

PROPS: Cut down 3PO pieces (Sc. 406pt.)

ART DEPT: Window section required for Sc. 61pt.

ELECTRICAL: 1. Systems and engine lights to dim out.
                2. Possible sunset fx. Sc. 434 and S431.

SPECIAL FX: 1. Laser/flak hit fx. required.
                2. Spark fx. required.
                3. S/BY with remote Artoo to tow 3PO pieces.

---

2. INT. CARBON FREEZING CHAMBER: Sc. 376:

BILLY DEE WILLIAMS		LANDO	90	FROM ABOVE	
DAVE PROWSE		VADER	133	S/BY FROM	10 a.m.
MILTON JOHNS		VADER'S AIDE	131	9.00	10.00
JOHN HOLLIS		LANDO'S AIDE	Hammer Hse	S/BY FROM	10 a.m.
TONY FRIER		HOGMAN	TBA	S/BY FROM	10 a.m.
JOHN GAVAM		HOGMAN	TBA	S/BY FROM	10 a.m.

STAND-INS:
A.N. OTHER	for	Mr. Dee Williams	FROM ABOVE	
ROY EVERSON	for	Mr. Prowse	10.20	11.00

STUNT ARTISTES:
PETER DIAMOND	)	
COLIN SKEAPING	)	S/BY FOR REHEARSALS FROM 8.30 a.m.
BOB ANDERSON	)	

CROWD ARTISTES:
ALAN HARRIS	LANDO GUARD	10.30	11.00
QUENTIN PIERRE	LANDO GUARD	10.30	11.00
4 STORMTROOPERS		10.30	11.00

PROPS: Tools for workers. Weapons for Stormtroopers

WARDROBE: Gloves required for Hogman.

                                                          .../contd.

```
                    CHAPTER II PRODUCTIONS LTD.              Call Sheet No: 62
                                                                  (Studio)

  PRODUCTION:     "THE EMPIRE STRIKES BACK"        DATE:    Tuesday, 12th June, 1979.
  DIRECTOR:       IRVIN KERSHNER                    UNIT CALL:      08:30 hrs.
  SETS:                                             STAGE 4:
  INT. CARBON FREEZING CHAMBER                      Sc:   379
  _____

  ARTISTE  :                   CHARACTER:      D/R:        M/UP:           READY:
  _____

  CARRIE FISHER                LEIA            76/78       7.30            9.00
  HARRISON FORD                HAN             86/88       8.30            9.00
  BILLY DEE WILLIAMS           LANDO           90          7.30            9.00
  ANTHONY DANIELS              THREEPIO        129         S/BY FROM       8.30
  PETER MAYHEW                 CHEWBACCA       92          8.00            8.30
  DAVE PROWSE                  DARTH VADER     133         8.00            8.30
  JEREMY BULLOCH               BOBA FETT       378         8.00            8.30
  JOHN HOLLIS                  LANDO'S AIDE    Hammer Hse  8.15            8.30
  MILTON JOHNS                 VADER'S AIDE    379         8.15            8.30
  EILEEN BAKER                 HOGMAN (1)      133         7.45            8.30
  JOHN GAVAM                   HOGMAN (2)      Mobile      7.45            8.30
  TONY FRIER                   HOGMAN (3)      Mobile      7.45            8.30
  MIKE EDMUNDS                 HOGMAN (4)      Mobile      7.45            8.30
  MIKE COTTRELL                HOGMAN (5)      Mobile      7.45            8.30
  JOHN LUMMIS                  HOGMAN (6)      Mobile      7.45            8.30

  STAND-INS:
  JANE HENLEY         for     Miss Fisher      )
  JACK DEARLOVE       for     Mr. Ford         )
  LEROY GOLDING       for     Mr. Dee Williams )
  A.N. OTHER          for     Mr. Daniels      )      8.00            8.30
  STEVEN MEEK         for     Mr. Mayhew       )
  ROY EVERSON         for     Mr. Prowse       )

  STUNT ARTISTE:
  PETER DIAMOND               Arranger/Stormtrooper (1)   )
  COLIN SKEAPING              Stormtrooper (2)   )
  REG HARDING                 Stormtrooper (3)   )      8.00            8.30
  TONY SMART                  Stormtrooper (4)   )
  MALCOLM WEAVER              Stormtrooper (5)   )
  BOB ANDERSON                TO S/BY ON SET FROM      8.30 a.m.

  CROWD ARTISTES:
  ALAN HARRIS                 LANDO GUARD  )            8.00            8.30
  ROBERT YOUNG                LANDO GUARD  )
  5 STORMTROOPERS                                      8.00            8.30
```

PROPS: "Little tools" for Hogmen. Weapons for Boba Fett and Stormtroopers.
                Dummy weapons for fight. Binders for Chewie and Han. Lando's
                box register. Mobile control unit. Cut down 3PO.

ART DEPT: 1. Han's coffin required.
                2. Mechanical grab required.

SP.FX: 1. Steam /CO_2 fx. required.
                2. Hydraulic light fx.

MAKEUP: Tears for Leia Sc. 379.

WARDROBE: 1. Repeat costumes required for Han.
                2. Gloves required for Hogmen.

STUNT ARRANGEMENTS: 1. S/BY with falling rigs.
                      2. S/BY with trampoline fx.

.../contd.

(Billy Dee Williams and Harrison Ford on the Cloud City Exterior Landing Platform set-up ©1979 LFL)

June 13th, 1979

Irvin Kershner and Harrison Ford go over the script prior to shooting the scene where Han and Leia kiss before he's put into Carbon Freeze.
The two made several dialogue changes including Han's infamous "I know" line.

June 14th, 1979

• Carrie Fisher feels sick and so production is cut short this day.

• Date of invoice from Elstree Studios to Chapter II Productions for the renting of stages for production on *Empire* in the total amount of £9,100.

June 15th, 1979

• PRODUCTION CALL SHEETS ON PAGES 122-123.

June 18th, 1979

• Irvin Kershner shoots the Millennium Falcon in the asteroid cave scene while 2nd Unit shoots Mark Hamill X-wing cockpit scenes against blue screen.

• Listed on internal ILM memo as date needed for "Snowspeeder #2" model.

June 19th, 1979

• PRODUCTION CALL SHEETS ON PAGES 124-125.

```
                         CHAPTER II PRODUCTIONS LTD.              Call Sheet No: 65
                                                                      (Studio)

PRODUCTION:     "THE EMPIRE STRIKES BACK"          DATE:   Friday, 15th June, 1979.
DIRECTOR:       IRVIN KERSHNER                     UNIT CALL:        08:30 hrs.
SETS:                                              STAGE:  "STAR WARS" STAGE
EXT. LANDING PLATFORM                              Sc: 406 ... .... Dusk
                                                       353. ..... Day
```

ARTISTE :		CHARACTER:	D/R:	M/UP:	READY:
CARRIE FISHER		LEIA	76/78	7.30	9.00
HARRISON FORD		HAN	86/88	S/BY AT HOME	
BILLY DEE WILLIAMS		LANDO	90	7.00	9.00
ANTHONY DANIELS		THREEPIO	129	S/BY AT HOME	
PETER MAYHEW		CHEWBACCA	92	8.30	9.00
JOHN HOLLIS		LANDO'S AIDE	Hammer Hse	TO BE ADVISED	

```
DOUBLE:
DEEP ROY            for    Artoo                      FROM 2ND UNIT


STAND-INS:
JANE HENLEY         for    Ms. Fisher      )
JACK DEARLOVE       for    Mr. Ford        )
LEROY GOLDING       for    Mr. B.D. Williams )          8.00          8.30
ALAN HARRIS         for    Mr. Daniels     )
STEVEN MEEK         for    Mr. Mayhew      )


CROWD:
6 CONTINUITY LANDO GUARDS                             TO BE ADVISED


STUNT ARTISTE:
PETER DIAMOND       )
COLIN SKEAPING      )                                 TO S/BY FROM 8.30 a.m.
```

PROPS:	Weapons for Han and Leia and Chewie. Brain Augmentor. Cut down 3PO.
SFX:	1. S/BY with wind/breeze fx. 2. S/BY with atmosphere fx. 3. S/BY with Laser Hit fx. (Sc. 406).
MAKEUP:	Change of hairstyle for Leia (Sc. 353pt.)
ELECTRICAL:	Dusk fx. (Sc. 406).
CAMERA:	Vistavision fx. required.
CATERING:	AM & PM breaks for 120 persons (2 trolleys) on STAR WARS Stage pls.

```
                                                   DAVID TOMBLIN
                                                   Assistant Director
```

```
2nd UNIT                    CHAPTER II PRODUCTIONS LTD.          Call Sheet No: 65A
                                                                      (Studio)

PRODUCTION:    "THE EMPIRE STRIKES BACK"      DATE:    Friday, 15th June, 1979.
DIRECTOR:      HARLEY COKLISS                  UNIT CALL:        08:30 hrs.
SETS:                                          STAGE 8:
1.  INT. COCKPIT LUKE'S X-WING (Blue Screen)  Scs: 228, 230, 270, 378, 232,
                                                   265, 269, 375, 228, 230 to
                                                                     complete

2.  INT. FALCON COCKPIT                        Scs: 61pt.
3.  INT. COCKPIT CORRIDOR                       Scs: Artoo drags 3PO + 406 pt.
```

ARTISTE :		CHARACTER:	D/R:	M/UP:	READY:
MARK HAMILL		LUKE	80/82	TO BE ADVISED	
PETER MAYHEW		CHEWBACCA		FROM MAIN UNIT	
DOUBLE:					
DEEP ROY	for	Artoo		TO BE ADVISED	
STAND-IN:					
JOE GIBSON	for	Mr. Hamill	)	08.00	08.30
STEVEN CALCUTT	for	Mr. Mayhew	)	08.00	08.30

```
ART DEPT./PROPS:    Cockpit dressing.  Joystick.
                    Breakdown 3PO pieces.  Eyes alight, arm moves.
                    Falcon dressing as required.  3PO net.

SFX:                1. Retro fx.
                    2. Crash fx.
                    3. Canopy to open.
                    4. Moving sun fx.
                    5. R/C Artoo.

EDITORIAL:          S/BY for rushes in Vistavision at 08.30
                    S/BY with reference footage for Sc. 61, 406 etc.

BLUE BACKING:       As per Stan Sayer.

CATERING:           AM & PM breaks for 50 persons on Stage 8 please.

TRANSPORT:          Roy Najda to collect Mr. Hamill as informed by
                    Asst. Directors.


                                            DOMINIC FULFORD
                                            Assistant Director
```

```
                    CHAPTER II PRODUCTIONS LTD.               Call Sheet No: 67
                                                                  (Studio)

PRODUCTION:    "THE EMPIRE STRIKES BACK"        DATE:    Tuesday, 19th June, 1979.
DIRECTOR:      IRVIN KERSHNER                    UNIT CALL:          08:30 hrs.
SETS:                                            STAGE:   "STAR WARS" STAGE
EXT. LANDING PLATFORM                            Sc: 353pt. . . . . . . . . . . Day
                                                     406 . . . . . . . . . . Dusk

_____

ARTISTE  :                      CHARACTER:   D/R:      M/UP:           READY:
_____

CARRIE FISHER                   LEIA         76/78     7.30            9.00
HARRISON FORD                   HAN          86/88     8.30            9.00
BILLY DEE WILLIAMS              LANDO        90        7.30            9.30
ANTHONY DANIELS                 THREEPIO     129       8.30            9.00
PETER MAYHEW                    CHEWBACCA    92        8.30            9.00


DOUBLE:
DEEP ROY             for    Artoo                     FROM 2ND UNIT


STAND-INS:
JANE HENLEY          for    Ms. Fisher        )
JACK DEARLOVE        for    Mr. Ford          )
LEROY GOLDING        for    Mr. B.D. Williams )       8.00            8.30
ALAN HARRIS          for    Mr. Daniels       )
STEVEN MEEK          for    Mr. Mayhew        )



STUNT ARTISTE:
PETER DIAMOND    )
COLIN SKEAPING   )                                    TO S/BY FROM 8.30 a.m.



PROPS:         Weapons for Han and Leia and Chewie.  Brain Augmentor.
               Cut down 3PO.

SFX:           1. S/BY with wind/breeze fx.      4. R/C Artoo
               2. S/BY with atmosphere fx.          from 2nd Unit.
               3. S/BY with Laser Hit fx. (Sc. 406).

MAKEUP:        Change of hairstyle for Leia (Sc. 406)

ELECTRICAL:    Dusk fx. (Sc. 406).

CAMERA:        Vistavision fx. required.


CATERING:      AM & PM breaks for 120 persons (2 trolleys) on STAR WARS Stage pls.


                                                    DAVID TOMBLIN
                                                    Assistant Director
```

```
2nd UNIT                  CHAPTER II PRODUCTIONS LTD.          Call Sheet No: 67A
                                                                   (Studio)

PRODUCTION:    "THE EMPIRE STRIKES BACK"       DATE:   Tuesday, 19th June, 1979.
DIRECTOR:      HARLEY COKLISS                  UNIT CALL:      08:30 hrs.
SETS:                                          STAGE 8:
1.  INT. COCKPIT LUKE'S X-WING ) Blue          1. Sc: 269D.
2.  INT./EXT. FALCON HULL      ) Screen        2. Sc: 423pt.
3.  INT. FALCON COCKPIT                        3. Sc: 61 pt.
4.  INT. COCKPIT CORRIDOR                      4. Sc: Artoo drags Threepio (406pt.)
```

ARTISTE :		CHARACTER:	D/R:	M/UP:	READY:
MARK HAMILL		LUKE	80/82	08.15	09.00
BILLY DEE WILLIAMS		LANDO		FROM MAIN UNIT	
PETER MAYHEW		CHEWBACCA		FROM MAIN UNIT	
DOUBLE:					
DEEP ROY	for	ARTOO		08.30	09.00
STAND-IN:					
JOE GIBSON	for	Mr. Hamill		08.00	08.30
A.N. OTHER	for	Mr. Dee Williams		08.00	08.30
A.N. OTHER	for	Mr. Mayhew		FROM MAIN UNIT	

```
ART DEPT./PROPS:        1.  X-Wing dressing
                        2.  "Roll-on" hull section.
                        3.  Lando's harness.
                        4.  Falcon dressing.
                        5.  Breakdown 3PO pieces.
                        6.  3PO eyes to light, arm to move.
                        7.  3PO dragnet rig.

SPECIAL FX:             Wind fx.
                        Remote control R2.

WARDROBE:               Luke's change (Sc. 423).

MAKEUP:                 Luke's change (Sc. 423).

EDITORIAL:              S/BY for rushes for 08.30 hrs.
                        Plus reference footage for all above scenes.

BLUE BACKING:           As per Stan Sayer.

CATERING:               AM & PM breaks for 50 persons on Stage 8 please.

TRANSPORT:              Roy Najda to collect Mr. Hamill at 07.30 to arrive by 08.15.

NOTE:                   ON COMPLETION OF THE ABOVE THE UNIT WILL MOVE TO STAGE 9
                        TO PREPARE & PRE-LIGHT FOR EXT. VERANDA - CLOUD CITY (Sc. 3620)

                                              DOMINIC FULFORD
                                              Assistant Director
```

(the Carbon Freezing Chamber set ©1979 LFL)

June 22nd, 1979

• Date of another invoice from Elstree Studios to Chapter II Productions for the renting of stages for production on *Empire* in the total amount of £9,100.

June 25th, 1979

• Nathan Elias Hamill is born to Mark and Marilou Hamill.

• Mark Hamill is asked to come in and film a final scene on a blue screen set in which Luke Skywalker leaps from his Snowspeeder as an AT-AT foot crushes it behind him.
During this scene Mark Hamill sprained his thumb and was rushed to the hospital.

• Date of internal Lucasfilm memo in which Production Coordinator Miki Herman states that ILM is over budget.

(the scene in which Mark Hamill sprains his thumb ©1979 LFL)

June 26th, 1979

• Due to Mark Hamill's sprained thumb 1st Unit is shut down for four days starting on this date.

The next day's call sheet listed 1st Unit production as the duel between Luke Skywalker and Darth Vader. Due to Hamill's injury it's most likely that only 2nd Unit shot that day while the duel was pushed back to the first week of July.

• Irvin Kershner continues filming 2nd Unit footage of Harrison Ford, Carrie Fisher, Peter Mayhew, and Anthony Daniels in the Millennium Falcon cockpit set.

June 27th, 1979

• PRODUCTION CALL SHEETS ON PAGES 128-129.

June 28th, 1979

• More filming of the main cast in the Millennium Falcon cockpit set.

• A special show-reel screening for the crew takes place with a buffet afterwards at the studio restaurant.

(Peter Mayhew, Anthony Daniels, Carrie Fisher, and Harrison Ford on the Millennium Falcon interior cockpit set ©1980 LFL)

CHAPTER II PRODUCTIONS LTD.

<u>Call Sheet No: 73</u>
(Studio)

<u>PRODUCTION</u>:	"THE EMPIRE STRIKES BACK"		<u>DATE</u>:	Wednesday, 27th June, 1979.	
<u>DIRECTOR</u>:	IRVIN KERSHNER		<u>UNIT CALL</u>:	08:30 hrs.	
<u>SET</u>:			<u>STAGE 4</u>:		
INT. CARBON FREEZING CHAMBER			Sc: 384, S391pt.		

ARTISTE :		CHARACTER:	D/R:	M/UP:	READY:

ARTISTE		CHARACTER	D/R	M/UP	READY
MARK HAMILL		LUKE	80/82	TO BE ADVISED	
DAVE PROWSE		DARTH VADER	133	8.00	8.30
<u>STAND-INS</u>:					
ROY EVERSON	for	Mr. Prowse	)		
JOE GIBSON	for	Mr. Hamill	)	TO BE ADVISED	
<u>STUNT ARTISTE</u>:					
PETER DIAMOND		Co-ordinator		S/BY FROM	8.30 a.m.
COLIN SKEAPING		Dble Luke		S/BY FROM	8.30 a.m.
BOB ANDERSON		Dble Vader		S/BY FROM	8.30 a.m.

<u>PROPS</u>:   Dummy weapons for fight. Laser swords.

<u>ART DEPT</u>:   Mechanical grab required.

<u>SFX</u>:
1. Steam /CO_2 fx. required.
2. Hydraulic lift fx. required.
3. Laser sword fx./Melting fx. for sword battle.

<u>STUNT DEPT</u>:   Arm and knee pads required for Sword battle.

<u>DEREK BOTELL</u>:   To S/BY for wire fx. from 8.30 a.m.

<u>CATERING</u>:   AM & PM breaks - TO BE ADVISED.

<u>TRANSPORT</u>:
1. R. Najda to P/UP Mr. Hamill - TO BE ADVISED.

<u>DAVID TOMBLIN</u>
Assistant Director

IMPORTANT NOTE
The special show reel screening/buffet for the crew will now take place
on Thursday, 28th June, 1979 instead of Wednesday, 27th as previously
advised. The venue will be the Admin. Theatre for the screening(at 6.30 p.m.) &
the studio restaurant for the buffet.

```
2ND UNIT                    CHAPTER II PRODUCTIONS LTD.           Call Sheet No: 73A
                                                                      (Studio)

PRODUCTION:     "THE EMPIRE STRIKES BACK"          DATE:    Wednesday, 27th June, 1979.
DIRECTOR:       HARLEY COKLISS                      UNIT CALL:        08:30 hrs.
SETS:                                               STAGE 8:
INT. FALCON COCKPIT (Blue Screen)                   Scs:  252, 261, 318, 319, 324,
                                                          V429, 431 (SPACE)
```

ARTISTE :		CHARACTER:	D/R:		M/UP:	READY:
CARRIE FISHER		LEIA	76/78	)	ALL ARTISTES TIMES	
HARRISON FORD		HAN	86/88	)	TO BE ADVISED BY	
BILLY DEE WILLIAMS		LANDO		)	ASSISTANT DIRECTORS	
ANTHONY DANIELS		THREEPIO	129	)	FROM SET.	
PETER MAYHEW		CHEWBACCA	92	)		
STAND-INS:						
JANE HENLEY	for	Ms. Fisher		)		
JACK DEARLOVE	for	Mr. Ford		)		
LEROY GOLDING	for	Mr. Dee Williams		)	8.00	8.30
ALAN HARRIS	for	Mr. Daniels		)		
STEVEN MEEK	for	Mr. Mayhew		)		

ART DEPT./PROPS: Cockpit loose dressing. S/BY cut down 3PO.

SFX: Cockpit practicals. Flash bulbs flash fx.

HAIR: S/BY Ms. Fisher's change. (Sc. V429).

EDITORIAL: S/BY with rushes at 08.15 hrs.
                        S/BY with reference footage for above scenes.

BLUE BACKING: As per Stan Sayer.

CATERING: AM & PM breaks for 50 persons on Stage 8 please.

                                                    DOMINIC FULFORD
                                                    Assistant Director

** IMPORTANT NOTE **
The screening of the special show reel for the crew, followed by the
buffet, will now take place on Thursday, 28th June and not Wednesday, 27th
as previously advised. The venue for the screening is the Admin. Theatre
at 6.30 p.m., followed by the buffet in the Studio Restaurant commencing
at approx. 7 p.m.
```
```

June 29th, 1979
• PRODUCTION CALL SHEET ON PAGE 131.

• Harrison Ford wraps filming.
He was anxious to leave the production due to the filming wearing him down both emotionally and physically.

• Alan Arnold interviews Harrison Ford, Mark Hamill, Irvin Kershner, Gary Kurtz, and Norman Reynolds for the book, *A Journal of the Making of the Empire Strikes Back*.

June 30th, 1979
• Listed on internal ILM memo as date "Snowspeeder #3" model needed.

July 1st, 1979
• Listed on internal ILM memo as date "Full-size Walkers (3)" models needed.

July 2nd-3rd, 1979
• The duel between Luke Skywalker and Darth Vader in the Carbon Freezing Chamber is shot.

July 3rd, 1979
• Revised storyboard of Darth Vader aboard his Star Destroyer completed by artist Nilo Rodis-Jamero.

July 4th, 1979
• Cast and crew gather to watch an *Empire* teaser trailer.
It was comprised mostly of Ralph McQuarrie's concept paintings and still shots of the cast in costume. They were also able to see about 15 minutes of shot footage.

July 5th, 1979
• Alan Arnold interviews 2nd Unit Director Harley Cokeliss and Gary Kurtz for the book, *A Journal of the Making of the Empire Strikes Back*.

• Peter Mayhew feels ill and is sent home for the day.

July 6th, 1979
• Alan Arnold interviews Mark Hamill and Irvin Kershner for the book, *A Journal of the Making of the Empire Strikes Back*.

```
                          CHAPTER II PRODUCTIONS LTD.              Call Sheet No: 75
                                                                        (Studio)

PRODUCTION:      "THE EMPIRE STRIKES BACK"          DATE:     Friday, 29th June, 1979.
DIRECTOR:        IRVIN KERSHNER                     UNIT CALL:        08:30 hrs.
SET:                                                STAGE 4:
INT. CARBON FREEZING CHAMBER                        Sc:   384, S391pt.
_____

ARTISTE  :                        CHARACTER:      D/R:        M/UP:          READY:
_____

MARK HAMILL                       LUKE            80/82      TO BE ADVISED
DAVE PROWSE                       DARTH VADER     133        S/BY FROM        8.30


STAND-INS:
ROY EVERSON           for    Mr. Prowse       )
JOE GIBSON            for    Mr. Hamill       )         S/BY FROM        8.30


STUNT ARTISTE:
PETER DIAMOND                     Co-ordinator             S/BY FROM        8.30
COLIN SKEAPING                    Dble Luke                S/BY FROM        8.30
BOB ANDERSON                      Dble Vader               S/BY FROM        8.30


PROPS:            Dummy weapons for fight. Laser swords.

ART DEPT:         Mechanical grab required.

SFX:              1.  Steam /CO₂ fx. required.
                  2.  Hydraulic lift fx. required.
                  3.  Laser sword fx./Melting fx. for sword battle.

STUNT DEPT:       Arm and knee pads required for Sword Battle.

DEREK BOTELL:     To S/BY for wire fx. from 8.30 a.m.

CATERING:         AM & PM breaks - TO BE ADVISED.

TRANSPORT:        R. Najda to P/UP Mr. Hamill at 7.15 a.m. to arrive by 8 a.m.


                                              DAVID TOMBLIN
                                              Assistant Director
```

July 6th, 1979 (cont.)

• The scene in which Vader requests his shuttle as he leaves Cloud City is shot.

• John Hollis (Lobot) wraps filming.

July 9th, 1979

• Listed on internal ILM memo as build start date of "Double Chili-Tie" (TIE Bomber) and Rebel Transport models.

• Listed on internal ILM memo as date "8ft. Stardestroyer model" needed.

• Listed on internal ILM memo as build start date of "Walker Snowscapes" set.

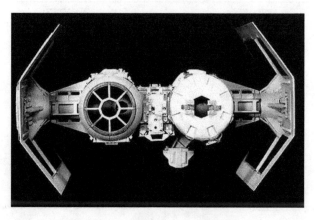

(TIE Bomber model ©1979 LFL)

July 10th, 1979

• Carrie Fisher is told that someone is planning to kidnap her.
The information was provided by Carrie's mother, Debbie Reynolds, who called Carrie after she had received an anonymous tip.

• Alan Arnold interviews Irvin Kershner and Billy Dee Williams for the book, *A Journal of the Making of The Empire Strikes Back.*

July 11th, 1979

• Shooting on *Empire* is 33 days over schedule.

• On this day Kershner moves production to the Medical Bay set where Luke Skywalker gets his mechanical hand and he and Princess Leia see Lando Calrissian and Chewbacca off as they leave to search for Han Solo.

• In response to her mother's warning the previous day about a kidnap attempt, Carrie Fisher arrives on set this day with security guards.

July 12th, 1979

• More scenes on the Medical Bay set are shot.

July 13th, 1979

• PRODUCTION CALL SHEETS ON PAGES 133-135.

CHAPTER II PRODUCTIONS LTD.   Call Sheet No: 85
                                                    (Studio)

PRODUCTION: "THE EMPIRE STRIKES BACK"   DATE: Friday, 13th July, 1979.
DIRECTOR: IRVIN KERSHNER   UNIT CALL: 08:30 hrs.
SETS:
1.   INT. FALCON HOLD   Stage 8: Additional Scenes
2.   INT. FALCON COCKPIT   Stage 9: 431pt.,419pt. (front angles)
3.   INT. CARBON FREEZING CHAMBER   Stage 4: 379pt. (Moving POV Leia)
                                                          (Threepio Dialogue)
                                                S391pt.

ARTISTE :		CHARACTER:	D/R:	M/UP:	READY:
1. INT. FALCON HOLD: Additional Scenes. (Stage 8)					
CARRIE FISHER		LEIA	76/78	7.30	9.00
MARK HAMILL		LUKE	80/82	8.00	9.00
STAND-INS:					
ERICA SIMMONDS	for	Ms. Fisher		8.00	8.30
JOE GIBSON	for	Mr. Hamill		8.00	8.30
PROPS:		Blanket for Luke.			
M/UP:		Damaged makeup for Luke.			

---

2. INT. FALCON COCKPIT: Front angle: Sc. 419pt. (Stage 9)					
CARRIE FISHER		LEIA	76/78	FROM ABOVE	
MARK HAMILL		LUKE	80/82	FROM ABOVE	
BILLY DEE WILLIAMS		LANDO	90	7.30	10.00
PETER MAYHEW		CHEWBACCA	92	FROM 2ND UNIT	
STAND-INS:					
ERICA SIMMONDS	for	Ms. Fisher		FROM ABOVE	
JOE GIBSON	for	Mr. Hamill		FROM ABOVE	
LEROY GOLDING	for	Mr. Dee Williams		8.30	9.00
STEVEN CALCUTT	for	Mr. Mayhew		FROM 2ND UNIT	
PROPS:		Blanket for Luke.			
SFX:		Flash bulb fx.			
M/UP:		Luke damaged M/UP.			
CAMERA:		Vistavision fx.			
BLUE SCREEN:		Stan Sayer to S/BY from 8.30 a.m.			

---

3. INT. CARBON FREEZING CHAMBER:		**Sc. 379pt. (Moving POV of Leia) (Stage 4)**			
		Sc. 379pt. (Threepio Dialogue)			
		Sc. S391pt.			
CARRIE FISHER		LEIA	76/78	FROM ABOVE	
MARK HAMILL		LUKE	80/82	FROM ABOVE	
ANTHONY DANIELS		THREEPIO	129	FROM 2nd UNIT	
PETER MAYHEW		CHEWBACCA	92	FROM ABOVE	
DAVE PROWSE		DARTH VADER	131	S/BY AT HOME 1 p.m.	

. . . / contd.

Call Sheet No: 85 (contd.)   Page 2.-

SET 3 (contd.)

STAND-INS:
ERICA SIMMONDS   for   Ms. Fisher   FROM ABOVE
JOE GIBSON   for   Mr. Hamill   FROM ABOVE
JACK DEARLOVE   for   Mr. Daniels   FROM 2nd UNIT
STEVEN CALCUTT   for   Mr. Mayhew   FROM ABOVE
ROY EVERSON   for   Mr. Prowse   10.30   11.00

CROWD:
4 STORMTROOPERS   IF REQUIRED FROM 2nd UNIT

STUNT ARTISTE:
COLIN SKEAPING   STORMTROOPER   )
PETER DIAMOND   CO-ORDINATOR   )   AS ADVISED
BOB ANDERSON   DBLE VADER   )

PROPS: Cut down 3PO. Binds for Chewie.

SFX: 1. Hydraulic lift fx.
                2. Steam /CO_2 fx.
                3. Laser sword/Melting fx.

DEREK BOTELL: To S/BY for wire fx. from 8.30 a.m.

_____

CATERING: AM Break for 85 persons on Stage 8 please.
                PM Break for 85 persons - venue to be advised.

                                              DAVID TOMBLIN
                                              Assistant Director

```
2ND UNIT                    CHAPTER II PRODUCTIONS LTD.          Call Sheet No: 85A
                                                                     (Studio)

PRODUCTION:     "THE EMPIRE STRIKES BACK"        DATE:    Friday, 13th July, 1979.
DIRECTOR:       HARLEY COKLISS                   UNIT CALL:          08:30 hrs.
SET:                                             STAGE 2:
EXT. EAST LANDING PLATFORM                        Scs: T391. 399pts. 405pts.
                                                      3908.(R/T)
```

ARTISTE :		CHARACTER:	D/R:	M/UP:	READY:

ANTHONY DANIELS		THREEPIO	129	8.30	9.00
PETER MAYHEW		CHEWBACCA	92	8.30	9.00
KENNY BAKER		ARTOO	131	8.30	9.00
STAND-INS:					
JACK DEARLOVE	for	Mr. Daniels	)	8.00	8.30
STEVE MEEK	for	Mr. Mayhew	)	"	"
CROWD:					
4 STORMTROOPERS				8.00	8.30
STUNTS:					
PETER DIAMOND				TO S/BY AS REQUIRED	
COLIN SKEAPING		TROOPER		8.30	9.00

```
ART DEPT./PROPS:            Weapons for Stormtroopers (practicals).
                           Lando's intercom.
                           Cut down 3PO.

SFX:                       R/C R2.
                           Computer socket + R2's arm.
                           Smoke fx.
                           R2's smokescreen.
                           Hits.

EDITORIAL:                 Moviola to Stage 2 with relevant footage please.
                           RUSHES AT 08.15 please.

CATERING:        AM & PM breaks for 50 persons on Stage 2 please.

TRANSPORT:
1.  D Cressy to collect Mr. Daniels at 8 a.m. to arrive by 8.30 a.m.
2.  P. Farretti to collect Mr. Mayhew at 6.45 a.m. to arrive by 7.30 a.m.


                                              DOMINIC FULFORD
                                              Assistant Director
```

July 15th, 1979

• George Lucas returns to London to help Irvin Kershner and Gary Kurtz due to the production being behind schedule and over budget.

July 16th, 1979

• PRODUCTION CALL SHEET ON PAGE 137.

• Listed on internal ILM memo as date "Vader's Stardestroyer model" needed.

• Listed on internal ILM memo as date "Double Chili-Tie" (TIE Bomber) model needed.

July 17th, 1979

• PRODUCTION CALL SHEET ON PAGE 139.

(Carrie Fisher and R2-D2 ©1979 LFL)

• Alan Arnold interviews Norman Reynolds for the book, *A Journal of the Making of The Empire Strikes Back*.

July 18th, 1979

• PRODUCTION CALL SHEET ON PAGE 140.

• Carrie Fisher wraps filming.

• Alan Arnold interviews Mark Hamill for the book, *A Journal of the Making of The Empire Strikes Back*.

July 19th, 1979

• PRODUCTION CALL SHEET ON PAGE 141.

• Alan Arnold interviews Gary Kurtz and George Lucas for the book, *A Journal of the Making of The Empire Strikes Back*.

```
                      CHAPTER II PRODUCTIONS LTD.              Call Sheet No: 86
                                                                   (Studio)

PRODUCTION:      "THE EMPIRE STRIKES BACK"        DATE:   Monday, 16th July, 1979.
DIRECTOR:        IRVIN KERSHNER                    UNIT CALL:      08.30 a.m.
SET:                                               STAGE 4:
INT. CARBON FREEZING CHAMBER                       Sc:   379pt.
```

ARTISTE :		CHARACTER:	D/R:	M/UP:	READY:
CARRIE FISHER		LEIA	76/78	7.30	9.00
MARK HAMILL		LUKE	80/82	FROM 2ND UNIT	
PPETER MAYHEW		CHEWBACCA	92	8.30	9.00
DAVE PROWSE		DARTH VADER	131	9.00	9.30
STAND-INS:					
ERICA SIMMONDS	for	Ms. Fisher		8.00	8.30
JOE GIBSON	for	Mr. Hamill		8.30	9.00
STEVEN CALCUTT	for	Mr. Mayhew		8.00	8.30
ROY EVERSON	for	Mr. Prowse		8.30	9.00

```
CROWD:
2 STORMTROOPERS                                   IF REQD. FROM 2ND UNIT

STUNT ARTISTES:
COLIN SKEAPING                 STORMTROOPER  )
PETER DIAMOND                  CO-ORDINATOR  )      S/BY FROM 8.30 a.m.
BOB ANDERSON                   DBLE VADER    )


PROPS:               Cut down 3PO.  Binds for Chewie.


SFX:                 1.  Hydraulic lift fx.
                     2.  Steam /CO₂ fx.
                     3.  Laser sword/melting fx.

DEREK BOTELL:        To S/BY on set from 8.30 a.m.

CATERING:            AM & PM breaks for 100 persons on Stage 8 please.


TRANSPORT:
1.  D. Cressy to collect Ms. Fisher at 6.50 a.m. to arrive by 7.30a.m.
2.  P. Ferretti to collect Mr. Mayhew at 6.45 a.m. to arrive by 8 a.m.




                                                   DAVID TOMBLIN
                                                   Assistant Director
```

(Mark Hamill (r) duels with Bob Anderson (l) for the Luke vs Vader lightsaber duel ©1979 LFL)

(Darth Vader on the Reactor Control Room set ©1979 LFL)

CHAPTER II PRODUCTIONS LTD.   Call Sheet No: 87
                                                       (Studio)

PRODUCTION: "THE EMPIRE STRIKES BACK"   DATE: Tuesday, 17th July, 1979
DIRECTOR: IRVIN KERSHNER   UNIT CALL: 08.30 a.m.
SET: STAGE 4:
INT. CARBON FREEZING CHAMBER   Sc. 391pt.

ARTISTE :		CHARACTER:	D/R:	M/UP:	READY:
MARK HAMILL		LUKE	80/82	8.00	8.45
DAVE PROWSE		DARTH VADER	131	8.30	8.45
STAND-INS:					
JOE GIBSON	for	Mr. Hamill		8.00	8.30
ROY EVERSON	for	Mr. Prowse		8.00	8.30

STUNT ARTISTE:
COLIN SKEAPING   STORMTROOPER)
PETER DIAMOND   CO-ORDINATOR)   S/BY FROM   8.30
BOB ANDERSON   DBLE VADER   )

PROPS: Laser swords.

SFX: 1. Hydraulic lift fx.
                         2. Steam /CO_2 fx.
                         3. Laser sword/melting fx.

DEREK BOTELL: To S/BY on set from 8.30 a.m.

CATERING: AM & PM Breaks for 100 persons on Stage   please.

TRANSPORT:
1, Roy Najda to collect Mr. Hamill at 7.15 a.m. to arrive by 8 a.m.

                                        DAVID TOMBLIN
                                        Assistant Director

CHAPTER II PRODUCTIONS LTD.   Call Sheet No: 88
                                                         (Studio)

PRODUCTION: "THE EMPIRE STRIKES BACK"   DATE: Wednesday, 18th July, 1979
DIRECTOR: IRVIN KERSHNER   UNIT CALL: 08.30 a.m.
SET: STAGE 4:
INT. CARBON FREEZING CHAMBER   Sc. 391pt.

ARTISTE :		CHARACTER:	D/R:	M/UP:	READY:
MARK HAMILL		LUKE	80/82	8.00	8.45
DAVE PROWSE		DARTH VADER	131	8.30	8.45
STAND-INS:					
JOE GIBSON	for	Mr. Hamill		8.00	8.30
ROY EVERSON	for	Mr. Prowse		8.00	8.30

STUNT ARTISTE:
COLIN SKEAPING   STORMTROOPER   )
PETER DIAMOND   DBLE LUKE   )   S/BY FROM   8.30
BOB ANDERSON   DBLE VADER   )

PROPS: Laser swords.

SFX: 1. Hydraulic lift fx.
                          2. Steam /CO_2 fx.
                          3. Laser sword/melting fx.

DEREK BOTELL: To S/BY on set from 8.30 a.m.

CATERING: AM & PM Breaks for 100 persons on Stage 4 please.

TRANSPORT:
1, Roy Najda to collect Mr. Hamill at 7.15 a.m. to arrive by 8 a.m.

                                                DAVID TOMBLIN
                                                Assistant Director

CHAPTER II PRODUCTIONS LTD.   Call Sheet No: 89
                                                    (Studio)

PRODUCTION: "THE EMPIRE STRIKES BACK"   DATE: Thursday, 19th July, 1979.
DIRECTOR: IRVIN KERSHNER   UNIT CALL: 08.30 a.m.
SET: STAGE 1:
INT. REACTOR CONTROL ROOM   Sc. U391

ARTISTE :		CHARACTER:	D/R:	M/UP:	READY:
MARK HAMILL		LUKE	80/82	8.30 for reh. then M/UP	
DAVE PROWSE		DARTH VADER	131	8.30 for reh.	
STAND-INS:					
JOE GIBSON	for	Mr. Hamill		8.00	8.30
ROY EVERSON	for	Mr. Prowse		8.00	8.30
STUNT ARTISTES:					
COLIN SKEAPING				FROM 2ND UNIT	
PETER DIAMOND				8.30 TO S/BY	
BOB ANDERSON		Dble Vader		8.30 TO S/BY	

PROPS: Laser swords. Small 'Tools' and equipment for throwing.

SFX: 1. To S/BY for flying machinery fx. with repeats.
                    2. Wind/air mortar fx. through window.

CAMERA: Vistavision camera required.

DEREK BOTELL: To S/BY on set from 8.30 a.m. for flying machinery fx.

ART DEPT: To S/BY for rubber window replacement T.B.A.

CATERING: AM & PM breaks for 80 persons on Stage 1 please.

TRANSPORT:
Roy Najda to collect Mr. Hamill at 7.45 to arrive by 8.30 a.m.

DAVID TOMBLIN
Assistant Director

CHAPTER II PRODUCTIONS LTD.   Call Sheet No: 90
                                                      (Studio)

PRODUCTION:	"THE EMPIRE STRIKES BACK"		DATE:	Friday, 20th July, 1979.
DIRECTOR:	IRVIN KERSHNER		UNIT CALL:	8.30 a.m.
SET:			STAGE 1:	
INT. REACTOR CONTROL ROOM			Sc. U391pt.	

ARTISTE :		CHARACTER:	D/R:	M/UP:	READY:
MARK HAMILL		LUKE	80/82	8.00	8.45
DAVE PROWSE		DARTH VADER	131	8.30	8.45
STAND-INS:					
JOE GIBSON	for	Mr. Hamill		8.00	8.30
ROY EVERSON	for	Mr. Prowse		8.00	8.30
STUNT ARTISTES:					
COLIN SKEAPING		Dble Vader		8.30	9.30
PETER DIAMOND		Dble Vader		8.30 TO S/BY	
BOB ANDERSON		Dble Vader		8.30 TO S/BY	

PROPS: Laser swords. Small 'Tools' and equipment for throwing.

SFX: 1. Wind/air mortar fx. through window.
                        2. S/BY with atmosphere fx.

CAMERA: Vistavision camera required.

DEREK BOTELL: To S/BY on set from 8.30 a.m. for flying machinery fx.

ART DEPT: To S/BY for rubber window replacement during morning.

CATERING: AM & PM breaks for 80 persons on Stage 1 please.

TRANSPORT:
Roy Najda to collect Mr. Hamill at 7.15 to arrive by 8.00 a.m.

                                            DAVID TOMBLIN
                                            Assistant Director

PERSPECTIVE YODA FITTING:

12 noon . . . . . . Deep Roy . . . . Feet fitting . . . . Art Dept.

July 20th, 1979
• PRODUCTION CALL SHEET ON PAGE 142.

• Joe Johnston completes revised storyboards for the crash of Luke's Snowspeeder in the path of an AT-AT walker.

July 23rd, 1979
• More revisions are made to the shooting script by Director Irvin Kershner and the cast.

• Some of Luke's training scenes with Yoda are cut from the script including a scene in which Luke must slice a metal bar with his lightsaber and fight seeker balls (devices similar to the training ball used by Ben Kenobi aboard the Millennium Falcon in *Star Wars*).

• Listed on internal ILM memo as build start date of "Boba Fett Ship" model.

July 24th, 1979
• The scene in which Luke Skywalker confronts Darth Vader in Dagobah's "tree of evil" is filmed.

(Luke Skywalker (Mark Hamill) in the "tree of evil" on Dagobah ©1979 LFL)

• A credit agreement with First National Bank of Boston is signed.
This was a refinancing of Lucasfilm's loan with Bank of America due to BofA not extending anymore credit to the production company once they started going over budget. The new loan allotted the production company $31 million with Twentieth Century Fox guaranteeing $3 million in exchange for additional distribution money. [4]

July 26th, 1979
• The scene in which Darth Vader tries to seduce Luke Skywalker to the Dark Side of the Force is shot including the moment in which Vader reveals that he is Luke's father. To keep the news of Luke and Vader's lineage a secret the script used during production stated Vader tells Luke that Obi-Wan killed his father. Irvin Kershner told Mark Hamill just prior to filming this scene the real dialogue so that his reaction would be accurate in the final film. Kershner went on to explain that only he, Lucas, and Kurtz knew the secret and that Hamill

was in the loop as well. That way if it leaked they would have known who the culprit was.

David Prowse was not told of the dialogue difference. Irvin Kershner stated that at the London premiere of the film David Prowse, who was sitting directly behind him, tapped Kershner on the shoulder during the scene and asked him why he wasn't told because he would have performed the scene differently (which further supports Prowse's claim that he had no idea Vader was really Luke's father even though he said as much during interviews in 1978).

(Darth Vader (David Prowse) and Luke Skywalker (Mark Hamill) during one of the film's most dramatic and iconic scenes ©1979 LFL)

July 27th, 1979
• PRODUCTION CALL SHEET ON PAGE 145.

• 1st Unit continues filming the confrontation between Darth Vader and Luke Skywalker, specifically after Luke loses his hand.

• Listed on internal ILM memo as build start date of "Probot (Imperial Probe Droid)" model.

• Listed on internal ILM memo as build start date of "Probot Snowscapes" set.

```
2ND UNIT                  CHAPTER II PRODUCTIONS LTD.           Call Sheet No: 95A
                                                                    (Studio)


PRODUCTION:     "THE EMPIRE STRIKES BACK"      DATE:    Friday, 27th July, 1979.
DIRECTOR:       HARLEY COKLISS                  UNIT CALL:       8.30 hrs.
SETS:                                           STAGE 8:
EXT. LUKE'S X-WING (Blue Backing)              Scs: 232. 265. 269pt. 375.
INT. BLACK VELVET                                    Leia's POV Mynock
_____

ARTISTE  :                    CHARACTER:     D/R:      M/UP:        READY:
_____

KENNY BAKER                   ARTOO          133       10.00       AS REQD.


ART DEPT./PROPS:              Cockpit dressing.
                             Rocking fx.
                             Mynock fx.


SFX:                         Cockpit practicals.
                             Artoo practicals.
                             S/BY readouts.
                             S/BY cable release fx.
                             Artoo's probe.
                             Harley's wallet to open.

CAMERA:     (*)              Vistavision fx.

BLUE SCREEN:                 Via Stan Sayer.

(*) IN THE EVENT OF VISTAVISION FX. BEING RE-POSSESSED BY 1ST UNIT, S/BY:

                             INSERT OF SNOWSPEEDER CABLE RELEASE
                             HAND INSERTS FOR SNOWSPEEDER
                             INSERT OF ARTOO - PROBING DOOR CONTROL


EDITORIAL                    Moviola on set.
                             Footage as reqd.


CATERING:                    AM & PM breaks for 50 persons on Stage 8 please.




                                          DOMINIC FULFORD
                                          Assistant Director
```

(Junk Room set where Chewbacca fights the Ugnaughts for C-3PO's body parts ©1979 LFL)

July 30th, 1979

• PRODUCTION CALL SHEET ON PAGE 147.

• Irvin Kershner is hit in the head by a cable gun.
He had headaches for the next several days.

July 31st, 1979

• PRODUCTION CALL SHEET ON PAGE 148.

• Footage of Luke Skywalker's leap from the gantry to escape Darth Vader is shot.

August, 1979

• Matte artist Harrison Ellenshaw begins working part-time at ILM.
Ellenshaw worked at Walt Disney Studios early in his career. He joined ILM to work on *Star Wars* after which he returned to Disney. In addition to *Star Wars* and *Empire* his film credits include *Tron*, *The Black Hole,* and *Dick Tracy*.

```
                    CHAPTER II PRODUCTIONS LTD.              Call Sheet No: 96
                                                                 (Studio)

PRODUCTION:     "THE EMPIRE STRIKES BACK"          DATE:   Monday, 30th July, 1979.
DIRECTOR:       IRVIN KERSHNER                      UNIT CALL:          8.30 a.m.
SET:                                               STAGE 2:
1.  INT. JUNK ROOM                                 Scs:  S360.
2.  EXT. SNOW-WALKER INSERT                   for   Sc:   173
```

ARTISTE :		CHARACTER:	D/R:	M/UP:	READY:

---

1. INT. JUNK ROOM . . . . . . Sc. 360:

PETER MAYHEW		CHEWBACCA	92	8.30 for rehearsal	

SPECIAL ARTISTES:

5 HOGPERSONS			86/88/90	8.30 for rehearsal	

STUNT ARTISTES:

PETER DIAMOND		HOGPERSON 6		S/BY FROM 8.30	

STAND-INS:

STEPHEN CALCUTT	for	Mr. Mayhew		8.00	8.30

PROPS:	Junk/Molten dressing. Cut down 3PO pieces. Lightweight 3PO leg.
ART DEPT:	Conveyor belt fx. reqd.
WARDROBE:	S/BY with arm and knee pads for Hogpersons.
SFX:	S/BY with atmosphere fx.

---

2. EXT. SNOW-WALKER (insert for Sc. 173):

ART DEPT:	Cable gun and hook.
CAMERA:	Reverse mag required.
SFX:	Atmosphere fx. required.

CATERING:	AM & PM break for 80 persons rqd. On Stage 2 please.
TRANSPORT:	Dan Cressy to P/UP Mr. Mayhew at 6.30 a.m. to arrive by 8.30 a.m.

DAVID TOMBLIN
Assistant Director

NOTE: 'YODA' HAND FITTING . . . . 3 children from Corona . . . . . 2.15 p.m. in
                                                                              M/UP Lab.

```
2ND UNIT              CHAPTER II PRODUCTIONS LTD.         Call Sheet No: 97A
                                                             (Studio)


PRODUCTION:     "THE EMPIRE STRIKES BACK"         DATE:    Tuesday, 31st July, 1979.
DIRECTOR:       HARLEY COKLISS                    UNIT CALL:      08:30 hrs.
SETS:                                             STAGE 8:
1.  EXT. UNDER CLOUD CITY (Blue Screen)           Scs:  418pt., 419, S422, 422.
2.  INT. MAIN HANGER      (Blue Screen)           Scs:  T209pt.
3.  EXT. LANDING PLATFORM (Blue Screen)           Scs:  S409pt.
4.  EXT. BATTLEFIELD      (Blue Screen)           Trooper Inserts
5.  INT. CLOUD CITY       (Insert)                Scs:  399pt. (Artoo)
6.  INT. CLOUD CITY JUNK ROOM                     STAGE 2:  Sc. 360pt.
```

ARTISTE :		CHARACTER:	D/R:	M/UP:	READY:
MARK HAMILL		LUKE		FROM MAIN UNIT	
DAVE PROWSE		DARTH VADER		FROM MAIN UNIT	
KENNY BAKER		ARTOO		S/BY AS REQD.	
STUNT DOUBLE:					
COLIN SKEAPING	for	Mr. Hamill		AS REQD.	
SPECIAL ARTISTE:					
JANE BUSBY		Hogperson		10.00	AS REQD.
STAND-INS:					
CHRIS PARSONS	for	Mr. Hamill		08.00	08.30
DAVID ALLEN	for	Mr. Prowse		08.00	08.30
CROWD:					
3 REBEL TROOPERS				08.30	09.00

```
ART DEPT.:      Weapons for troopers. Junk dressing as usual:

SFX:            S/BY wind fx.  S/BY ice fx.  R2 probe fx.

WIRE FX:        D. Dotell to S/BY from 08.30 hrs.

CAMERA:         Vistavision fx. required.

EDITORIAL:      Relevant footage as requested please.

CATERING:       AM & PM breaks for 50 persons on Stage 8 please.

MEDICAL:        S/BY massage for Keith Vowles.




                                                DOMINIC FULFORD
                                                Assistant Director
```

August 1st, 1979

• PRODUCTION CALL SHEET ON PAGE 150.

• The previous day's footage of Luke Skywalker leaping from the gantry to escape Darth Vader is ruined during development of the film stock.

• Listed on internal ILM memo as build start date of "4 ft. Walker & HS legs", "exploding head model", and date "Walker Snowscapes" set needed.

• Alan Arnold interviews Irvin Kershner and Gary Kurtz for the book, *A Journal of the Making of The Empire Strikes Back*.

August 2nd, 1979

• Peter Mayhew wraps filming.

August 3rd, 1979

• PRODUCTION CALL SHEET ON PAGE 151.

• Alan Arnold interviews Irvin Kershner for the book, *A Journal of the Making of The Empire Strikes Back*.

• David Prowse wraps filming.

August 4th, 1979

• Date of revised Star Wars Sequel Fact Sheet containing names of the actors, crew, locations, financing, and merchandising information as well as a brief synopsis of the film which states: *A continuation of STAR WARS I. More emphasis on the characters; the screenplay will be based on the overall "Adventures of Luke Skywalker." The romantic rivalry will be resolved.*

• Director of Fan Relations Craig Miller hosts an *Empire* presentation at San Diego Comic-Con premiering the film's first trailer weeks before its theatrical debut. The trailer was such a hit that Miller ended up showing it twice.

CHAPTER II PRODUCTIONS LTD.   Call Sheet No: 98
(Studio)

PRODUCTION: "THE EMPIRE STRIKES BACK"   DATE: Wednesday, 1st August, 1979.
DIRECTOR: IRVIN KERSHNER   UNIT CALL: 08.30 a.m.
SET: STAGE 2:
INT. BLACK VELVET (Hologram)   Sc. 280pt.

ARTISTE :		CHARACTER:	D/R:	M/UP:	READY:
MICHAEL CULVER		CAPT. NEEDA		8.00	8.30
STAND-IN:					
ROY EVERSON	for	Mr. Culver		8.00	8.30

EXTRA ARTISTES:
9 VADER CAPTAINS

PROPS: Weapons for officers.

EDITORIAL: Continuity footage/Moviola required on Stage 2.

CATERING: AM & PM breaks for 80 people on Stage 2 please.

DAVID TOMBLIN
Assistant Director

```
2ND UNIT                    CHAPTER II PRODUCTIONS LTD.          Call Sheet No: 100A
                                                                      (Studio)

PRODUCTION:     "THE EMPIRE STRIKES BACK"           DATE:     Friday, 3rd August, 1979.
DIRECTOR:       HARLEY COKLISS                      UNIT CALL:      8:30 a.m.
SETS:
1.  EXT. GANTRY - PINNACLE                          STAGE 1:  Scs. 398pt. 400 P/UPS.
2.  EXT. UNDER CLOUD CITY (Blue Screen)             STAGE 2:  Scs. 418pt. 419. 422. S422.
                                                              (Scs. to complete).
3.  EXT. BLACK VELVET (Cockpit P.O.V.)              STAGE 2:  Sc. 296pt.
4.  INT. CARBON FREEZING (Inserts)                  STAGE 2:  S391.
```

ARTISTE :		CHARACTER:	D/R:	M/UP:	READY:
MARK HAMILL		LUKE	80/82	FROM MAIN UNIT	
DAVE PROWSE		VADER	131	FROM MAIN UNIT	
STUNT DOUBLE:					
COLIN SKEAPING	for	Mr. Hamill		S/BY FROM 8.30 a.m.	
STAND-IN:					
CHRIS PARSONS	for	Mr. Hamill		08.00	08.30
DAVID ALLEN	for	Mr. Prowse		08.00	08.30

```
ART DEPT./PROPS:        Continuity props for fight sequence. Hand props.
                        Mynock discharge effects. Mynock head fx.
                        KY jelly via Keith Vowles. Mynock wing fx.

SFX:                    Atmosphere smoke fx.
                        Ridley boxes.
                        S/BY wind fx.

WIRE FX:                Derek Botell to S/BY from 08.30 a.m.

CAMERA:                 Vistavision fx.

EDITORIAL:              Moviola to Stage 2 please.
                        Relevant footage to be available.

BLUE SCREEN:            As per Dennis Bartlett.

CATERING:               PM Breaks for 50 persons on Stage 2 please.


???T NOTE:              Please don't forget the Sparks' Soiree tonight in
                        celebration of our hundredth call sheets.  A
                        magnificent century!




                                                  DOMINIC FULFORD
                                                  Assistant Director
```

(David Prowse and Jeremy Bulloch (as Boba Fett) on the set of Darth Vader's Star Destroyer ©1979 LFL)

August 6th, 1979

• Frank Oz films his first scenes for *Empire* puppeteering Yoda opposite Mark Hamill inside of Yoda's hut.

• Drawing of Cloud City reactor shaft gantry camera angle set-up done by draftsman, Ted Ambrose.

• Listed on internal ILM memo as build start date of "Oversized Snowspeeder-Luke's" and "2nd Oversized Snowspeeder" models.

• Alan Arnold interviews Irvin Kershner for the book, *A Journal of the Making of The Empire Strikes Back*.

August 8th, 1979

• Mark Hamill shoots footage in Yoda's hut, specifically the scene in which he tells Yoda, "I'm not afraid" to which Yoda replies, "You will be. You will be."

• Alan Arnold interviews Mark Hamill, Gary Kurtz, and animal trainer Mike Culling for the book, *A Journal of the Making of The Empire Strikes Back.*

(Mark Hamill shares a scene with Yoda, puppeteered by Frank Oz ©1979 LFL)

August 9th, 1979
• PRODUCTION CALL SHEETS ON PAGES 154-155.

August 10th, 1979
• Shooting on the Dagobah set, Luke Skywalker's introduction to Yoda is filmed.

• Date of internal Lucasfilm Memo from Joan Eisenberg to Pat Carr forwarding a revised edition of the *Star Wars* sequel fact sheet.

• *Variety* announces that artist Harrison Ellenshaw would be leaving Disney to work at ILM to oversee its matte painting shop for *Empire*.
Ellenshaw's matte paintings included (among many others) Cloud City exteriors, Boba Fett's Slave 1 as it appears on the Bespin landing platform, and Dagobah swamp exteriors.

<u>CHAPTER II PRODUCTIONS LTD.</u>   <u>Call Sheet No: 104</u>
                                                                (Studio)

<u>PRODUCTION</u>:   "THE EMPIRE STRIKES BACK"   <u>DATE</u>:   Thursday, 9th August, 1979.
<u>DIRECTOR</u>:   IRVIN KERSHNER   <u>UNIT CALL</u>:   8.30 a.m.
<u>SET</u>:   <u>STAR WARS STAGE</u>:
EXT. BOG CLEARING   Scs: 283 . . . . Dusk
                                                       284pt. . . . . . Dusk

---

ARTISTE :		CHARACTER:	D/R:	M/UP:	READY:
MARK HAMILL		LUKE	76/78	AS AVAILABLE FROM 2nd Unit	
FRANK OZ		YODA	80/82	S/BY FROM 8.30 a.m. @ EMI	
KENNY BAKER		ARTOO	133	S/BY FROM 8.30 a.m. @ EMI	
<u>HAND DOUBLE</u>:					
RACHEL HUNT + CHAPERONE				S/BY AT STUDIO FROM 9 a.m.	
<u>STAND-IN</u>:					
JOE GIBSON	for	Mr. Hamill		8.00	8.30

<u>PROPS</u>:   Equipment boxes, Luke's light sabre, Luke's equipment,
                            fusion furnace, power unit and cable, container of
                            processed food, spoon, case prepared for Yoda.
                            Tiny power lamp.

<u>ANIMALS/ART DEPT</u>:   Large snakes etc. as discussed to S/BY from 8.30 a.m. on set.

<u>SFX</u>:   Fusion furnace fx., power cable plugs into R2,
                            R2 are to grab power lamp, fog, mist, steam, atmosphere fx.
                            + remote R2 + Kenny Baker R2 on set from 8.30 a.m.

<u>VIDEO FX</u>:   Samuelson video engineer to S/BY and monitors etc., 8am on set.
                            plus Frank Oz personal video setup (in Frank Oz caravan).

<u>PRODUCTION</u>:   Caravan 1: (Katmobile) Frank Oz
                            Caravan 2: Mark Hamill D/Room
                            Caravan 3: Director.   * SFX drying hut as
                            Cinefood kitchen mobile.   arranged with
                                                                Roy Button
<u>FIREMAN/NURSE</u>:   To S/BY from 8.30 a.m.

<u>CATERING</u>:   AM & PM breaks for 150 persons on Star Wars Stage please
                            + running buffet for 150 people from 5.30 p.m. - Mobile by SW Stage

<u>TRANSPORT</u>:   Roy Najda to collect Mr. Hamill at 7.15 to arrive studio 8 a.m.
                            (as arranged by 2nd Unit)

<u>PRODUCTION NOTE</u>:   PROTECTIVE FOOTWEAR IS AVAILABLE IN WARDROBE 1/2, SEE
                            TINY NICHOLLS OR FRANK VIHALL, AS THE SET IS DIRTY.

                                                        DOMINIC FULFORD
                                                        Assistant Director

<u>PRODUCTION NOTE</u>:   Frank Oz is available <u>all day</u> on Thursday, 9th August.

```
2ND UNIT                    CHAPTER II PRODUCTIONS LTD.          Call Sheet No: 104A
                                                                    (Studio)

PRODUCTION:     "THE EMPIRE STRIKES BACK"        DATE:    Thursday, 9th August, 1979.
DIRECTOR:       HARLEY COKLISS                   UNIT CALL:          8:30 a.m.
SETS:
1.  EXT. GANTRY FIN (Luke C/UP)                  STAGE 1:  Sc. 398pt.
2.  INT. X-WING (Luke's POV of Artoo)            STAGE 8:  Sc. 230pt.
3.  INT. X-WING (POV's)                          STAGE 8:  Scs. 228. 266.
4.  BLUE BACKING (C/UP Rebel Troops)             STAGE 8:
5.  CLOUD CITY BACKING                           STAGE 8:  (2 Stormtroopers walking)
6.  EXT. BLACK VELVET (Cockpit POV)              STAGE 8:  Sc. 296pt.
```

ARTISTE :		CHARACTER:	D/R:	M/UP:	READY:
MARK HAMILL		LUKE	76/79	8.00	8.45
RICHARD JONES		ARTOO	133	S/BY FROM 8.30 a.m.	
STAND-IN:					
A.N. OTHER	for	Mr. Hamill		08.00	08.30
CROWD:					
CHRIS PARSONS		STORMTROOPER		8.30	9.00
ALLAN HARRIS		STORMTROOPER		8.30	9.00
A.N. OTHER		REBEL TROOPER		8.30	9.00

ART DEPT./PROPS:	1. Mynock discharge fx.
	2. Head & wing fx.
	3. Weapons for Stormtroopers.
	4. Weapons for Luke.
	5. Walking rostrum for stormtroopers.
MAKEUP:	Luke bloodied from Vader fight.
SFX:	Artoo robot required.
WIRE FX:	Derek Botell to S/BY - TIME TO BE ADVISED.
CAMERA:	Vistavision fx.
EDITORIAL:	Moviola on Stage 1 & 8.
	Footage to be available as requested.
BLUE SCREEN:	As per Dennis Bartlett.
CATERING:	AM break for 50 persons on Stage 1.
	PM break for 50 persons on Stage 8. please.
TRANSPORT:	Roy Najda to collect Mr. Hamill at 7.15 to arrive 8 a.m.

STEVE LANNING
Assistant Director

(Yoda tries to take Luke's lamp while R2 sneakily attempts to reclaim it ©1979 LFL)

(Mark Hamill receives direction from Irvin Kershner for the scene in which Luke Skywalker first arrives on Dagobah ©1979 LFL)

August 13th, 1979
• PRODUCTION CALL SHEET ON PAGE 158.

• Scenes shot on this day include Luke Skywalker's arrival on Dagobah and Darth Vader and Luke's confrontation on Cloud City.

• Listed on internal ILM memo as date "Probot model", "Rebel Fleet", and "Probot Snowscapes" set needed.

• Miki Herman notes on this day that the construction of the stop-motion stage at ILM is completed.

• The US Patent for the Boba Fett action figure is filed.

August 13th-15th, 1979
• The scene in which Luke decides to leave Dagobah is shot including Yoda's revelation that "there is another."

August 16th, 1979
• ILM finishes filming Darth Vader's Super Star Destroyer model.

August 17th, 1979
• The Muppets visit the Dagobah set.
Jim Henson arrived with some friends; Miss Piggy and Kermit the Frog.

August 20th, 1979
• Listed on internal ILM memo as date "Boba Fett Ship" model needed.

• Alan Arnold interviews Stunt Coordinator Peter Diamond for the book, *A Journal of the Making of The Empire Strikes Back*.

(Mark Hamill enjoys a set visit from Miss Piggy and Kermit the Frog ©1979 LFL)

CHAPTER II PRODUCTIONS LTD.   Call Sheet No: 106
                                                      (Studio)

PRODUCTION: "THE EMPIRE STRIKES BACK"   DATE: Monday, 13th August, 1979.
DIRECTOR: IRVIN KERSHNER   UNIT CALL: 8.30 a.m.
SET:
1. EXT. BOG CLEARING   1. Scs: 283 to complete . . . . Dusk
                                                 284pt. . . . . Dusk
2. EXT. BOG: X-WING CLEARING   2. Scs: S368 . . . . Dusk
                                                 S340
                                                 314pt.

ARTISTE :		CHARACTER:	D/R:	M/UP:	READY:
MARK HAMILL		LUKE	76/78	8.00	8.45
FRANK OZ		YODA	80/82	S/BY FROM 8.30 a.m. @ EMI	
KENNY BAKER		ARTOO	133	S/BY FROM 8.30 a.m. @ EMI	
DOUBLE:					
JOHN TATHAM	for	BEN KENOBI		S/BY FROM 8.30 ON SET	
HAND DOUBLE:					
RACHEL HUNT + CHAPERONE				S/BY AT HOME	
STAND-IN:					
JOE GIBSON	for	Mr. Hamill		8.00	8.30

PROPS: Equipment boxes; Luke's light sabre; Luke's equipment;
                    fusion furnace; power unit and cable; containers etc. for loading;
                    tiny power lamp.

ANIMALS/ART DEPT: Large snakes etc. as discussed to S/BY from 8.30 a.m. on set.
                      X-wing covered in mud etc.? R2 in position in X-wing.
                      Full X-wing in position

SFX: Fog; mist; steam; atmosphere fx; + remote R2 + Kenny Baker R2 on
                    set from 8.30 a.m. + R2 for water jet (Sc. 340) + pipaing etc.
                    Practical X-wing cockpit.

VIDEO FX: Samuelson video engineer to S/BY and monitors etc. 8 a.m. on set
                    plus Frank Oz personal video setup (in Frank Oz caravan).

PRODUCTION: Caravan 1: (Kabmobile) Frank Oz.
                    Caravan 2: Mark Hamill D/Room
                    Caravan 3: Director.
                    Cinefood kitchen mobile

ELECTRICAL: Landing lights on X-wing come on.

FIREMAN/NURSE: To S/BY from 8.30 a.m.

CATERING: AM & PM Breaks for 150 persons on Star Wars Stage please
                    + running buffet for 150 people from 5.30 p.m. - Mobile by SW Stage.

TRANSPORT: Roy Najda to collect Mr. Hamill at 7.15 to arrive studio 8 a.m.

PRODUCTION NOTE:
1. PROTECTIVE FOOTWEAR IS AVAILABLE IN WARDROBE 1/2.   SEE TINY NICHOLLS.
2. FRANK OZ WILL BE AVAILABLE ALL DAY ON MONDAY, 13TH AUGUST.

                                             DOMINIC FULFORD
                                             Assistant Director

August 20th-22nd, 1979
• Scenes filmed during this time include Luke standing atop his X-wing when he first arrives on Dagobah as well as his search for R2 after the droid is spit out of the water by the swamp monster.

August 23rd, 1979
• Jeremy Bulloch wraps filming as Boba Fett.

August 23rd-24th, 1979
• The scene in which Luke attempts to lift his X-wing using the Force is filmed.

August 23rd-27th, 1979
• Slideshow presentation of *The Empire Strikes Back* at Season/World Science Fiction Convention in Brighton, England presented by Lucasfilm Ltd.

August 24th, 1979
• PRODUCTION CALL SHEET ON PAGE 162.

• The shooting script continues to be revised by George Lucas, Irvin Kershner, and the actors including the final scene on Dagobah where Luke converses with Obi-Wan Kenobi and Yoda before leaving to help his friends.

• Sir Alec Guinness confirms that he will be reprising his role as Obi-Wan Kenobi.

• *Empire* Production Supervisor Bruce Sharman sends a memo to Make-Up and Special Creature Designer Stuart Freeborn informing him of the date of his contract termination with Lucasfilm.

August 25th, 1979
• George Lucas leaves London and flies back home to California.

August 28th, 1979
• The scene in which Luke Skywalker senses the Dark Side of the Force on Dagobah and approaches the "tree of evil" is shot.

(actor Deep Roy as Yoda for walking shots of the Jedi Master ©1979 LFL)

August 30th, 1979

• PRODUCTION CALL SHEET ON PAGE 163.

August 31st, 1979

• A dinner party on the Dagobah set is held for the cast and crew, coordinated by Gary Kurtz's wife, Meredith.

• Local and trade papers announce the deal between RSO Records and Lucasfilm for the release of the *Empire* Soundtrack.

September, 1979

• Lucasfilm's Los Angeles offices officially move to 3855 Lankershim Boulevard in North Hollywood, CA.

• Ralph McQuarrie paints a fitting image for the Lucasfilm announcement.

(Ralph McQuarrie's painting reflecting the Lucasfilm move ©1979 LFL)

September 1st, 1979

• Listed on internal ILM memo as build start date of "Walker Oversize Foot" model.

September 3rd, 1979
• PRODUCTION CALL SHEETS ON PAGES 164-165.

• Alan Arnold interviews Irvin Kershner for the book, *A Journal of the Making of The Empire Strikes Back.*

September 3rd-5th, 1979
• Mark Hamill finishes his scenes on the weather vane beneath Cloud City.

September 4th, 1979
• A new design for the Rebel Cruiser is approved at ILM.

(Mark Hamill sits atop the weather vane beneath Cloud City in one of the film's final scenes ©1979 LFL)

CHAPTER II PRODUCTIONS LTD.   Call Sheet No: 116
                                                      (Studio)

PRODUCTION: "THE EMPIRE STRIKES BACK"   DATE: Friday, 24th August, 1979.
DIRECTOR: IRVIN KERSHNER   UNIT CALL: 8.30 a.m.
SET: "STAR WARS" STAGE:
EXT. BOG SWAMP   Sc. U313, 311, S313 S311pt.
X-Wing section (½ scale)   V313, 340pt., S310, 359pt.
                                                    283pt.

ARTISTE :	CHARACTER:	D/R:	M/UP:	READY:

MARK HAMILL   LUKE   80/82   8.45 for reh. then M/UP
KENNY BAKER   ARTOO   133   S/BY @ STUDIO FROM 8.30
DEEP ROY   PERSPECTIVE YODA   8.30 for Rehearsal

STUNT ARTISTES:
PETER DIAMOND   )
COLIN SKEAPING   )   S/BY FROM 8.30 a.m. @ EMI

STAND-IN:
JOE GIBSON   8.00   8.30

CAMERA: Poss. Vistavision shot - camera as available from 2nd Unit.

PROPS: Luke's equipment, etc. Waders. Silver bar. Yoda bag etc.
                 Large Yoda stick for Perspective Yoda.

ANIMALS/ART DEPT: Various snakes etc.; Wing section ½ scale; muddy R2 dressing.

SFX: Possible practical cockpit opening; dashboard lights etc.
                 Water creature; periscope fx. in water; remote R2;
                 Kenny Baker R2; R2 in water; R2 ejecting muddy water;
                 poss. bubble fx. in water; R2 flying out of water fx.;
                 radio controlled Yoda on set (Ref. Ron Hone). Fog/mist/
                 smoke/'atmosphere' fx.; wet suits; air bottles, etc.
                 + X-wing moving rigs. Rocks Sc. S310; silver bar cutting fx.;

DEREK BOTELL: Possible flying rig R2. S/BY studio from 8.30 a.m.

WARDROBE: Mark in Orange flying suit with dry repeats. Poss wetsuit
                 underneath. Towels, etc.

ELECTRICAL: Landing lights on X-wing in water.

PRODUCTION: Caravan 1: Production.
                 Caravan 2: Mark Hamill.
                 Caravan 3: Director.
                 SFX. drying room as per Roy Button - Dave Watkins.
                 Cinefood kitchen.

MAKEUP: Tree monster in place - practical.

FIREMAN & NURSE: To S/BY from 8.30 a.m.
CATERING: AM & PM breaks for 150 persons on "Star Wars" Stage please.
                 Sandwiches for 150 persons at 5.30 p.m. on SW Stage please.

TRANSPORT: R. Najda to P/UP Mr. Hamill at 8.00to arrive by 8.45 a.m.

PRODUCTION NOTE: PROTECTIVE FOOTWEAR IS AVAILABLE IN WARDROBE 1/2, SEE
                     TINY NICHOLLS OR FRANK VIHALL, AS THE SET IS DIRTY.

                                          DOMINIC FULFORD
                                          Assistant Director

```
                    CHAPTER II PRODUCTIONS LTD.              Call Sheet No: 120
                                                                 (Studio)

PRODUCTION:    "THE EMPIRE STRIKES BACK"      DATE:    Thursday, 30th August, 1979.
DIRECTOR:      IRVIN KERSHNER                 UNIT CALL:        8.30 a.m.
SET:                                          "STAR WARS" STAGE:
EXT. BOG SWAMP                                Sc. U313, 311, S313 S311pt.
X-Wing section (½ scale)                         V313, 340pt., S310, 359pt.
                                                 283pt.
_____

ARTISTE  :                    CHARACTER:    D/R:      M/UP:           READY:
_____

MARK HAMILL                   LUKE          80/82     8.45 for reh. then M/UP
KENNY BAKER                   ARTOO         133       S/BY @ STUDIO FROM 8.30


STUNT ARTISTES:
PETER DIAMOND       )
COLIN SKEAPING      )                                 S/BY FROM 8.30 a.m. @ EMI

STAND-IN:
JOE GIBSON                                            8.00            8.30
```

EDITORIAL: Moviola + relevant footage on SW Stage from 8.30 please.

CAMERA: Poss. Vistavision shot – camera as available from 2nd Unit.

PROPS: Luke's equipment, etc. Waders. Silver bar. Yoda bag etc.
Large Yoda stick for Perspective Yoda.

ANIMALS/ART DEPT: Various snakes etc.; wing section ½ scale; muddy R2 dressing.

SFX: Possible practical cockpit opening; dashboard lights etc.
Water creature; periscope fx. in water; remote R2;
Kenny Baker R2; R2 in water; R2 ejecting muddy water;
poss. bubble fx. in water; R2 flying out of water fx.;
radio controlled Yoda on set (Ref. Ron Hone). Fog/mist/
smoke/'atmosphere' fx.; wet suits; air bottles, etc.
+ X-wing moving rigs. Rocks Sc. S310; silver bar cutting fx.;

DEREK BOTELL: Possible flying rig R2. S/BY studio from 8.30 a.m.
& hanging rig for Luke Sc. 359.

WARDROBE: Mark in Orange flying suit with dry repeats. Poss wetsuit
underneath. Towels, etc.

ELECTRICAL: Landing lights on X-wing in water.

PRODUCTION: Caravan 1: Production.
Caravan 2: Mark Hamill.
Caravan 3: Director.
SFX. drying room as per Roy Button – Dave Watkins.
Cinefood kitchen.

MAKEUP: Tree monster in place – practical.

FIREMAN & NURSE: To S/BY from 8.30 a.m.
CATERING: AM & PM breaks for 150 persons on "Star Wars" Stage please.
Sandwiches for 150 persons at 5.30 p.m. on SW Stage please.

TRANSPORT: R. Najda to P/UP Mr. Hamill at 7.15 to arrive by 8 a.m.

DOMINIC FULFORD
Assistant Director

CHAPTER II PRODUCTIONS LTD.   Call Sheet No: 122
                                                    (Studio)

PRODUCTION: "THE EMPIRE STRIKES BACK"   DATE: Monday, 3rd September, 1979.
DIRECTOR: IRVIN KERSHNER   UNIT CALL: 8:30 a.m.
SETS:
1. EXT. EXHAUSE PIPE & WEATHERVANE   STAGE 4: Sc. 407pt.
2. EXT. ROTUNDA   STAGE 4: Sc. 398pt.
3. EXT. EXHAUST PIPE WEATHERVANE   STAGE 8: Sc. 407pt.
        (Blue Backing)

ARTISTE :	CHARACTER:	D/R:	M/UP:	READY:
MARK HAMILL	LUKE	80/82	8.00	8.45

STAND-IN:
JOE GIBSON   for   Mr. Hamill   S/BY FROM 8.30 ON SET

STUNT ARTISTE:
PETER DIAMOND   S/BY FROM 8.30 ON SET
COLIN SKEAPING   S/BY FROM 8.30 ON SET

SPECIAL FX: Heavy wind fx. Large VW fans reqd. Door fx. on porthole.

ART DEPT: On completion of Stage 4 weathervane sequence, weathervane
                        moves to Blue Backing (Stage 8).

CAMERA: Vistavision camera required on Stage 8.

BLUE BACKING: Stan Sayer to S/BY from 8.30 a.m. re Stage 8 Blue Backing setup
MAKEUP: Luke scarred from Vader fight. No hand.

WARDROBE: Mark in beige suit - various conditions. Long-sleeve jacket
PROPS: Luke's weapons + boxes, mattresses, etc.   to S/BY.

DEREK BOTELL: To S/BY with wire rig from 8.30 a.m. + Mark's harness.
                        + S/BY with hanging rig for Stage 8 (Blue Backing).

CATERING: AM break for 80 persons on Stage 4 please.
                        PM break for 80 persons - venue T.B.A.
                        Sandwich break at 5.30 p.m. for 80 persons - venue T.B.A.

TRANSPORT: Roy Najda to collect Mr. Hamill at 7.15 to arrive 8 a.m.
                                            DOMINIC FULFORD
                                            Assistant Director

NOTE: On completion of Sets (1) and (2) Unit will move to Stage 8 for blue
       backing sequence.

2ND UNIT | CHAPTER II PRODUCTIONS LTD. | Call Sheet No: 122A (Studio)

PRODUCTION: "THE EMPIRE STRIKES BACK"
DIRECTOR: HARLEY COKLISS
SET:
EXT. BOG SWAMP

DATE: Monday, 3rd September, 1979.
UNIT CALL: 8.30 a.m.
"STAR WARS" STAGE:
Sc. 291 Dusk + 310pt., 359pt., V313pt., Z313pt. to complete + various inserts

ARTISTE :	CHARACTER:	D/R:	M/UP:	READY:
MARK HAMILL	LUKE	80/82	TO BE ADVISED	
KENNY BAKER	ARTOO	133	S/BY AT STUDIO FROM 8.30	
STUNT ARTISTES:				
PETER DIAMOND)				
COLIN SKEAPING)			S/BY FROM MAIN UNIT	
STAND-IN:				
CHRIS PARSONS			8.00	8.45

EDITORIAL: Moviola + relevant footage on SW Stage from 8.30 please.

PROPS: Luke's equipment, etc. Waders. Yoda bag etc. Large Yoda stick for Perspective Yoda.

ANIMALS/ART DEPT: Various snakes etc.: muddy R2 dressing. Yoda house in position.

SFX: Remote R2; Kenny Baker R2; R2 in water; radio controlled Yoda on set (Ref. Ron Hone). Fog/mist/smoke/'astmosphere' fx.; wet suits; air bottles, etc; X-wing moving rigs; Rocks Sc. S310; Rain fx. on Yoda house + flying boxes, R2 etc. Sc. 359.

DEREK BOTELL: Possible flying rig R2; S/BY studio from 8.30 a.m. + hanging rig for Luke Sc. 359.

WARDROBE: Mark in Orange Flying Suit with dry repeats. Poss. wetsuit underneath. Towels, etc. and beige suit.

PRODUCTION: Caravan 1: Production.
Caravan 2: Mark Hamill.
Caravan 3: Director.
SFX. drying room as per Roy Button - Dave Watkins.
Cinefood kitchen.

MAKEUP: Tree monster in place - practical.

FIREMAN & NURSE: To S/BY from 8.30 a.m.
CATERING: AM & PM breaks for 150 persons on "Star Wars" Stage please.
Sandwiches for 150 persons on SW Stage at 5.30 p.m. please.

PAT CLAYTON
Assistant Director

REMINDER: To all 2nd Unit Personnel who have not yet had the happy experience of working on the Bog Planet set - please remember to bring your wellies!

(Mark Hamill and Sir Alec Guinness during the filming of Obi-Wan's Force ghost scenes ©1979 LFL)

September 5th, 1979

• Sir Alec Guinness arrives at Elstree Studios.
Mark Hamill greeted Guinness and fed him his lines during the shoot which took only six hours to complete.

• Final day of 1st Unit principal photography.

September 6th-7th, 1979

• The scene in which Luke stands on his hands during his Jedi training with Yoda is filmed.

September 7th, 1979

• The scene in which Yoda uses the Force to lift Luke's X-wing from the swamp is filmed.

• Listed on internal ILM memo as build start date of "Cloud Car" model.

• Stuart Freeborn's contract with Lucasfilm is terminated.

September 9th, 1979
• Irvin Kershner returns to the United States.

September 10th, 1979
• Date of the contract between Sir Alec Guinness and Lucasfilm for one quarter of one percent of the film's gross – his compensation for filming his scenes for *Empire*.

September 11th, 1979
• Mark Hamill wraps filming after 103 days of production.

September 13th, 1979
• Mark Hamill, his wife, Marilou, and their baby son, Nathan, leave London and head home to the United States.

September 14th, 1979
• Kenny Baker wraps filming.

(Kenny Baker (l) as Artoo-Detoo next to Mark Hamill's stand-in Joe Gibson (r) on the Dagobah set ©1979 LFL)

September 14th, 1979 (cont.)

• Dennis Muren photographs shot M-137 - a stop-motion scene featuring AT-ATs progressing through the snow.

September 17th, 1979

• Listed on internal ILM memo as date "4 ft. Walker & HS legs" and "exploding head model" needed.

• 2nd Unit continues filming scenes on the Dagobah set over the next few days including shots with puppeteer Dave Barclay taking over for Frank Oz and additional shots of actor Deep Roy as Yoda.

September 19th-27th, 1979

• Scenes of the Imperial Fleet assembling is storyboarded with revisions to be made in the following months.

September 24th, 1979

• 2nd Unit photography finishes on *Empire*.
The final scenes that were filmed included an insert of Luke on Hoth (portrayed by Mark Hamill's stand-in, Joe Gibson), coverage in the "tree of evil" on Dagobah and the slicing open of the Tauntaun's belly. The hand holding the lightsaber during the belly shot was Producer Gary Kurtz.

The film then entered post-production at ILM where George Lucas oversaw the special effects and editing of the film. Lucas also directed a handful of additional blue screen and insert shots.

September 26th, 1979

• Dennis Muren photographs the Hoth backdrop used for the AT-AT scenes.

September 27th, 1979

• The AT-AT set-up is torn down with the lights left in position for the next set-up.

• Reference Polaroids are taken of an unpainted Cloud Car model.

September 29th, 1979

• Alan Arnold interviews Irvin Kershner for the book, *A Journal of the Making of The Empire Strikes Back*.

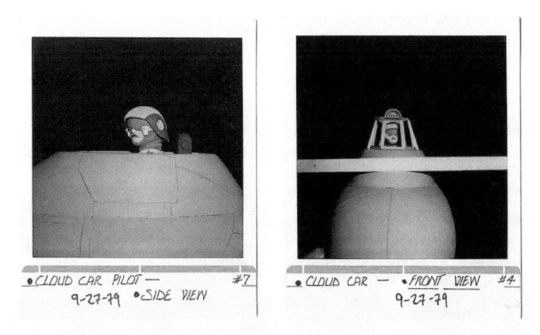

(Polaroid photos of the unpainted Cloud Car model ©1979 LFL)

October 1st, 1979

• Harrison Ellenshaw begins work at ILM full-time as head of the matte paintings shop.

• Listed on internal ILM memo as date "Walker Oversize Foot", "Cloud Car", "Rebel Cruiser (redress Princess)", "Slug & Teeth", "Oversized Snowspeeder-Luke's", and "2nd Oversized Snowspeeder" needed.

• "The Medical Frigate" is added to ILM's list of required model ships.

October 2nd, 1979

• A memo is sent from John Shepherd (Chief Accountant) to Ron Phipps (Accountant for Chapter II Productions) regarding charges for First Aid services.

October 5th-7th, 1979

• Slideshow presentation of *The Empire Strikes Back* at Windycon in Chicago, Illinois presented by Lucasfilm Ltd.

October 15th, 1979

• An internal Lucasfilm memo outlines *Empire*'s promotional plan with licensing from companies including Kenner, General Mills®, Coca-Cola®, Topps®, and Nestlè®.

October 15th, 1979 (cont.)

• Joe Johnston completes a sequence of four storyboards that showcase a new opening for the film (the scene where a Star Destroyer launches Probe Droids from its underbelly into space) as well as a storyboard featuring the Emperor.

October 15th, 22nd & 29th, 1979

• Palitoy's national press and television campaign promotional dates for the *Empire* toy line.

October 15th, 25th & 31st, 1979

• Three separate screenings of the first cut of the film where Lucas dictates 31 pages of editorial notes to Assistant Editor Duwayne Dunham.

October 18th, 1979

• Lucasfilm Director of Fan Relations Craig Miller goes to the home of Harrison Ford to interview him for the Bantha Tracks Fan Club Newsletter.
The interview appeared in the autumn 1979 issue.

October 24th, 1979

• Sound effects recorder Randy Thom visits two metal-working factories in Oakland, CA to record the sound of metal being cut mechanically which would be used for the sound of the Imperial Walker's heavy footsteps.

October 26th, 1979

• George Lucas and Joe Johnston make adjustments to the opening scene of the film with the Star Destroyer.

October 29th, 1979

• George Lucas proclaims that he is leaving for Japan to work on the film *Kagemusha* by Akira Kurosawa of which he is executive producer.

October 31st, 1979

• Alan Arnold interviews Joe Johnston and Norman Reynolds for the book, *A Journal of the Making of The Empire Strikes Back*.

November, 1979

• *The Empire Strikes Back* theatrical advance one-sheet poster is distributed to US theaters in anticipation of the sequel.
The poster featured Darth Vader's helmet against a starry background with the *Empire* logo

and the film credits beneath it. At the bottom edge read: "Coming to your galaxy this Summer."

• Frank Oz's contract with Lucasfilm is finalized for his vocal performance as Yoda. Oz was not George Lucas' first choice as the voice of Yoda, but was eventually chosen for the role.

November 1st, 1979

• Listed on internal ILM memo as date "Giant Ball-shaped Cannon", "Gun Turret", "Glowing Seeker Balls", and "Luke & Vader Fight Debris" models needed.

• Date of handwritten dialogue on yellow legal pad pages for the exchange between Darth Vader and Luke Skywalker where Vader reveals he is Luke's father.
The pages were titled "Revised Secret Pages."

(EMPIRE advance one-sheet poster ©1979 LFL)

November 2nd, 1979

• Alan Arnold is on hand at Irvin Kershner's home in Marin County as the director collects a variety of LPs and plays bits and pieces as he compiles the types of music he wants for specific scenes in the film to present to composer John Williams.

• Original date of the ADR (Automated Dialogue Replacement) session for Clive Revell as the Emperor.
The session was pushed back to an undetermined later date.

November 4th, 1979

• Revisions are made to the musical score over the film's opening.

November 5th, 1979

• Duwayne Dunham provides notes from George Lucas to Music Editor Ken Wannberg regarding editorial changes to music cues.

November 10th, 1979

• ILM films a shot of the AT-AT Walker's feet.

November 12th, 1979
• George Lucas and Joe Johnston make more adjustments to the film's opening scene.

November 14th, 1979
• Alan Arnold interviews ILM personnel, Jon Berg, Richard Edlund, Dennis Muren, Lorne Peterson, and Phil Tippett for the book, *A Journal of the Making of The Empire Strikes Back*.

November 15th, 1979
• Alan Arnold interviews Lorne Peterson, rotoscope supervisor Peter Kuran, and Brian Johnson for the book, *A Journal of the Making of The Empire Strikes Back*.

November 16th, 1979
• ILM storyboard artist Dave Carson completes a series of storyboard images of a Snowspeeder attacking an AT-AT.

November 17th, 1979
• Alan Arnold interviews composer John Williams at his Los Angeles home for the book, *A Journal of the Making of The Empire Strikes Back*.

November 19th, 1979
• ILM shoots the stop-motion Tauntaun against a blue screen for the scene in which Han Solo searches for Luke on Hoth.

November 23rd-25th, 1979
• Slideshow presentation of *The Empire Strikes Back* at Creation Con in New York, NY presented by Lucasfilm Ltd.

November 27th, 1979
• Joe Johnston completes a storyboard of Darth Vader conferring with the Emperor.

December, 1979
• Carrie Fisher, Mark Hamill, Harrison Ford, Anthony Daniels, and James Earl Jones record voice messages as their respective characters for *The Empire Strikes Back* 1-800 number promotion.
Prior to the film's release Director of Fan Relations Craig Miller wrote and produced ads for a toll free number that fans could call and listen to the characters from the film talk about what they could expect in the upcoming sequel. The number was 1-800-521-1980 (5/21/1980 being the release date of the film). Characters included Princess Leia, Han Solo, Luke Skywalker, C-

3PO, and Darth Vader.

December 3rd, 1979

• A. Johnston completes a storyboard of the Millennium Falcon flying into the asteroid cave to escape the Empire.

December 11th, 1979

• Producer Gary Kurtz sends his letter of resignation to George Lucas.

There is much speculation as to what transpired between Lucas and Kurtz during *Empire*'s production and Kurtz's eventual departure from Lucasfilm, but many sources cite the film's inflated budget and extended production schedule as being a major problem for Lucas who blamed Kurtz for allowing Kershner to take too long to shoot the film.

Kurtz stated in later interviews that Lucasfilm had turned in to a giant corporation that he didn't want to be a part of and had mentioned that towards the end he wasn't even able to speak to Lucas personally without going through his assistant.

Lucas has gone on record blaming himself for *Empire*'s troubled production saying that because he wasn't on set enough that he wasn't able to make sure the film stayed on schedule and within budget.

(ILM films the AT-AT foot crushing Luke's Snowspeeder on Hoth ©1979 LFL)

December 18th, 1979

• Hand-written ILM memo to Jim Bloom from Visual Effects Editor Michael Kelly specifies the addition of TIE Fighters to specific shots.

• ILM films the AT-AT Walker "foot shot" – the scene in which a Walker's foot crushes

Luke's Snowspeeder.

December 27th-29th, 1979

• *The Empire Strikes Back* Soundtrack begins recording during eighteen sessions at Anvil Studios in London over three days.
The music was performed by the London Symphony Orchestra and was conducted by John Williams who also wrote the score.

Part of the soundtrack was recorded briefly at Abbey Road Studios, but the majority of recording took place at Anvil.

December 29th, 1979

• ILM films the matte painting of Cloud City used for the Millennium Falcon's approach to the city.

(artist Harrison Ellenshaw with one of many matte paintings of Cloud City ©1979 LFL)

1980

1980

• Burger King's® *The Empire Strikes Back* promotional tie-in begins.
Customers could buy four different collector glasses, similar to the *Star Wars* promotion in 1978. Glasses included Darth Vader, R2-D2 and C-3PO, Luke Skywalker, and Lando Calrissian.

• Burger Chef's *The Empire Strikes Back* promotional tie-in begins featuring exclusive posters by artist Boris Vallejo.
Posters included scenes from Dagobah, Hoth, and Cloud City.

(Boris Vallejo TESB promotional poster ©1980 LFL)

• Burger King's *The Empire Strikes Back* promotional tie-in – Super Scene Collection begins.
This promotion featured a fold-out chart where you could place 48 stamps that, when completed, made up 12 scenes from *Empire*. This promotion continued into 1981.

• *The Empire Strikes Back* Super 8mm Reels are released for home viewing.

• Release of *The Empire Strikes Back* Play-Doh® Action Set.

• O-Pee-Chee and Topps release *The Empire Strikes Back* trading cards.
Topps also released *The Empire Strikes Back* Photo Cards - oversized 5"x7" trading cards of promo stills and images from the film.

(THE EMPIRE STRIKES BACK logo used for all Kenner toy packaging ©1980 LFL / Kenner)

January, 1980

• Mark Hamill, Anthony Daniels, and Peter Mayhew film their episode of *The Muppet Show* which features Luke Skywalker, C-3PO, Chewbacca, and R2-D2 in various skits throughout.

• *Toy and Hobby World* runs a Kenner ad for *The Empire Strikes Back* toys.
The ad featured early prototypes including 12" action figures from *Empire* of Luke and Leia in their Bespin outfits, Han in his Hoth outfit, as well as Lando Calrissian – none of which were ever released.

January 1st, 1980

• *Star Wars The Empire Strikes Back Mix or Match Storybook* by Wayne Barlowe is published by Random House®.

January 3rd, 1980

• A hand-written production memo to Jim Bloom regarding film stock dated 1-03-80.

January 7th-10th, 1980

• *The Empire Strikes Back* Soundtrack recording sessions continue.

January 15th, 1980

• Richard Edlund films effects of the AT-AT walker's head exploding.

The explosion was filmed at the San Francisco Armory.

January 17th-18th, 1980

• *The Empire Strikes Back* Soundtrack recording sessions continue and are completed.

The score was orchestrated by Herbert W. Spencer, recorded by engineer Eric Tomlinson and edited by Kenneth Wannberg with supervision by Lionel Newman.

John Williams himself took over duties as record producer from George Lucas.

January 18th, 1980

• Additional pick-up shots are completed with Mark Hamill at Elstree Studios in England.

January 25th, 1980

• Dennis Muren completes shot M-141 which is a scene in which an AT-AT fires its cannons.

January 29th, 1980

• The patents for the X-wing Starfighter and TIE Fighter toys are issued by the US Patent Office to George Lucas.

February 1st, 1980

• *The Empire Strikes Back* 1-800 telephone line goes into operation.

The pre-recorded messages were written and produced by Craig Miller who had the actors from the film record them in character.

The number was only available in the United States.

February 2nd, 1980

• ILM films more of the stop-motion Tauntaun with Han Solo as he searches for Luke on Hoth.

February 5th, 1980

• Lucasfilm General Manager Jim Bloom sends a letter to actress Marjorie Eaton with the Emperor's lines included for her to memorize.

Eaton was filmed at ILM as the Emperor later in the month. Unfortunately her performance was not what they were looking for and so she was replaced by Elaine Baker (wife of special FX make-up artist Rick Baker) in a full facial prosthetic mask designed by her husband. These are the final shots that are used in the film with chimpanzee eyes superimposed over Baker's.

((l to r) Harrison Ellenshaw, Ralph McQuarrie, and Michael Pangrazio in costume for their cameos in EMPIRE ©1979 LFL)

February 9th, 1980

• George Lucas, Gary Kurtz, and Irvin Kershner come together at ILM to film a pick-up shot in which Joe Johnston, Harrison Ellenshaw, Michael Pangrazio, and Ralph McQuarrie all appear together as Rebel soldiers.

The scene, which depicted Rebels prepping for the Empire's attack on Hoth, was originally shot in London during production on *Empire*, but Lucas did not like the look of it and decided to reshoot it and have the film's production artists as the Rebel soldiers.

The scene featured a painting of the Rebel Hangar by McQuarrie as the background. The only one to speak any lines was Joe Johnston.

February 11th, 1980

• Date of Kenner 1980 Advertising Plans brochure with an emphasis on the *Empire* toy line.

February 18th, 1980

• Memo from ILM Senior Staffer Patty Blau to Director of Publications Carol Titelman with an attached film strip that showcases the work being done on the lightsaber effects by "two or more outside animation people."

February 19th, 1980

• George Lucas directs insert shots of Luke Skywalker.

The scenes shot included a close-up of Luke releasing his harness to fall from the AT-AT and Luke's feet frozen to the ceiling of the Wampa cave. Standing in for Mark Hamill in both shots was Jim Bloom.

February 21st, 1980

• Irvin Kershner is interviewed by *Starlog* Magazine as he is working on *Empire* – specifically, "looping dialogue."

The term refers to the process of ADR (Automated Dialogue Replacement) where actors overdub their lines in a recording studio. Usually this is done to replace bad audio recorded on set or sometimes just to get a better take of a line after filming has completed.

• Air date for *The Muppet Show* episode 417 which features Mark Hamill (who appears as both Luke Skywalker and himself during the episode), R2-D2, C-3PO, and Chewbacca.

February 23rd, 1980

• Joe Johnston completes revised storyboards of the AT-ST "Chicken Walker" for its late inclusion in the film where it appears in two different shots.

March 2nd, 1980

• An ad appears in *The Los Angeles Times* for Kenner's Star Wars Sweepstakes.
The ad stated that First Prize winners were awarded a trip to Washington D.C. to see the premiere of the film on May 18th, although the screening was actually held on May 17th. Secondary prizes included *Empire* toys from Kenner and *Empire* patches.

March 3rd, 1980

• ILM films test shots of the stop-motion Tauntaun running.

March 5th, 1980

• ILM films the stop-motion version of Luke riding his Tauntaun across the snow plains of Hoth for the opening sequence of the film.

March 11th, 1980

• Hand-written ILM production sheet bears this date for a composite shot of a Y-Wing for the final scene of the film where we see the Rebel Fleet.

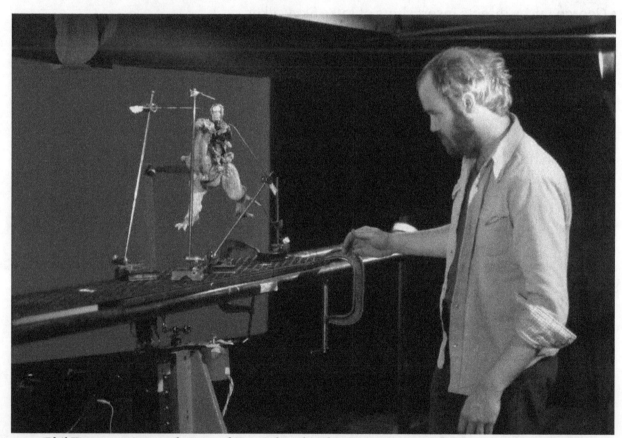

(Phil Tippett animates footage of Han Solo riding his Tauntaun against blue screen ©1979 LFL)

March 13th, 1980

• ILM shoots more footage of the stop-motion version of Han Solo riding his Tauntaun on Hoth.

March 20th, 1980

• Lucasfilm internal memo from Miki Herman to Duwayne Dunham stating: "George would like you to make a list of which outside opticals are missing from these reels."

• *Starlog* magazine interviews Producer Gary Kurtz in Los Angeles, CA for an exclusive interview that appears in issue #36.

March 22nd, 1980

• A screening of the film is held for executives at Twentieth Century Fox on the Fox Studios lot.

March 25th, 1980

• Nilo Rodis-Jamero creates four drawings that plot out the final scene of the movie.

March 27th, 1980

• Production sheet regarding art matte composite shot is dated 3/27/80. Shot #CC36.

March 31st, 1980

• Extended expiration date for Kenner's Boba Fett mail-away offer.
With four proofs of purchase you could send in for a free Boba Fett action figure. Included with the figure was an insert sheet that mentioned Boba Fett's first appearance in the Star Wars Holiday Special (listed as "A Wookie Holiday" [sic]) as well as the character playing a major role in the next Star Wars movie, "The Empire Strikes Back."

The promotion showcased a spring-launched plastic rocket that would fire out of Boba Fett's back, however, Kenner scrapped the idea due to "safety reasons" and included an apology letter along with the figure allowing those who received the figure the option to return it and have it replaced with any Star Wars mini-action figure of their choice. Existing cardbacks with the Boba Fett offer had stickers placed over the expiration date showcasing the new expiration date. This would happen again as the expiration date was eventually extended until December 31st.

• A photoshoot is held at London's Oxford Street with Darth Vader and two Stormtroopers.
The Vader costume was a licensed replica manufactured by N. J. Farmer Associates.

March 31st, 1980 (cont.)

• UK toy company Chad Valley launches an in-store promotion giving away a Boba Fett action figure with three purchases of any other Star Wars action figures.

• ILM's internal completion date for *Empire*.

April 1st, 1980

• According to George Lucas' agreement with Twentieth Century Fox for *Empire*, Lucasfilm and Fox's split on the sequel would change to 90/10 in favor of Lucasfilm on this date.

• Expiration date for *The Empire Strikes Back* Sweepstakes contest.

April 4th, 1980

• Internal ILM memo listing final shots to be completed.

April 9th, 1980

• Memo to secretary Chrissie England asking to have documents signed by Ralph McQuarrie notarized.

• BBC program *The Risk Business* features *Empire* and discusses the business side of the film industry and the affect of shooting big budget Hollywood movies in the UK. The episode featured interviews with the cast and crew and behind-the-scenes footage from the film exclusive to this program.

April 11th, 1980

• Harrison Ellenshaw, Ralph McQuarrie, and the rest of the ILM matte team complete all paintings on this day.

April 12th, 1980

• *The Empire Strikes Back* novelization by Donald F. Glut is published by Del Rey. It sold 2 million copies during its first week of release.

• *The Empire Strikes Back* Storybook by Shep Steneman is published by Random

House.

April 14ᵗʰ, 1980

• The TV program *Film 1980* features *The Empire Strikes Back*.

April 16ᵗʰ, 1980

• The final reel of the film is delivered.

April 17ᵗʰ, 1980

• George Lucas puts into place an employee bonus plan which enables qualified staff to share in the profits of *Empire*.

• *The Hollywood Reporter* prematurely states that the film is "done."

April 18ᵗʰ, 1980

• The US Patent for the Tauntaun toy is filed.

April 19ᵗʰ, 1980

• George Lucas previews *Empire* for a small audience at the Northpoint Theater in San Francisco – the same theater where he previewed *Star Wars* years earlier.
Those who attended the screening were asked to fill out questionnaires and whose responses were mostly positive.

April 21ˢᵗ, 1980

• The "Action Negative" of the film is delivered to DeLuxe for coloring.

April 23ʳᵈ, 1980

• Luke's rescue from beneath Cloud City is finalized in post-production.

• *The Sun* newspaper in the UK begins an *Empire* serialization of the story utilizing promotional photographs - some pulled from the *Empire* novelization.

April 29ᵗʰ, 1980

• "Yoda's Theme" and "The Imperial March" premiered on this day during John

Williams' first concert as official conductor-in-residence of the Boston Pops Orchestra.

C-3PO made an appearance at this event.

• The Dolby stereo optical soundtrack negative is delivered.

May, 1980

• First appearance of Boba Fett in comic book form in the Marvel Comics graphic novel adaptation of *The Empire Strikes Back*.

• *Sunday Times Magazine* in the UK showcases *Empire* with an article titled "A New Empire of Illusion" featuring an interview with Producer Gary Kurtz.

(1ˢᵗ wave of Kenner's Empire Strikes Back action figure line
©2019 Kim D. M. Simmons / themanwhoshotlukeskywalker)

• 1ˢᵗ wave of Kenner's *Empire Strikes Back* action figure line is released.

This first wave featured 10 new characters from *Empire* including Princess Leia (Bespin

Gown), FX-7 Medical Droid, Imperial Stormtrooper (Hoth Battle Gear), Hoth Rebel Soldier, Bossk, IG-88, Luke Skywalker (Bespin Fatigues), Han Solo (Hoth Outfit), Lando Calrissian, and Bespin Security Guard. An action figure of Yoda was supposed to have been released at this time, but Lucasfilm wanted Kenner to wait to introduce the character until after the film had premiered so as not to spoil the surprise. Yoda was released later in the year after *Empire* had already been seen by the masses.

Kenner released a total of 32 new action figures in 1980 on *Empire* cardbacks. Similar to the *Star Wars* line there were variations to the back of the cards that featured different layouts of the figure images as well as different vehicles, playsets, and promotional offers showcased on the lower portion of the card. New vehicles and playsets were also introduced from *The Empire Strikes Back* including the Snowspeeder, Hoth Ice Planet Action Playset, Darth Vader's Star Destroyer Action Playset, and the Imperial Attack Base. Kenner also released the Droid Factory - an item not seen in any of the films - where kids could build their own droids from a variety of available toy parts.

One of the most notable items released this year was the Darth Vader Collector's Case, a three dimensional likeness of Darth Vader's head and shoulders that would open up to reveal storage slots for 31 action figures and a special weapon and accessory storage chamber. These collector cases were first released only through store catalogs such as Sears Roebuck and Montgomery Ward, but were later available on store shelves. They became one of the most popular Kenner Star Wars items ever made and are to this day one of the most recognizable.

(Darth Vader Collector's Case ©1980 LFL)

• *The Empire Strikes Back* Official Collector's Edition book is released to coincide with the film and is sold in movie theaters as a movie program and also at newsstands. It featured many behind-the-scenes photos, stills from the movie, interviews with the cast and crew, and interesting tidbits about the film's production.

• First issue of *The Empire Strikes Back Official Poster Monthly* magazine is published featuring character info, behind-the-scenes info about the film, and a giant full-color poster every month.

May 1st, 1980

• Release date of *Empire* as listed in the original sequel contract between Lucasfilm and Twentieth Century Fox.

May 3rd-4th, 1980

• Special screenings of the film for cast and crew members of *Empire* are held in London at the Odeon Cinema in Leicester Square beginning at 10:15am on both dates.

May 5th, 1980

• Harrison Ford, Carrie Fisher, Mark Hamill, Billy Dee Williams, David Prowse, Anthony Daniels, and Peter Mayhew attend an autograph signing at Selfridges Department Store in London.

May 6th, 1980

• A press screening of *Empire* is held at Odeon Cinema in Leicester Square in London where the film would premiere later that month.
Another screening was held at the Dominion Theater, also in London.

May 9th, 1980

• BBC2 re-airs the *Empire* episode of *The Risk Business* in which host Michael Rodd visits the film's production.

May 16th, 1980

• Release date of the soundtrack to *The Empire Strikes Back* on the RSO Record Label.
The album was released on vinyl, cassette, and 8-track formats.

May 17th, 1980

• *The Empire Strikes Back* premieres at The Kennedy Center in Washington, D.C. as a Special Olympics Children's World Premiere event.
In attendance were Carrie Fisher, Mark Hamill,

(TESB Soundtrack ©1980 LFL / RSO Records)

Harrison Ford, Billy Dee Williams, Frank Oz, Kenny Baker, David Prowse, Peter Mayhew, Irvin Kershner, Gary Kurtz, and Lawrence Kasdan along with over 600 children and their chaperones.

(the cast of EMPIRE at the Kennedy Center Premiere of the film ©1980 LFL)

May 18th, 1980

• BBC2 airs *Star Wars: Music by John Williams*, a special that focuses on composer John Williams' career and most notably his score for *Empire*.

The special included interviews with Irvin Kershner, Gary Kurtz, George Lucas, Steven Spielberg, and Ben Burtt. It also included behind-the-scenes footage of scoring the scene between Han Solo and Princess Leia in the carbon-freezing chamber where it is presented with and without music.

• Mark Hamill, Carrie Fisher, Billy Dee Williams, and Harrison Ford fly from

Washington DC to England to attend the London premiere of *Empire*.

May 19th, 1980

• A press screening of the film is held in New York City at the Loew's State Theater. Irvin Kershner attended this screening.

• Exclusive screenings of *Empire* were held for Kenner salaried employees on May 19th and 20th at Showcase Cinemas in Springdale, OH.
The May 19th screening was held at 3 pm while the following day's screening was held at 9:30 am.

It was stipulated that employees were not expected to come to work before the screening on May 20th, but were expected to come in after. Employees were allowed to bring 1 guest each.

• *Time* magazine features Darth Vader on the cover for their story about *The Empire Strikes Back* written by Gerald Clarke.
Clarke described Empire as "...a better film than *Star Wars*." The article confirmed that the film was dubbed as *Episode V* with the first Star Wars film being confirmed as *Episode IV*.

• The UK television program *Clapperboard* airs a special on *Empire* where host Chris Kelly interviews David Prowse, Anthony Daniels, and ILM FX supervisor Brian Johnson.

• A final press/promotional screening of *Empire* is held at the Dominion Theater in London.

• Harrison Ford, Mark Hamill, Carrie Fisher, David Prowse, Kenny Baker, and Peter Mayhew pose for photographs with Imperial Stormtroopers outside of the Savoy Hotel.

May 20th, 1980

• The Royal Charity Premiere in London at the Odeon Cinema in Leicester Square.
The special event was dubbed "Empire Day," a playful take on the British Commonwealth Day holiday (known as Empire Day prior to 1958).
Celebrity attendees included Harrison Ford, Carrie Fisher, Mark Hamill, Billy Dee Williams, Kenny Baker, Peter Mayhew, Anthony Daniels, Sir Alec Guinness, Irvin Kershner, Gary Kurtz,

Steven Spielberg, Paul Simon, Art Garfunkel, Martin and Janet Sheen, Sid Ganis, and the Countess of Snowdon, Princess Margaret.

• A special screening of *Empire* is held at the Northpoint Theater in San Francisco, CA. The flyer for the screening read: The Northern California Benefit Preview to help match the National Endowment for the Arts Challenge Grant to the University Art Museum, Berkeley/Pacific Film archive. Tickets for this screening were $20 and included a specially designed, limited edition collector's T-shirt.

• Another special screening of *Empire* is held in Los Angeles, CA at the former Avco Center Cinema on Wilshire Blvd for the Crossroads School in West LA.
Each invitation to the screening was a die-cut Darth Vader head. After the screening a buffet dinner was held where attendees received a carved Lucite sparkling star with "The Empire Strikes Back" imprinted inside. The star was placed inside of a blue velvet bag.

(EMPIRE advance theatrical poster ©1980 LFL)

May 21st, 1980

• *The Empire Strikes Back* is released theatrically in the United States and the United Kingdom.

Empire's initial US release was limited to 127 theaters and was released on 70mm prints. It broke 125 house records for its opening day and achieved the highest single-day per theater grossing of all time with an opening 3-day weekend gross of $4.9 million. The film grossed a total of $181.4 million (domestic) in its initial run and at the time became the third largest grossing film behind *Star Wars* and *Jaws*. [5]

• *Empire* premieres in Seattle, WA at the Seattle International Film Festival (the festival's final year at The Moore Egyptian Theater).

• Both the Egyptian Theater in Los Angeles, CA and the UA Cinema 150 in Seattle, WA play the film for 24 hours straight opening day.

• After seeing the film with an audience George Lucas realizes that the ending may be a bit confusing to movie goers as they are missing key establishing shots that showcase the location of Lando and Chewie in relation to Luke, Leia, R2, and 3PO during their final interaction aboard the Medical Frigate.

Lucas contacted ILM General Manager Tom Smith about adding extra shots to the movie. Smith asked him if he was joking to which Lucas stated that he wasn't. Joe Johnston sketched the shots into storyboards and faxed them over to Smith. ILM quickly put the shots together in time for the 35mm wide release the following month.

There were many other minor changes and tweaks between the 70mm and 35mm versions of the film including some scene edits, shot omissions, special fx updates, dialogue changes, and other various items to improve the overall look and feel of the movie.

May 23rd, 1980

• UK based newspaper *The Telegraph* publishes a review of *Empire* by critic Eric Shorter who criticizes the film for *"the usual emphatic pride in machinery and paucity of characterization that marks so much space fiction."*

May 25th, 1980

• A benefit screening of *Empire* is held at the Egyptian Theater in Hollywood, CA at 6:30pm.

Souvenirs were presented at the door as a thank you for contributions.

May 26th, 1980

• President Jimmy Carter invites Defense Secretary Harold Brown and Chinese Vice Premiere Geng Biao to a special White House screening of *Empire*.

May 27th, 1980
• Writer Joy Gould Boyum reviews *Empire* for *The Wall Street Journal*.
Her review was a mixed bag of good and bad, but the byline summed it up: *A Dazzling Sequel That Loses Charm of the Original.*

• *US* magazine features *Empire* with a small photo of Leia and Chewie from the cockpit of the Millennium Falcon on the cover.
The magazine featured interviews with Carrie Fisher, Harrison Ford, Mark Hamill, Billy Dee Williams, and matte artist, Harrison Ellenshaw.

May 28th, 1980
• George Lucas receives a letter from the DGA (Director's Guild of America) demanding $250,000 in fines for placing the director's name at the end of the film and not at the beginning as well as other assorted credit issues.
Since the film had been made by Lucasfilm's European Production Company it was not subject to the DGA's rules and regulations. In spite of this the DGA fined Director Irvin Kershner $25,000. This made Lucas furious and he immediately resigned from the DGA and paid Kershner's fine himself. [4]

It has been rumored that Steven Spielberg was asked to direct *Return of the Jedi*, but could not due to his membership with the DGA.

May 29th, 1980
• Marvel Comic's *Star Wars Weekly* UK comic is renamed *The Empire Strikes Back Weekly* in issue #118 and is the first issue of the comic adaptation of the film.

May 31st, 1980
• Original expiration date of Kenner's Secret Star Wars Action Figure promotion. With four proofs of purchase you could send in for a new action figure from *The Empire Strikes Back*. The identity of the figure was kept a secret during the promotion to not only incite interest among kids and collectors, but also to keep the sequel film's details under wraps.

The promotion appeared on Kenner's *Star Wars* 20-back and 21-back action figure packaging as

(Kenner promotional offer on ESB 21-back action figure card back ©1980 LFL)

well as the *Empire Strikes Back* 21-back action figure packaging.

The promotion was extended until December 31st and stickers were placed on existing packaging to reflect the date change.

The secret figure was later revealed to be the alien bounty hunter, Bossk.

June, 1980
• Ballantine Books releases *The Empire Strikes Back Sketchbook*, a large size collection of concept art from the film including drawings by Joe Johnston and Nilo Rodis-Jamero.

• *Starlog* magazine features *The Empire Strikes Back* on the cover with a photo of Darth Vader on his Star Destroyer and the tagline: *Darth Vader Returns!*
The issue featured interviews with Special F/X Supervisor Brian Johnson and Billy Dee Williams (Lando Calrissian), an Empire color "Pin-Up" section, and an article discussing the newly reformed Star Wars Fan Club featuring quotes from Lucasfilm publicist Craig Miller discussing how Lucasfilm had taken the Fan Club out of the hands of a third party company and ran it directly.

• *Starburst* magazine volume 2 #10 features *Empire* on the cover with a photo of Chewbacca and an insert photo of Princess Leia and the 2-1B Medical Droid. The tagline reads: *The Return of Chewbacca!*
The issue featured a making of article.

• *American Cinematographer* magazine features *The Empire Strikes Back* with two paintings by Ralph McQuarrie adorning the cover.

• *Photoplay* magazine features Darth Vader on the cover and the interior article includes quotes from Carrie Fisher, George Lucas, and Gary Kurtz.

• Kenner launches a national and local television promo campaign in the United States for the Hoth Ice Planet Action Playset.

June 3rd, 1980
• Marvel Comic's Star Wars comic book series begins its six issue adaptation of *Empire* with issue #39 (dated as September on the cover).
It was written by Archie Goodwin and drawn by artists Al Williamson and Carlos Garzon. Simultaneously Marvel released a paperback version of the entire adapted story. The paperback version included an early concept version of Yoda drawn by Ralph McQuarrie that Lucasfilm originally provided Williamson and Garzon prior to the final design by Stuart

Freeborn. Freeborn's revised version of the Jedi Master appeared corrected in the monthly comic.

The comic also contained differing dialogue than the final film as it was written based on an early draft of the script that had certain lines changed during production by Irvin Kershner and the cast.

June 9th, 1980
• *People* magazine features Yoda on the cover and has an interview with puppeteer Frank Oz.

June 12th, 1980
• *Rolling Stone* magazine Issue #319 features an interview with George Lucas about *Empire*. The cover features Edward M. Kennedy with additional story titles: "Journey" and "Star Wars II George Lucas Talks."

June 14th, 1980
• *Billboard* magazine features a 2-page ad for the *Empire* soundtrack from RSO Records.

June 15th, 1980
• *New York Times* writer Vincent Canby reviews *Empire* for the paper.
His review was not kind and he criticized the movie for being bland and lifeless. Summing up his opinion of the movie towards the end of the article read as such:
""The Empire Strikes Back" is about as personal as a Christmas card from a bank."

June 17th, 1980
• The Star Wars comic strip features a storyline that fleshes out the relationship between Han Solo and Boba Fett in "The Frozen World of Ota."

June 18th, 1980
• The 35mm version of *Empire* expands the release to 115 more theaters and includes the new F/X shots that Lucas had ILM add to the final sequence of the movie.

June 20th, 1980
• *Empire* expands to 116 more theaters.

June 27th, 1980
• Ireland theatrical release date of *Empire*.

June 28th, 1980
• Israel and Japan theatrical release date of *Empire*.

July, 1980
• Burger King begins its 4-week *Empire* promotion which features four different *Empire* themed drinking glasses with characters and ships frosted over the glass as well as four different 12x16 glossy posters illustrated by artist, Boris Vallejo.

• An over-sized and illustrated reader's edition of *The Empire Strikes Back* novel from Ballantine Books is released.

• *Famous Monsters* magazine #165 features *Empire* on the cover with a photo of bounty hunters, Bossk, Boba Fett, and IG-88.
Articles included interviews with Don Glut, writer of *The Empire Strikes Back* novelization, and David Prowse (Darth Vader).

• *Starburst* magazine #23 features *The Empire Strikes Back* on the cover with photos of Darth Vader and Boba Fett.

• *Starlog* magazine #36 features *Empire* on the cover along with a host of other sci-fi movies.
The photo used for the cover was Darth Vader and Boba Fett in the carbon freezing chamber on Bespin. The issue included feature interviews with Gary Kurtz and David Prowse.

• *The Electric Company Magazine* issue #14244 features *The Empire Strikes Back* with a drawing of Darth Vader on the cover.

• Kenner launches its promotional network and local television ad campaign in the United States for the Snowspeeder toy.

(The Electric Company magazine cover ©1980 Children's Television Workshop)

July 1st, 1980
• Kenner launches a national and local television promo campaign in the United States for the Darth Vader Collector's Case, Snowspeeder, and Millennium Falcon.

July 7ᵗʰ, 1980
• Mark Hamill, Harrison Ford, Carrie Fisher, and Billy Dee Williams appear on the cover of *People* magazine.

July 18ᵗʰ, 1980
• Special premiere of *Empire* at the Westwood Cinema in Jackson, MI.
The 11am screening of the film was presented by the local AM radio station, WKHM, and sponsored by Montgomery Ward.

July 22ⁿᵈ, 1980
• Mark Hamill appears on the cover of *US* magazine as Luke Skywalker in his Bespin outfit with smaller photos of Han Solo, Chewbacca, and Yoda.

July 26ᵗʰ, 1980
• *Billboard* magazine reports that Freddie Mercury ends a Queen concert by riding on the shoulders of a stagehand dressed as Darth Vader.

(Freddie Mercury and Darth Vader ©1980 photo credit unknown)

August, 1980
• *Starlog* magazine #37 features *The Empire Strikes Back* on the cover with photos of the Millennium Falcon escaping a Star Destroyer from *Empire* as well as an insert photo of Han Solo and Princess Leia on Bespin. The tagline reads: "Will Han Solo Return?"
The issue featured an interview with Harrison Ford and a review of the film's soundtrack by Dennis Ahrens who called it a "masterpiece of film music."

• *Famous Monsters* magazine #166 features *Empire* on the cover with photos of Boba Fett, Darth Vader, and C-3PO.
The issue contained an article that revealed an insider's scoop on the film months prior to its release which ended up being false information that *Famous Monsters* never printed for fear of retaliation from Lucasfilm. Also included are quotes from George Lucas, Harrison Ford, Billy Dee Williams, and Mark Hamill.

• *Cinefex* magazine features *The Empire Strikes Back* on the cover with an image of AT-ATs on Hoth.

August 1st, 1980

• Kenner launches national and local television promo campaigns in the United States for the Tauntaun, Imperial Attack Base Playset, Star Destroyer Playset, Twin-Pod Cloud Car, and 'The Force' Lightsaber toys.

August 9th, 1980

• Norway theatrical release date of *Empire*.

August 12th, 1980

• Mass Market Paperback edition of *Once Upon a Galaxy: A Journal of the Making of Star Wars: The Empire Strikes Back* by Alan Arnold is published.

• *Star Wars The Empire Strikes Back: A Pop-Up Book* by Patricia Wynne is published by Random House.

August 22nd, 1980

• Boba Fett makes an in-store appearance at Gammon Toys in Lowestoft, England. Many costumed performers made toy store appearances in both the US and the UK including Boba Fett, Darth Vader, and Imperial Stormtroopers.

September, 1980

• Mark Hamill appears as Luke Skywalker on the cover of *Dynamite* magazine #76.

September 1st, 1980

• Kenner launches national and local television promo campaigns in the United States for the Droid Factory playset, X-wing Fighter, TIE-Fighter, Darth Vader TIE-Fighter, and Imperial Troop Transporter.

October, 1980

• Irvin Kershner is named Director of the Year by the National Association of Theater Owners.

• While appearing on the David Letterman Show science fiction author Isaac Asimov proclaims that he enjoyed *The Empire Strikes Back* and laments that he will probably be dead before they finish the last few Star Wars movies.
Asimov died in 1992.

• *Empire* begins screening at U.S. military base theaters in England for the first time.

• *Famous Monsters* magazine #167 features *Empire* on the cover with photos of Yoda, Darth Vader, Boba Fett, Luke Skywalker, C-3PO, Chewbacca, Lando Calrissian, R2-D2, and AT-AT Walkers.
The issue featured a glowing review of the film by magazine Editor Forrest J. Ackerman:
"I gotta tell ya, friends, I like THE EMPIRE STRIKES BACK even better than STAR WARS."

• A 35mm film print of *The Empire Strikes Back* is acquired by the Library of Congress for copyright purposes.

November, 1980

• *Starlog* magazine #40 features *Empire* on the cover with a photo of Luke Skywalker and Yoda on Dagobah.
The issue featured an interview with Mark Hamill.

• *The Empire Strikes Back Notebook* by Diana Attias (Editor) is published by Ballantine Books.
The book featured the script of the film combined with storyboards as well as quotes from Director Irvin Kershner and Script writer Lawrence Kasdan.

• *Cracked* magazine features *Empire* on the cover with a cartoon depiction of characters on Hoth including Darth Vader, Luke Skywalker on a reindeer, Chewbacca, R2-D2, and Yoda on a sled.

November 25th, 1980

• *Woman's Day* magazine features two *The Empire Strikes Back* do-it-yourself Star Wars playsets allowing kids and parents to build together a Hoth-based structure and a Dagobah swamp utilizing common household items.
The Hoth playset featured the Wampa ice cave, the "Rebel station", and a "Personnel launcher", which consisted of a rubber glove and an embroidery hoop that kids could bounce their Star Wars figures off of, launching them into the air.

The Dagobah playset consisted of a "swamp", a volcano-like structure with rocks and various swamp-esque features such as vines, and a river made of plastic wrap.

December, 1980

• *Cinefex* magazine features *The Empire Strikes Back* again on the cover with an image of Luke riding his Tauntaun taken from the stop-motion scene at the beginning of the film.

December 31st, 1980

• Extended end date of Kenner's Boba Fett action figure mail-away promotion and Secret Star Wars Action Figure promotion.

(PEOPLE magazine cover ©1980 Meredith Corporation/Mark Sennet Photography)

1981

1981

• Magnetic releases *The Making of Star Wars* and *SPFX: Special Effects of The Empire Strikes Back* documentaries on Laserdisc.

• Release of the Yoda Play-Doh Set.

• Release of Kenner's *Yoda: The Jedi Master Game*.

• Launch of Burger King's *The Empire Strikes Back* Promotional Tie-In – Everybody Wins Game.
Prizes included 36 trading cards from *The Empire Strikes Back* and *Star Wars*, a *TESB* Frisbee®, and food and drinks. Top prize was an Atari® 2600 game system.

• Yoda appears on the cover of *LIFE* magazine's special1980 "Year in Pictures" issue.

January-April, 1981

• Kenner releases its 2nd wave of *Empire Strikes Back* action figures.
Included were the figures Dengar, Imperial Commander, Rebel Commander, AT-AT Driver, Ugnaught, Leia Organa (Hoth Outfit), Lobot, Han Solo (Bespin Outfit), 2-1B, and Yoda (which had already been released the year prior).

Throughout 1981 Kenner released an assortment of new vehicles, playsets, and roleplay toys including the Turret & Probot Playset, the Dagobah playset, new Mini-Rigs, the Electronic Laser Rifle, the Yoda hand puppet, Boba Fett's Slave 1 ship, the Twin Pod Cloud Car vehicle, and the Imperial AT-AT Walker.

The Electronic Laser Rifle was the same toy rifle released for *Star Wars*, but did not have the '3-position' feature: a swinging plastic handle that could be positioned to the rear as a shoulder stock for "Laser Battle" mode, to the front as a handle underneath the gun's barrel for "Standing Guard" mode or the handle swung up for "Sneak Attack" mode. Kenner removed this feature from the *Empire* version of the toy by simply eliminating the swinging plastic handle altogether. The name was changed from '3-Position Laser Rifle' to 'Electronic Laser Rifle.'

(2ⁿᵈ wave of Kenner's Empire Strikes Back action figure line
©2019 Kim D. M. Simmons / themanwhoshotlukeskywalker)

January, 1981

• *MAD* Magazine releases Issue #220 which features the satire, "The Empire Strikes Out."
Lucasfilm threatened to sue the magazine to which *MAD* responded with a fan letter written by George Lucas himself in which Lucas praised artist Mort Drucker and writer Dick Debartolo as "the Leonardo Da Vinci and George Bernard Shaw of satire."

January 1ˢᵗ, 1981

• Expiration date for Canada's York Peanut Butter Darth Vader "Action Poster" promotional offer.

January 2ⁿᵈ, 1981

• German magazine *Gong* features *The Empire Strikes Back* on the cover utilizing photos from *Star Wars* of the main cast with a photo of the Star Destroyer and Millennium Falcon from *Empire.*

January 15th, 1981

• Uruguay theatrical release date of *Empire*.

February 5th, 1981

• Taiwan theatrical release date of *Empire*.

February 12th, 1981

• Peru theatrical release date of *Empire*.

February 15th, 1981

• *The Washington Post* publishes an article about the upcoming Academy Awards. Written by Peter H. Brown, the article went on to discuss Twentieth Century Fox's campaign for Frank Oz to be nominated for an Oscar for his portrayal as the Jedi Master, Yoda:

Some campaigns were merely funny, such as Twentieth Century-Fox's flashy campaign for Yoda, and Muppet of "The Empire Strikes Back," and for Darth Vader in the same picture. Should a Muppet, a puppet or a robot actually be nominated, Academy officers would have to run to their rule books. Darth Vader, which uses the voice of James Jones and the body of British actor David Prowse, would be ruled out before even a single vote was counted since the Oscar rules forbid entries whose voice is supplied by other actors. However, Frank Oz, who is both the voice and the muppeteer of Yoda, is eligible and might, given the right circumstances, be nominated.

March 5th, 1981

• The People's Choice Awards televised ceremony features *The Empire Strikes Back* as the #1 movie of 1980.
There to accept the award were Irvin Kershner, Mark Hamill, and Billy Dee Williams.

March 9th, 1981

• Internal Lucasfilm memo from Anne-Marie Stein to all employees stating that *Empire* was voted the #1 movie of 1980 by the People's Choice Awards.

March 31st, 1981

• At the 53rd Annual Academy Awards *The Empire Strikes Back* wins the Academy Award for Best Sound Mixing which is awarded to Bill Varney, Steve Maslow, Gregg Landaker, and Peter Sutton.
The film received the Special Achievement Academy Award for Best Visual Effects awarded to Brian Johnson, Richard Edlund, Dennis Muren, and Bruce Nicholson. Composer John Williams was also nominated for the Academy Award for Best Original Score, and Norman Reynolds, Leslie Dilley, Harry Lange, Alan Tomkins, and Michael Ford were nominated for the

Academy Award for Best Production Design. Lucasfilm and Twentieth Century Fox submitted Sound Designer Ben Burtt's name along with *Empire*'s sound team, but the Academy refused to acknowledge the credit of Sound Designer as a valid one so it was not allowed.

((l to r) Brian Johnson, Richard Edlund, Dennis Muren and Bruce Nicholson
©1981 Academy of Motion Picture Arts and Sciences)

May 31ˢᵗ, 1981
• Expiration date of Kenner's Survival Kit mail-away offer.
With five proofs of purchase you could send in for a pack of action figure weapons and accessories including two Hoth backpacks, Luke's Jedi training harness for Yoda, a grappling hook, three gas masks to reenact the Mynock/asteroid scene, and five assorted laser pistols and blasters. The promotion appeared on Kenner's *Empire Strikes Back* 41-back action figure packaging.

July, 1981
• Kenner photographer Kim D. M. Simmons photographs images of the toy AT-AT which will be used for the retail box and promotional imagery.

• *Starlog* magazine #48 (5ᵗʰ Anniversary Spectacular) includes a photo of Luke Skywalker and Yoda on the cover.
The issue featured interviews with George Lucas and Harrison Ford.

(AT-AT image for Kenner retail box ©1981 Kim D. M. Simmons / themanwhoshotlukeskywalker)

July 4th, 1981

• During the annual Lucasfilm Company Picnic a time capsule is filled with Star Wars and Lucasfilm memorabilia and placed into the cornerstone of the main building at Skywalker Ranch.

A commemorative ceremony was held where George Lucas placed several items inside the time capsule including the 8mm version of *The Empire Strikes Back*, a miniature AT-AT Walker in a "rosebud" crystal ball, *The Art of The Empire Strikes Back* book, and other assorted items including Frank Marshall's *Raiders of the Lost Ark* cast and crew hat.

July 23rd, 1981

• The longest theatrical run of *Empire* comes to an end in Seattle, WA at the United Artists Cinema 150 after a total of 61 weeks.

July 30th, 1981

• End date of Burger King's *The Empire Strikes Back* Everybody Wins game.

(George Lucas at the 1981 Lucasfilm Company Picnic ©1981 LFL)

July 31st, 1981

• The first theatrical re-release of *Empire*.

The film returned to movie theaters for a five-week engagement in 1,000 theaters in the US and Canada.

The re-release grossed an additional $28 million. [5]

September, 1981

• *Famous Monsters* magazine Issue #177 features *The Empire Strikes Back* with Yoda on the cover along with the title: an interview with Boba Fett.

The magazine featured an interview with writer Donald Glut, author of the *Empire* novelization, and an interview with actor Jeremy Bulloch (Boba Fett).

September 4th, 1981

• Seattle's *Bumbershoot* Festival holds free screenings of both *Star Wars* and *Empire* for the first time together as a double bill.

The screenings were free to the public and made possible by George Lucas himself who gave the prints to the festival for the screenings – the reason being that *Empire*'s theatrical run lasted longer in Seattle than anywhere else in the United States. Two screenings of the films were planned with a third announced the same day to accommodate as many fans as possible.

(EMPIRE theatrical re-release poster ©1981 LFL)

1982

1982

• Twentieth Century Fox re-releases *The Making of Star Wars* and *SPFX: Special Effects of The Empire Strikes Back* documentaries on Laserdisc (with new packaging), CED (Capacitance Electronic Disc), VHS, and Beta formats.

• Kenner launches the Star Wars Micro Collection, a series of miniature metal die-cast characters, vehicles, ships, and playsets from the first two films.

January 28th, 1982

• Hungary theatrical release date of *Empire*.

(photographer Kim D. M. Simmons sets up the iconic promotional image for the Kenner EMPIRE toy line ©1982 Kim D. M. Simmons / themanwhoshotlukeskywalker)

February, 1982

• Photographer Kim D. M. Simmons creates and shoots the iconic Kenner Toys Hoth battle scene promotional image utilizing an assortment of 3.75" and die-cast versions of the AT-AT, AT-ST, X-wing, Rebel Transport, and Snowspeeder toy vehicles. The image was used for in-store displays, print advertising, and general promotional purposes.

(final photo before laser effects added ©1982 Kim D. M. Simmons / themanwhoshotlukeskywalker)

February 15th, 1982

• Kenner 1982 Advertising Plans booklet bears this date and includes the *Empire* standard toy line and Micro Collection toy line television advertising campaign dates.

April, 1982

• Marvel UK's *The Empire Strikes Back* comic series (formerly titled *Star Wars Weekly*) features a five page story in issue #155 written by Alan Moore (Watchmen) and artist John Stokes.

April 20th, 1982

• National Public Radio and Lucasfilm announce *The Empire Strikes Back* radio drama.

April 27th, 1982

• US Patent created for the Boba Fett action figure.

U.S. Patent   Apr. 27, 1982   Sheet 1 of 4   Des. 264,109

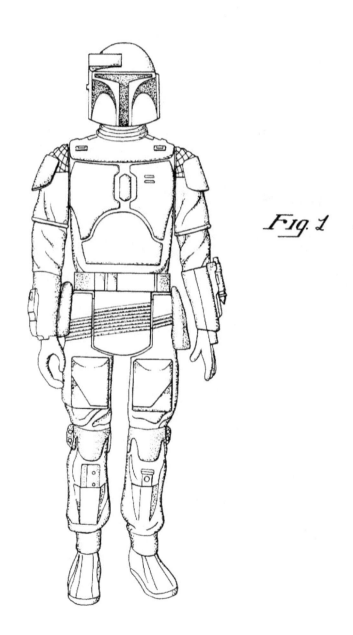

Fig. 1

May, 1982
• British theaters begin showing both *Star Wars* and *Empire* as a double-bill.
A poster was created for the event combining elements of individual posters by Tom Chantrell (*Star Wars*) and Tom Jung (*Empire*).

(STAR WARS and EMPIRE double bill poster ©1982 LFL)

May 16th, 1982
• An L. A. Times article reports that products from both *Star Wars* and *Empire* have sold more than 1.5 billion dollars' worth in retail sales worldwide.

May 31st, 1982
• Expiration date of Kenner's Display Arena mail-away offer.
For 10 proofs of purchase and $2.00 you could send in for a display stand for your Star Wars action figures. You received four "L" shaped display stands that could interconnect in a variety of shapes and patterns. The display stands included four different backdrops depicting scenes from *Empire*.
The offer appeared on Kenner's *Empire Strikes Back* 45-back action figure packaging.

June, 1982
• A handful of the original cast of *Empire* spend 10 days at A&R Studios in New York

City recording their parts for the audio of *The Empire Strikes Back Radio Drama*. Included in the sessions were *Empire* actors Mark Hamill (Luke Skywalker), Anthony Daniels (C-3PO), and Billy Dee Williams (Lando Calrissian).

The characters of Han Solo, Princess Leia, Darth Vader, Obi-Wan Kenobi, Yoda, and others were portrayed by different actors than the original film including John Lithgow (Yoda) and Perry King (Han Solo).

• Over the summer Kenner releases the AT-ST toy vehicle as well as the X-wing Fighter and TIE Fighter Micro Collection ships.

June 22nd, 1982
• The patents for the Ugnaught action figure and Tauntaun toy are issued by the US Patent Office to George Lucas.

July 6th, 1982
• The patents for the Snowtrooper and IG-88 action figures are issued by the US Patent Office to George Lucas.

August 3rd, 1982
• The patent for the Cloud Car toy is issued by the US Patent Office to George Lucas.

August 10th, 1982
• The patents for the Yoda action figure and Darth Vader's TIE Fighter are issued by the US Patent Office to George Lucas.

August 31st, 1982
• Expiration date for Kenner's Free 4-LOM mail-away offer.
For five proofs of purchase you would receive a free 4-LOM Bounty Hunter action figure through the mail. The promotion appeared on the *Empire Strikes Back* 47-back action figure packaging.

Worth noting is Kenner's mistake in mixing up the names for this figure and two other bounty hunter characters, Zuckuss and Dengar. Zuckuss (the original name was Tuckuss in the shooting script, but was changed at the last minute) was the name Lucasfilm had given to the humanoid bounty hunter covered in armor and bandages. This character would mistakenly be labeled by Kenner as Dengar. Because of this Kenner decided to use the name Zuckuss for another bounty hunter figure – a droid bounty hunter that Lucasfilm had already named 4-LOM (the name being an acronym of "for the love of money"). Having already named the first two figures incorrectly, Kenner had no choice but to release the final insectoid bounty hunter character with the name 4-LOM.

These mistakes were never corrected throughout the entire run of Kenner's vintage Star Wars line and these would be the names most would attribute to the characters for many years until learning of the mistake second hand – many through the Star Wars Roleplaying Game.

(as designated by Kenner – (l to r) 4-LOM, Dengar, and Zuckuss
©2019 Kim D. M. Simmons / themanwhoshotlukeskywalker)

September, 1982

• Release of *The Empire Strikes Back* video game on the Atari 2600 gaming console published by Parker Brothers®.

The game was a left-to-right side scrolling battle simulation in which the player piloted a Snowspeeder over the snow plains of Hoth.

The object of the game was to shoot down enemy AT-AT Walkers before they reached your base.

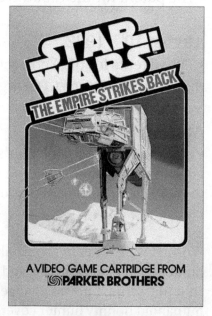

(©1982 Atari)

October, 1982

• Kenner releases its 3rd wave of *Empire Strikes Back* action figures.

Included were the figures Cloud Car Pilot, Bespin Security Guard (black), AT-AT Commander, Luke Skywalker (Hoth Battle Gear), C-3PO (Removable Limbs), R2-D2 (with Periscope), Tie Fighter Pilot, Zuckuss, and 4-LOM.

(3rd wave of Kenner's Empire Strikes Back action figure line
©2019 Kim D. M. Simmons / themanwhoshotlukeskywalker)

October 12th, 1982

• *The Jedi Master's Quiz Book* is released by Del Rey which features trivia questions about *Star Wars* and *The Empire Strikes Back* including obscure questions derived from the film's novels.

The book was written by then 11-year old Rusty Miller from Florida.

November 2nd, 1982

• The patent for the AT-AT Walker toy is issued by the US Patent Office to George Lucas.

November 19th, 1982

• *Empire* is again re-released in theaters grossing an additional $13,276,241.00. [5]

• The name of Darth Vader's Super Star Destroyer, the Executor, is revealed for the first time in the Star Wars daily comic strip.

While the name appeared in *The Empire Strikes Back Sketchbook* this was the first time it appeared in story-form as it was absent from the film, the novel, and the comic adaptation.

November 23rd, 1982
• The patent for the Snowspeeder toy is issued by the US Patent Office to George Lucas.

(Kenner Snowspeeder with Tauntaun and assorted action figures
©1980 Kim D. M. Simmons / themanwhoshotlukeskywalker)

1983

1983
• Release of *The Empire Strikes Back* video game on the Intellivision gaming console published by Parker Brothers.

January, 1983
• Turkey theatrical release date of *Empire*.

• *Famous Monsters* magazine #190 features *Empire* on the cover with a portion of the film's movie poster as the imagery.
The issue discusses the re-release of *Empire* in theaters prior to the release of *Return of the Jedi*.

(©1982 Warren Publishing)

January 31ˢᵗ, 1983
• Expiration date for Kenner's Build Your Armies mail-away offer.
This promotion was specifically for Kenner's Star Wars Micro Collection from the *Empire Strikes Back* line. For two Micro Collection proofs of purchase you would receive six die cast figures (three Hoth Rebel soldiers and three Imperial Snowtroopers).
This promotion appeared only on Kenner's Micro Collection packaging.

February 17ᵗʰ-18ᵗʰ, 1983
• *The Empire Strikes Back Radio Drama* airs for the first time on National Public Radio in the United States.
This 10-part radio adaptation of the original film, *Star Wars: Episode V: The Empire Strikes Back*, was written by Brian Daley and directed by John Madden. The radio drama expands on the movie's storyline and incorporated new scenes such as an Imperial attack on a Rebel convoy taking place before the film's original opening and a conversation between Han Solo and Luke Skywalker in their make-shift shelter while stranded in the cold at night on Hoth.

National Public Radio promoted the series in part by getting Craig Claiborne (long-time food editor and restaurant critic for *The New York Times*) to create his version of Yoda's root leaf stew recipe, which the Jedi Master serves Luke in his hut on Dagobah. The recipe ran in magazines and newspapers across the country.

March 8ᵗʰ, 1983
• The patents for the TIE Bomber and Rebel Transport toys are issued by the US Patent Office to George Lucas.

April 17ᵗʰ-23ʳᵈ, 1983
• The iconic Yoda READ poster is launched at libraries all over the world as part of National Library Week.
The poster showed a photo of Yoda from *The Empire Strikes Back* holding a book and stated: "READ and the Force is with you."

April 26ᵗʰ, 1983
• The patent for Boba Fett's Slave 1 ship toy is issued by the US Patent Office to George Lucas.

May 5ᵗʰ, 1983
• Australia theatrical re-release of *Empire*.

(©1983 LFL)

May 10ᵗʰ, 1983
• The patents for the Imperial Probe Droid toy and the 2-1B medical droid action figure are issued by the US Patent Office to George Lucas.

May 25ᵗʰ, 1983
• The third installment of the Star Wars saga, *Return of the Jedi*, premieres worldwide. Originally titled *Revenge of the Jedi*, the name was changed at the last minute by George Lucas even after Lucasfilm had publicly announced the original title.

Many promotional items carried the original title including Kenner's *Revenge of the Jedi* action figure promotion, movie posters, press kits, and other assorted imagery tied to the film. The Star Wars fan club eventually sold *Revenge* posters which now fetch quite a bit on the collector's market. Bootlegged versions have littered the market for quite some time.

December 3ʳᵈ, 1983
• The documentary *From Star Wars to Jedi: The Making of a Saga* is broadcast for the

first time on PBS.

The special featured behind-the-scenes interviews and video footage from all three Star Wars films with a heavy focus on *Return of the Jedi* as well as an exclusive interview with George Lucas.

It was written and directed by Richard Schickel and narrated by Mark Hamill.

December 13th, 1983

• The patent for the Rebel Escort/Medical Frigate toy is issued by the US Patent Office to George Lucas.

The toy would be released for the first time many years later as part of Galoob's Micro Machines line in 1995.

United States Patent [19]

Lucas, Jr. et al.

[11] **Des. 271,780**

[45] ∗∗ **Dec. 13, 1983**

[54] **TOY SPACE VEHICLE**

[75] Inventors: George W. Lucas, Jr., San Anselmo; Joseph E. Johnston, Fairfax; Nilo Rodis-Janero, San Jose, all of Calif.

[73] Assignee: Lucasfilm, Ltd., North Hollywood, Calif.

[∗∗] Term: **14 Years**

[21] Appl. No.: **260,469**

[22] Filed: **May 4, 1981**

[51] Int. Cl. .... D21—01
[52] U.S. Cl. D21/87
[58] Field of Search .... D21/87, 88, 89, 128; D12/319, 320, 321, 12; 46/74 A, 74 B, 76 R, 76 A, 79

[56] **References Cited**

U.S. PATENT DOCUMENTS

D. 157,535 2/1950 Quick D21/87
D. 260,789 9/1981 Probert D21/87
D. 263,856 4/1982 Probert D21/87

Primary Examiner—Charles A. Rademaker
Attorney, Agent, or Firm—Townsend & Townsend

[57] **CLAIM**

The ornamental design for a toy space vehicle, substantially as shown and described.

DESCRIPTION

FIG. 1 is a side perspective view of a toy space vehicle showing our new design;
FIG. 2 is a right side elevational view thereof;
FIG. 3 is a top plan view thereof;
FIG. 4 is a bottom plan view thereof;
FIG. 5 is a rear elevational view thereof;
FIG. 6 is a front elevational view thereof;
FIG. 7 is a cross-sectional view thereof taken along line 7—7 in FIG. 2; and,
FIG. 8 is a cross-sectional view thereof taken along line 8—8 in FIG. 2.

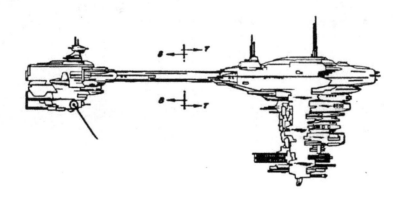

(REVENGE OF THE JEDI poster by artist Drew Struzan ©1983 LFL)

1984

1984

• Artist Lee Seiler files a multi-million dollar lawsuit against George Lucas, Lucasfilm, Industrial Light and Magic, Joe Johnston, and Twentieth Century Fox claiming the AT-ST 'Chicken Walker' design was stolen from him.
Ralph McQuarrie, who began sketching Armored Tank Walkers in late 1977, was asked to provide evidence for the hearing.

In addition to monetary compensation Seiler demanded that all instances of the walkers be removed from film prints of both *The Empire Strikes Back* and *Return of the Jedi*. The case went to court in 1986 and due to lack of evidence to support Seiler's claims the district court granted summary judgment to Lucas at the evidentiary hearing.

April 23rd, 1984

• Bulgaria theatrical release date of *Empire*.

September 2nd-3rd, 1984

• The entire Star Wars trilogy is screened at the 42nd World Science Fiction Convention in Los Angeles, CA.
1,100 patrons of the marathon were given a button that proclaimed "I sat through the Trilogy."

September 5th, 1984

• Ralph McQuarrie is sent a subpoena to testify in court regarding the Seiler v. Lucasfilm case.

September 10th, 1984

• The court date given to Ralph McQuarrie regarding the Seiler v. Lucasfilm case, although McQuarrie was told to ignore this date and call Lucasfilm's attorneys to obtain an 'appropriate time and place.'

November 13th, 1984

• *The Empire Strikes Back* is released on VHS, Beta, Laserdisc, and CED formats with the VHD format released only in Japan.

CBS/FOX paid $15 million for the video cassette rights to *Empire* and the film went on to reach the number one spot for video rentals and sales.

(THE EMPIRE STRIKES BACK original VHS cassette tape and sleeve ©1980 LFL / CBS/FOX)

1985

1985
• Re-release of *The Empire Strikes Back* on Laserdisc in Standard Play as opposed to the previously released version which was Extended Play (time compressed).

• First release of *The Empire Strikes Back* soundtrack on CD via Polydor Records.

February 20th, 1985
• The song "Yoda", by parody artist and musician "Weird" Al Yankovic, is recorded. The song appeared on his third album, *Dare to Be Stupid* (1985), and was a parody of the song "Lola" by the Kinks. Inspired by the events of the movie *The Empire Strikes Back*, the song was told from the perspective of Jedi-in-training Luke Skywalker and concerned his dealings with Master Yoda on the planet Dagobah. The song was initially written and recorded in 1980 around the original release of *The Empire Strikes Back* and achieved success on radio via *The Dr. Demento Show*, however, securing permission from both Star Wars creator George Lucas and "Lola" songwriter Ray Davies delayed the physical release of the song for about five years.

"Yoda" was never released as a single and no music video was ever made for it. Nevertheless the parody went on to be one of Yankovic's most famous songs. It was re-released twice in 1994 on both *Greatest Hits Volume II* and the box set, *Permanent Record*. The song also appeared on the 2009 compilation, *The Essential "Weird Al" Yankovic*.

The song has been a consistent staple of his live shows for many years.

March, 1985
• Atari releases *The Empire Strikes Back* vector-based arcade game, which is simply a conversion kit for the original *Star Wars* vector-based arcade game.
The game was also released in 1988 by Domark for various home computer systems including the Commodore 64, Atari ST, Amiga, BBC Micro, and others. The game is also included as an unlockable extra on *Star Wars Rogue Squadron III: Rebel Strike* on Nintendo's® GameCube system.

March 28th, 1985
• The entire Star Wars Trilogy is released for the first time as a triple-bill in a one-day,

eight-city event across the United States in select cities including Los Angeles, New York, Chicago, Seattle, and Denver as well as screenings in Canada, the UK, France, Germany, and Australia.

The films were shown in 70mm and all US screenings began at 4pm.

April 12th, 1985

• *The Empire Strikes Back: Step-Up Movie Adventure* hardcover is published by Random House.

This book geared towards children featured color photos from the film with an adaptation of the script by Larry Weinberg.

June 12th, 1985

• Paperback printing of *The Empire Strikes Back* by LucasBooks.

June 18th, 1985

• The music album *Dare To Be Stupid* by "Weird" Al Yankovic is released featuring the song "Yoda".

*(STAR WARS TRILOGY Triple Bill Ad in the New York Times
©1985 LFL/Twentieth Century Fox)*

1986

1986

• Re-release of *The Empire Strikes Back* on VHS with an included 10th Anniversary trailer.

• Re-release of *The Empire Strikes Back* on Laserdisc in Japan as full-screen and non-time compressed.

February 1st, 1986

• *The Empire Strikes Back* on cable television channels HBO, Prism, and The Movie Channel.

February 2nd, 1986

• *The Empire Strikes Back* on cable television channels Showtime and Home Theater Network.

February 4th, 1986

• *The Empire Strikes Back* on HBO.

February 7th, 1986

• *The Empire Strikes Back* on cable television channels The Movie Channel and Z Channel.

February 8th, 1986

• *The Empire Strikes Back* on Showtime, Z Channel, and Home Theater Network.

February 9th, 1986

• *The Empire Strikes Back* on HBO and Z Channel.

February 10th, 1986

• *The Empire Strikes Back* on Z Channel.

February 11th, 1986
- *The Empire Strikes Back* on Showtime and Z Channel.

February 12th, 1986
- *The Empire Strikes Back* on Z Channel.

February 13th, 1986
- *The Empire Strikes Back* on The Movie Channel and Z Channel.

February 16th, 1986
- *The Empire Strikes Back* on The Movie Channel.

February 17th, 1986
- *The Empire Strikes Back* on HBO, Showtime, Prism, and Home Theater Network.

February 21st, 1986
- *The Empire Strikes Back* on Showtime.

February 22nd, 1986
- *The Empire Strikes Back* on HBO and Prism.

February 23rd, 1986
- *The Empire Strikes Back* on First Choice, Super Channel, and Prism.

February 26th, 1986
- *The Empire Strikes Back* on Showtime, Super Channel, and Home Theater Network.

February 27th, 1986
- *The Empire Strikes Back* on HBO.

February 28th, 1986
- *The Empire Strikes Back* on Prism and First Choice.

1987

(THE EMPIRE STRIKES BACK Special Collection Laserdisc from Japan ©1986 LFL / CBS/FOX)

1987

• Re-release of *The Empire Strikes Back* on Laserdisc in Japan as widescreen 'Special Collection' version.

This re-release was formatted in CAV (Constant Angular Velocity) allowing for clear freeze framing and slow motion playback. The release had each disc in its own separate sleeve with chapter descriptions and the "Special Collection" letters on the packaging printed in gold. This was the first letterbox version of the film on home video.

1987 (cont.)
• The original trilogy is re-released on home video for the 10th Anniversary of *Star Wars*.

May, 1987
• Reissue of all three Original Trilogy novels as a single trade paperback book titled *The Star Wars Trilogy*.

(Gene Roddenberry (l) with George Lucas (r) - photo by Lee Forbes ©1987 Starlog Magazine)

May 24th, 1987
• *Starlog* magazine hosts a screening of *Empire* at the *STARLOG Salutes Star Wars* 10th Anniversary convention event in Los Angeles, CA at the Stouffer Concourse Hotel's Grand Ballroom.
Irvin Kershner introduced the film and fielded questions from attendees prior to the screening. Gary Kurtz, Anthony Daniels, Billy Dee Williams, Dennis Muren, Charles Lippincott, and Lorne Peterson were also in attendance at the convention as was George Lucas who did a fan Q&A – something that Lucas has rarely ever done.

Gene Roddenberry (creator of *Star Trek*) was also in attendance and appeared for the first time on stage together with Lucas. The event was written and directed by *Starlog* publisher Kerry O'Quinn.

October 2nd-4th, 1987

• The Star Wars Trilogy is screened in 70mm as part of the Twentieth Century Fox Film Retrospective.

This three day event marked the opening of the AMC Century 14 Theater at the Century City Shopping Center in Los Angeles, CA. The Film Retrospective occurred due to the fact that the property on which the theater was built was previously part of the Twentieth Century Fox production lot.

Many Twentieth Century Fox films from the 30s, 40s, 50s, 60s, 70s, and 80s were screened during the event including the Star Wars Trilogy. *Empire* was screened daily at 7:15pm.

The AMC Century 14 closed its doors on December 13th, 2005.

November 12th, 1987

• *Star Wars: The First Ten Years Movie Storybook Trilogy* is published by Random House.

A compilation of the original *Star Wars*, *The Empire Strikes Back*, and *Return of the Jedi* movie storybooks.

November 22nd, 1987

• *The Empire Strikes Back* Network Television Premiere on NBC® – ranked 32nd for the week with a 14.5 rating.

The premiere was an NBC *Sunday Night at the Movies* presentation and featured an introduction by Darth Vader (voiced by James Earl Jones).

The opening of the broadcast was "interrupted" by the Empire with a message that read "WE INTERCEPT YOUR EARTH BROADCAST IN THE NAME OF THE GALACTIC EMPIRE" followed by a montage of scenes from the film with the following voiceover from Darth Vader:

"Welcome. Through this intergalactic broadcast, your planet, and thousands like it, are witnessing the glorious victory of the Galactic Empire. Tonight, we will finally crush Luke Skywalker and his Rebel Alliance. This time, there will be no escape from the Dark Side of the Force when the Empire strikes back."

(TV Guide ad for THE EMPIRE STRIKES BACK Network Television Premiere on NBC ©1987 TV Guide)

1988

1988

• Domark re-releases *The Empire Strikes Back* vector-based arcade game for various home computer systems including the Commodore 64, Atari ST, Amiga, BBC Micro, and others.

February, 1988

• Soviet Union release date of *Empire* as part of the Days of US Cinema in the USSR Film Festival.

October, 1988

• West End Games releases *Assault on Hoth*, a board game that recreates *Empire*'s Battle of Hoth scene - specifically the Rebel Snowspeeders VS the Imperial AT-ATs. *Assault on Hoth* was the second Star Wars board game from West End Games, the first being *Star Warriors* released in 1987 – the same year the company acquired the Star Wars license. West End Games declared bankruptcy in 1998 and lost the license which was picked up by Wizards of the Coast in 2000 and retained until 2010.

The license is currently held by Fantasy Flight Games who acquired it in August of 2011.

(ASSAULT ON HOTH board game box art ©1988 West End Games)

1989

1989
• Re-release of *The Empire Strikes Back* on Laserdisc in the USA as wide-screen extended play version (non-time compressed).

January-February, 1989
• Wargamer Magazine Vol. 2 issue #10 features West End Games' *Assault on Hoth* on the cover.

April 22nd, 1989
• The Star Wars Trilogy is screened together for the first time in Utah at the Mann Theatre in Salt Lake City.
70mm versions of the movies were screened for one day only and started at 10am. The event was a benefit for The Primary Children's Medical Center and was hosted by local radio station, KCPX.

May, 1989
• Reissue of all three Original Trilogy novels as a single hardcover and trade paperback book titled *Classic Star Wars Trilogy*.

September 1st, 1989
• *The Empire Strikes Back RPG Galaxy Guide 3* by Michael Stern and Pablo Hidalgo is published by West End Games.

(Star Wars: The Roleplaying Game Galaxy Guide 3: THE EMPIRE STRIKES BACK
©1989 West End Games)

1990

1990
• Soviet Union theatrical wide release of *Empire*.

March 19th-20th, 1990
• John Williams conducts the Skywalker Symphony Orchestra (a group of 95 musicians from the San Francisco Bay Area) who perform music from the original trilogy for a special recording session at Skywalker Sound using 20-bit technology.
It was the first digital recording of any Star Wars music and was later released as *John Williams Conducts John Williams: The Star Wars Trilogy* by Sony® Classical.

May, 1990
• The Star Wars Fan Club releases an exclusive *Empire* poster for the film's 10th Anniversary featuring unused artwork by artist Lawrence Noble done during the film's original theatrical release.

(10ᵗʰ Anniversary Limited Edition Poster by Lawrence Noble ©1990 LFL)

1991

December 30th, 1991

• North American release date of *Star Wars: The Empire Strikes Back* video game for the Nintendo® Entertainment System.

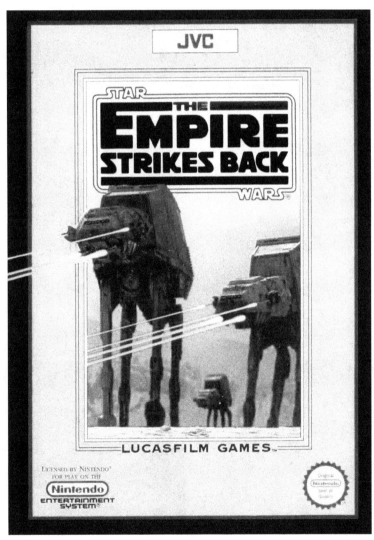

(STAR WARS: THE EMPIRE STRIKES BACK game cover artwork for the NES ©1991 Nintendo)

1992

● ━━━━━━ ● ━━━━━━━━━━ ● ━━━━━━━ ● ━━━━━━ ●

1992

• Re-release of *The Empire Strikes Back* as part of the Special Letterbox Collector's Edition Widescreen box set on VHS.

• Reissue of *The Empire Strikes Back* on Laserdisc in full-screen with FOX/CBS logo as opposed to CBS/FOX – the film is also time-compressed again on this release.

May 10th, 1992

• North American release date of *Star Wars: The Empire Strikes Back* video game for the Nintendo Game Boy.

June, 1992

• Paperback edition of *Empire* published by Del Rey/Ballantine Books.
The red cover version with the 'Gone with the Wind' style poster as the book's cover art.

December, 1992

• LucasArts, JVC and *Electronic Gaming Monthly* magazine launch a contest for the *Super Star Wars: The Empire Strikes Back* video game.
The contest was a multiple choice questionnaire appearing in volume 5, number 12, issue 41 of *EGM* for which the Grand Prize was to have the winner's likeness appear in the *Empire* video game.

The winner was Jeff Crosno who had his face digitally added to a Hoth soldier in one of the game's cut-scenes. Additional prizes included a Darth Vader mask, *From Star Wars to Jedi* VHS tapes, and a Star Wars T-shirt.

(Electronic Gaming Monthly magazine's Super Star Wars: The Empire Strikes Back contest
©1992 Electronic Gaming Monthly)

1993

1993
• Toy maker Galoob introduces the Star Wars Micro Machines line – a collection of small sized Star Wars ships and vehicles from the Original Trilogy.

March, 1993
• Reissue of all three Original Trilogy novels as a single paperback book titled *The Star Wars Trilogy*.

March 12th, 1993
• Japan release date of *Star Wars: The Empire Strikes Back* video game for the Nintendo Entertainment System and Nintendo Game Boy.

May 1st, 1993
• Special Collector's Limited Edition reissue of the *Star Wars* and *The Empire Strikes Back* NPR radio dramatizations.
The reissue was limited to 5,000 copies.

June 1st, 1993
• North American release of *Super Star Wars: The Empire Strikes Back* video game for the Super Nintendo Entertainment System.
The game received very positive reviews when it was released and was praised for its graphics.

September, 1993
• *Nintendo Power* magazine issue #52 features an article on the making of *Super Star Wars The Empire Strikes Back* game.

• Re-release of *The Empire Strikes Back* as part of the The Definitive Collection (Widescreen

(Super Star Wars The Empire Strikes Back game ©1993 LucasArts / Nintendo)

Collector's Edition) box set on standard play Laserdiscs – THX remastered.

October, 1993
• *Nintendo Power* magazine issue #53 features a 10-page feature article about *Super Star Wars The Empire Strikes Back* including a visual walk-through of each level of the game.

November, 1993
• *Super Star Wars: The Empire Strikes Back: Official Game Secrets* by Rusel DeMaria, Jeronimo Barrera, and Tom Stratton is published by Boxtree.
This official strategy guide to the *Super Star Wars: The Empire Strikes Back* game for the Super Nintendo game system featured a complete level-by-level walkthrough, strategies, techniques, and more.

November 1st, 1993
• Audio of *The Empire Strikes Back* NPR Radio Dramatization is released on CD.

November 23rd, 1993
• The Star Wars Trilogy soundtrack licenses revert back to Lucasfilm and Twentieth Century Fox Film Scores releases a special four-CD box set: *Star Wars Trilogy: The Original Soundtrack Anthology*.
This anthology included the soundtracks to all three of the original *Star Wars* films in separate discs.

The disc dedicated to *The Empire Strikes Back* restored almost all of the original seventy-five minutes from the 1980 LP version and included new music cues never released before for a total of nineteen tracks.

On the fourth bonus disc, five additional tracks from *Empire* were included in a compilation of additional cues from all three films.

December 17th, 1993
• Japan release of *Super Star Wars: The Empire Strikes Back* video game for the Super Nintendo Entertainment System.

1994

●━━━━━●━━━━━●━━━━━●━━━━━●

January, 1994

• *Star Wars: The Empire Strikes Back* Movie Script Library and Premiere Magazine's Collector's Edition script is published by O. S. P. Publishing.

February 24th, 1994

• European release of *Super Star Wars: The Empire Strikes Back* video game for the Super Nintendo Entertainment System.

May 26th, 1994

• *Classic Star Wars: The Empire Strikes Back* audio book is released on cassette tape by Time Warner.

August 1st, 1994

• *Classic Star Wars: The Empire Strikes Back Volume 1* collects the first three issues of Marvel Comics' adaptation of *The Empire Strikes Back* - the first printing since the original release in 1980.

These reprints by Dark Horse Comics® featured brand new interior coloring as well as a new cover by original artist Al Williamson created specifically for this volume.

September 1st, 1994

• *Classic Star Wars: The Empire Strikes Back Volume 2* collects the final issues of Marvel Comics' adaptation of *The Empire Strikes Back* - the first printing since the original release in 1980.

October, 1994

• Reissue of *The Art of The Empire Strikes Back* by Deborah Call.

• Reissue of *The Empire Strikes Back* novel written by Donald F. Glut.
Retitled as *Classic Star Wars: The Empire Strikes Back*.

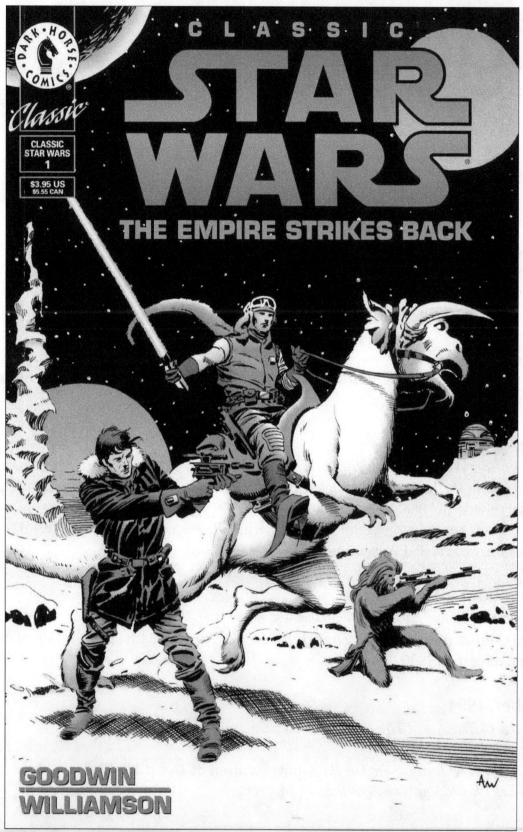

(cover of Classic Star Wars: The Empire Strikes Back Volume 1 ©1994 Dark Horse Comics)

1995

1995

• Topps releases *The Empire Strikes Back* Widevision, Widevision Finest Chromium, Mini-Posters, and Promos trading cards.

(Kenner/Hasbro's THE POWER OF THE FORCE line of toys branding ©Hasbro 1995)

• Having purchased Kenner in 1991, Hasbro® releases a new line of Star Wars toys dubbed *The Power of the Force*.
The 3.75" figures were bulkier than their Kenner predecessors and made from new molds while the ships and vehicles were copied almost directly from the original Kenner molds. The line included the Millennium Falcon, Landspeeder, AT-ST, X-wing Fighter, TIE Fighter, Snowspeeder, and Speeder Bike all with updated paint applications and new sticker designs. The packaging on figures, ships, and vehicles all featured the original Kenner logo on the back.

While being the top selling toy line of 1995, *The Power of the Force* eventually became the least valuable to collectors of any of the Star Wars toy lines. Collectors dubbed it *The Power of the Force 2* to differentiate it from the original 1985 Kenner *The Power of the Force* line.

• Release of *The Definitive Collection* widescreen Laserdisc Original Trilogy box set and the *Collector's Set* Original Trilogy Laserdisc boxset; both released only in Japan.

1995 (cont.)

• MGA (Micro Games of America) releases *The Empire Strikes Back* LCD handheld game.

May 23rd, 1995

• *The Empire Strikes Back* NPR Radio Dramatization script is published by Del Rey.

August 29th, 1995

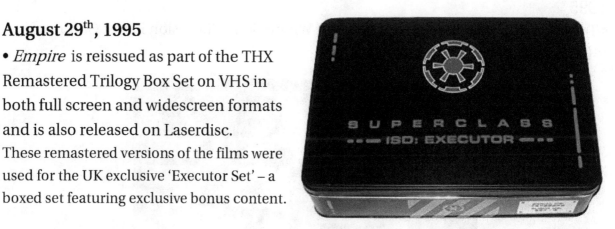

• *Empire* is reissued as part of the THX Remastered Trilogy Box Set on VHS in both full screen and widescreen formats and is also released on Laserdisc.
These remastered versions of the films were used for the UK exclusive 'Executor Set' – a boxed set featuring exclusive bonus content.

• Reissue of the hardcover version of *The Empire Strikes Back* novel written by Donald F. Glut published by Del Rey/Ballantine Books.

(the UK exclusive Executor boxed set featuring the reissued Trilogy on VHS ©1995 LFL)

The cover featured the same artwork as the VHS reissue.

October, 1995

• Energizer® releases a battery commercial featuring scenes from *The Empire Strikes Back* as well as new footage of Darth Vader battling the Energizer bunny in a mock-up of the Cloud City Carbon Freezing Chamber until his lightsaber dies because he uses generic "D" Batteries.
It was the first time a Star Wars character had been used to sell a non-licensed product in the United States.

November 21st, 1995

• *Classic Star Wars: The Empire Strikes Back* is published.
This reprint trade paperback collection includes both issues of the *Classic Star Wars: The Empire Strikes Back* comic book series by Archie Goodwin and Al Williamson.

1996

July, 1996

• *The Empire Strikes Back RPG Galaxy Guide 3* by Michael Stern and Pablo Hidalgo revised and expanded 2nd edition is published by West End Games.

November, 1996

• Lucasfilm launches the official Star Wars website, *www.starwars.com*.

1997

This year saw the release of the Special Edition versions of the original Star Wars trilogy films. Along with the theatrical re-releases came a barrage of new Star Wars marketing and merchandising ranging from toys, books, and games to fast-food and commercial tie-ins.

Of all three of the original films *Empire* had the fewest changes made to it by George Lucas. The most significant changes included new scenes shot of the Wampa in the Wampa cave, new CGI shots created for the Millennium Falcon's approach to Cloud City, Bespin city backgrounds removed and replaced with CGI exteriors, and the original Emperor replaced by new footage of Ian McDiarmid shot specifically for the Special Edition version.

1997

• Release of *The Empire Strikes Back* Special Edition as part of the Special Edition box sets available in both widescreen and full screen formats on VHS and also available on Laserdisc in widescreen.
This would be the last time any Star Wars film would be released on Laserdisc in the United States.

• RCA Victor releases a definitive two-disc set of the soundtrack to the Special Edition versions of the Original Trilogy to coincide with the theatrical releases.
This limited-edition set featured a thirty-two page black booklet that was encased inside of a protective outer slipcase. The covers of the booklet and the slipcase brandished the Star Wars Trilogy Special Edition poster art. The booklet was very detailed, providing extensive notes on each music cue as well as pictures of the main characters and action sequences from each film. Each disc bore a glittery laser-etched holographic Empire emblem.

The musical content featured the complete film score for the first time including all of the previously released tracks (restoring the Mynock Cave music which was left off the 1993 release) plus extended versions of five of those tracks with previously unreleased material and six brand new tracks of never before released music for a total of one hundred and twenty-four minutes.

All of the tracks were digitally remastered. They were rearranged and retitled from the previous releases to follow the film's story in chronological order. RCA Victor repackaged the Special Edition set later in 1997 offering it in slimline jewel case packaging as an unlimited edition, but without the original "black booklet" version's stunning presentation and packaging.

• Taco Bell® Special Edition Promotion is launched.
The promotion included drink toppers, toys, games, and figures.

• Topps releases *The Empire Strikes Back 3Di* trading cards.

• THQ re-releases the SNES *Super Star Wars: The Empire Strikes Back* video game to coincide with the Special Edition release of the film.
This version of the game was identical to the original 1993 release.

January, 1997
• Reissue of *The Empire Strikes Back* paperback novel written by Donald F. Glut.

• Reissue of all three Original Trilogy novels as a single paperback book titled *The Star Wars Trilogy*.

January 1st, 1997
• *The Empire Strikes Back: A Flip Book* by Walt Disney Company is published by Mouse Works.

January 14th, 1997
• Release of the Special Edition version of *The Art of The Empire Strikes Back* by Deborah Call which includes concept art and storyboards from the Special Edition scenes created for the revised version of the film.

• *The Empire Strikes Back* Read-A-Long storybook is reissued by Walt Disney Records on audio cassette.

January 28th, 1997
• Release of *The Empire Strikes Back* Special Edition Soundtrack.

February 2nd, 1997
• Publication date of *The Empire Strikes Back* Special Edition Comic-Book Adaptation from Dark Horse Comics.
This was a reprint trade paperback collection of the Classic Star Wars comics from Dark Horse that were already reissues of the original comic adaption of *Empire* from Marvel Comics.

February 15th, 1997
• Special screening of *The Empire Strikes Back* Special Edition for Lucasfilm, LucasArts, and Lucas Digital employees in various theaters around the San Francisco Bay Area.

February 21st, 1997
• *The Empire Strikes Back* Special Edition Theatrical release date.
The re-released film sat at the #1 spot in theaters for 2 weeks and grossed an additional $67,597,694 which brought its final domestic haul to $290,547,067 and its worldwide total to $538,375,067. [6]

From this point forward all screenings of the Original Trilogy films were of the Special Edition versions as George Lucas proclaimed them to be the only versions he considered as official. The only exception to this was a private screening of an original 1977 70mm print of *Star Wars* by the Academy of Motion Picture Arts & Sciences as part of a special presentation titled *Galactic Innovations: Star Wars and Rogue One* that focused on technology in film - specifically special effects.

The original 70mm version of the film was screened back to back with 2016's *Rogue One* two days after the presentation on June 29th, 2019.

April 1997
• *Star Wars Insider* magazine #33 features the Wampa from the Special Edition version of *Empire* on the cover and has an in-depth look at the reshoots done for the Special Edition.
The issue also featured interviews with Special Effects Technician Howie Weed who performed as the Wampa for the Special Edition revised shots, actor John Hollis who played Lobot, and Special Effects and stop-motion mastermind Phil Tippett.

April 4th, 1997
• Norway and Poland Special Edition release date.

April 7th, 1997
• Yugoslavia Special Edition release date.

April 9th, 1997
• France Special Edition release date.

April 10th, 1997
• Australia, New Zealand, Germany, Hungary, Hong Kong, and Czech Republic Special

Edition release date.

April 11th, 1997
• Austria, Brazil, Switzerland, Finland, United Kingdom, Greece, Ireland, Iceland, Italy, Mexico, Portugal, Sweden, Turkey, and South Africa Special Edition release date.

April 17th, 1997
• Argentina Special Edition release date.

April 18th, 1997
• Denmark Special Edition release date.

April 26th, 1997
• South Korea Special Edition release date.

June, 1997
• Italy Special Edition release date (Fantafestival).

June 12th, 1997
• Singapore Special Edition release date.

June 13th, 1997
• Estonia Special Edition release date.

July 5th, 1997
• Japan Special Edition release date.

August 13th, 1997
• *Star Wars: The Special Edition Box Set* is released by Dark Horse comics.
This box set was a collection of the *Star Wars Special Edition Trilogy* Trade paperback comics.

September 8th, 1997
• *Star Wars: The Annotated Screenplays* released by Del Rey featuring scripts of each film including *Empire* with quotes and notations by writer Laurent Bouzereau.

1998

March 24th, 1998

• *The Empire Strikes Back Illustrated Screenplay* is published by LucasBooks.

August 10th, 1998

• *Choose Your Own Star Wars Adventure: The Empire Strikes Back* by Christopher Golden and Phil Franke (illustrator) is published by Skylark.

This Choose Your Own Adventure style novel let you be Luke Skywalker and choose to follow the Light Side of the Force or join Darth Vader down the Dark Path.

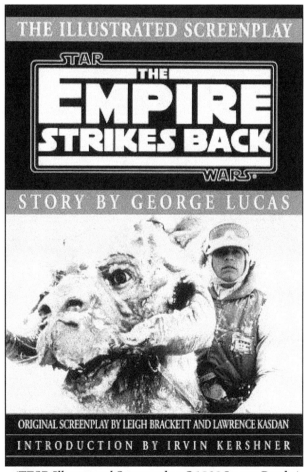

(TESB Illustrated Screenplay ©1998 Lucas Books)

1999

January 27th, 1999

• *Star Wars Manga: The Empire Strikes Back Volume 1* is published by Dark Horse.
It is the first volume in *The Empire Strikes Back* manga series and was illustrated by Toshiki Kudo and based upon the original story by George Lucas.

February 24th, 1999

• *Star Wars Manga: The Empire Strikes Back Volume 2* is published by Dark Horse.
The second volume in *The Empire Strikes Back* manga series and was illustrated by Toshiki Kudo and David Land and based upon the original story by George Lucas.

March 18th, 1999

• *The Empire Strikes Back: The Complete, Fully Illustrated Script* hardcover book is published by Virgin Books.
This version of the script included all scenes from the Special Edition version of the film.

March 31st, 1999

• *Star Wars Manga: The Empire Strikes Back Volume 3* is published by Dark Horse.
The third volume in *The Empire Strikes Back* manga series and was illustrated by Toshiki Kudo and based upon the original story by George Lucas.

April 28th, 1999

• *Star Wars Manga: The Empire Strikes Back Volume 4* is published by Dark Horse.
The fourth volume in *The Empire Strikes Back* manga series and was illustrated by Toshiki Kudo and David Land and based upon the original story by George Lucas.

August, 1999

• Reissue of *The Empire Strikes Back* paperback novel written by Donald F. Glut retitled as *Star Wars: The Empire Strikes Back*.

• Actor Morris Bush dies at the age of 69.
Bush portrayed the bounty hunter, Dengar in *Empire*. The British boxer-turned-actor appeared in many British films and TV series and was also a good friend of David Prowse.

December 31st, 1999

• *Star Wars: The Empire Strikes Back* Golden Book by Chris Angelilli is published. The book featured full-color photos from the film as well as water transfer tattoos.

(Morris Bush as Dengar in THE EMPIRE STRIKES BACK ©1979 LFL)

2000

2000

• Reissue of *The Empire Strikes Back* Special Edition as part of the Special Edition box set reissue in both widescreen and full screen formats on VHS.

This was the last time the Original Trilogy was released on VHS. This box set was also released on VCD in Malaysia and on Laserdisc in Japan.

May/June, 2000

• *Star Wars Insider* magazine #49 features a special issue focusing on the 20th Anniversary of *The Empire Strikes Back*.

The cover was inspired by the publication *The Empire Strikes Back Official Collector's Edition* (1980). The issue itself featured interviews with actor John Ratzenberger (Major Derlin), Director Irvin Kershner, writer Lawrence Kasdan, Billy Dee Williams (Lando Calrissian), James Earl Jones (voice of Darth Vader), Clive Revill (voice of The Emperor) and Donald F. Glut (author of *The Empire Strikes Back* novelization).

A section focusing on the bounty hunters included articles about and interviews with Jeremy Bulloch (Boba Fett), Jason Wingreen (voice of Boba Fett), Cathy Munroe (Zuckuss), Alan Harris (Bossk), Chris Parsons (4-Lom), and Morris Bush (Dengar). There is an article titled 'Ultimate Insider's Guide to The Empire Strikes Back' as well as articles about *Empire* related comic books, books, collectibles and more.

August 5th, 2000

• Sir Alec Guinness (Obi-Wan Kenobi) dies at the age of 86.

Guinness was a renowned Shakespearian stage actor who made the transition to film soon after World War II. In addition to his work on Star Wars Guinness was most well-known for his roles in *The Bridge on the River Kwai, Lawrence of Arabia, Doctor Zhivago,* and many others. His accolades include an Academy Award, a BAFTA, a Golden Globe, and a Tony Award. He was also knighted by Elizabeth II for his services to the arts and received a star on the Hollywood Walk of Fame.

(Harrison Ford (l), Sir Alec Guinness (c) and Kenny Baker (r) at the London premiere of EMPIRE ©1980 photo credit unknown)

2001

2001

• Hallmark releases *The Empire Strikes Back* Lunch Box and Drink Container two-piece set Keepsake ornament.

This ornament featured a miniaturized version of the original *Empire Strikes Back* metal lunchbox from the 80s with included mini thermos.

• Hasbro releases two *Empire* action figures on their *Power of the Jedi* cardbacks including FX-7 (Medical Droid) and Luke Skywalker (with Bacta Tank).

(Hasbro's POWER OF THE JEDI line Luke Skywalker Deluxe figure in Bacta Tank ©2001 Hasbro)

August 24th, 2001

• Kevin Smith's *Jay and Silent Bob Strike Back* is released to theaters.
Smith, a well-known Star Wars fan, made the film's title and logo homage to *The Empire Strikes Back* as well as a few key moments in the movie.

The film featured cameos by Carrie Fisher and Mark Hamill. Fisher portrayed a nun who gives the two title characters a ride during their trek to Hollywood to stop the movie about them from being made. Mark Hamill appeared as himself portraying the movie's villain, Cocknocker. He fought the film's heroes in a "bong saber" duel during which Cocknocker had his hand cut-off to which Hamill stated to the camera: "Not again."

During the bong saber duel Chris Rock's character (who is the director of the film) commented: "I think George Lucas gonna' sue somebody."

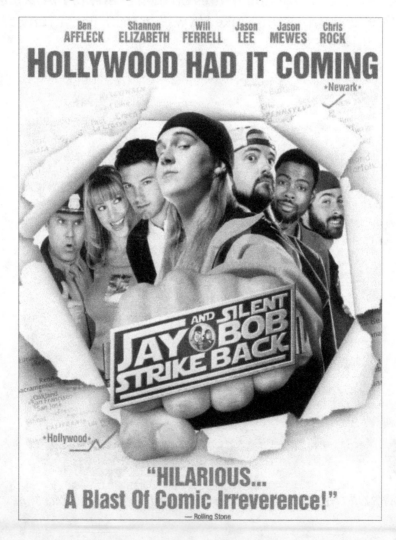

(JAY AND SILENT BOB STRIKES BACK movie poster ©2001 Miramax Films/View Askew Productions)

2002

June, 2002

• Reissue of all three Original Trilogy novels as a single hardcover book titled *The Star Wars Trilogy 25th Anniversary Collector's Edition*.

July 10th, 2002

• *Star Wars Infinites: The Empire Strikes Back Volume 1* by Dave Land is published by Dark Horse Comics.
A 'what if' storyline that deviated from the tale we all know and love.

August 28th, 2002

• *Star Wars Infinites: The Empire Strikes Back Volume 2* by Dave Land is published by Dark Horse Comics.

October 23rd, 2002

• *Star Wars Infinites: The Empire Strikes Back Volume 3* by Dave Land is published by Dark Horse Comics.

November 20th, 2002

• *Star Wars Infinites: The Empire Strikes Back Volume 4* by Dave Land is published by Dark Horse Comics.

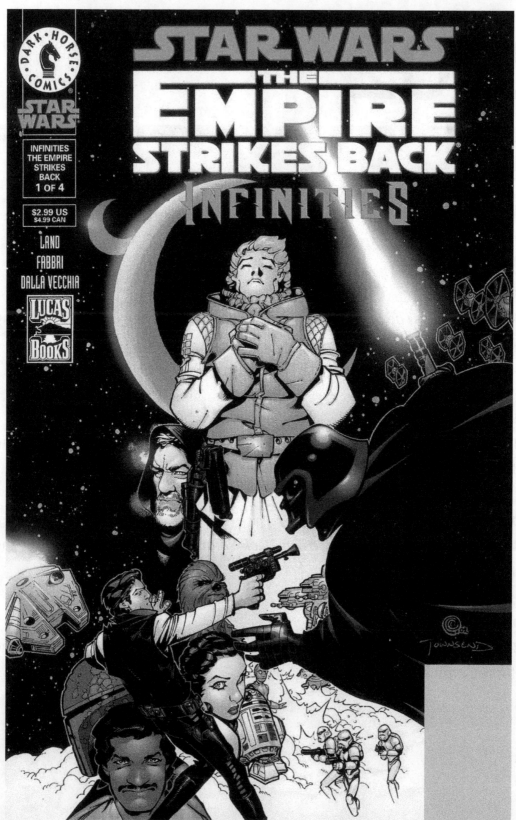

(Star Wars: The Empire Strikes Back Infinities comic cover Volume #1 ©2002 Dark Horse Comics)

2003

March 11th, 2003
• Hasbro releases a Han Solo action figure in his Hoth outfit in both blue and brown colors in reference to the fan debate over the actual color of his coat.
The parka appeared blue on screen due to the film's color correction yet was actually brown. A print ad was run by Hasbro which humorously used the controversy to promote the action figure.

April 2nd, 2003
• *Star Wars Infinites: The Empire Strikes Back* Trade Paperback by Dave Land is published by Dark Horse Comics and features all four volumes of the original comic series.

(Han Solo action figure ad ©2003 Hasbro)

2004

2004

• Sony Classical re-presses the 1997 RCA Victor release of the Special Edition Star Wars trilogy soundtrack including *The Empire Strikes Back.*

Sony Classical acquired the rights to the classic trilogy scores as it already had the rights to release the second trilogy soundtracks (*The Phantom Menace* and *Attack of the Clones*). This new set was released with the same art work as the DVD and was digitally remastered.

April 17th, 2004

• Actor Bruce Boa dies at the age of 74.

Boa portrayed General Reeikan in *Empire.*

August 24th, 2004

• *The Empire Strikes Back Step-Up Movie Adventure* hardcover is reissued by Random House.

September, 2004

• Reissue of all three Original Trilogy novels collected as a single volume trade paperback titled *The Star Wars Trilogy.*

September 8th, 2004

• A special press preview day of the Star Wars Trilogy on DVD for the first time.

The event was held at the Silent Movie Theater in Hollywood, CA and invitations were presented on the back of a Han Solo action figure cardback. The event included a THX home theater demo as well as a preview of the bonus material included in the set.

A Q&A panel was also held which included Irvin Kershner, Jim Ward, Kevin Burns, John Lowry, Rick Dean, and Van Ling. Mark Hamill was also in attendance as a special surprise guest.

Similar events took place on September 14th in Tokyo, Japan and on June 24th in the UK at the BAFTA Theatre in London. The invitation to the Japan event was presented on the back of a Luke Skywalker action figure cardback while the UK invitation was on a Princess Leia action figure cardback.

Attendees in the UK included Jim Ward, John Lowry, Gary Kurtz, Rick McCallum, and Anthony Daniels.

September 21st, 2004

• Re-release of *The Empire Strikes Back* Special Edition on DVD for the first time in a special box set of the Original Trilogy in both widescreen and full screen formats.

These versions of the films were further altered by George Lucas for this release.

(USA Press Screening Invitation for the Star Wars Trilogy on DVD ©2004 LFL)

October 1st, 2004

• *The Empire Strikes Back* Junior Novelization published by Scholastic®.
The junior novelization adaptation is written by Ryder Windham and contains sixteen pages of full-color photos from the motion picture.

2005

2005
• The 25th Anniversary of *The Empire Strikes Back*.

• Re-release of *The Empire Strikes Back* Special Edition on DVD in a special box set reissue with different packaging in both widescreen and full screen formats.

• Burger King's The Super Star Wars Collection promotional tie-in.
Included an assortment of toys, characters, monsters, and ships from all six movies including *The Empire Strikes Back*.

April, 2005
• Reissue of *The Empire Strikes Back* paperback novel written by Donald F. Glut.
Retitled as *Star Wars: Episode V: The Empire Strikes Back*.

August 31st, 2005
• Actor Michael Sheard dies at the age of 67.
Sheard portrayed Admiral Ozzel in *Empire*.

October 15th, 2005
• Author Pablo Hidalgo posts a blog on StarWars.com titled *The Falcon's Speculative Voyage from Hoth to Bespin*.
The blog broke down Hidalgo's speculation of the timeline of events between Han Solo and company's escape from Hoth and their arrival at Cloud City.

2006

September 12th, 2006

• *Empire* is reissued again on a separate two-disc Limited-Edition DVD for a brief time from September 12th, 2006 to December 31st, 2006.

All three Original Trilogy films were released this way. The first disc of each set was the Special Edition version of the film while the second disc featured the original, unaltered version as "bonus material."

Many fans were upset that these original versions of the films were released on DVD for the first time as non-anamorphic versions taken from a 1993 Laserdisc release and were not updated to reflect the remastered films used to create the Special Edition versions.

Original, unaltered versions of the films have never been officially released again since 2008 when these DVDs were re-released as a Trilogy box set on November 4th.

(EMPIRE DVD cover for the 2006 reissue ©2006 LFL)

2007

February 1st, 2007
• France screening at the Gérardmer Fantasticarts Film Festival of the Special Edition version of *Empire*.

November 6th, 2007
• The Music of Star Wars: 30th Anniversary Collector's Edition is released.
This seven disc set of CDs features John Williams' music from all six Star Wars films (Episodes I-VI) including *Empire*.

*(The Music of Star Wars 30th Anniversay Collector's Edition
©2007 Sony Music)*

2008

March 26th, 2008

• *Star Wars Episode V: The Empire Strikes Back Photo Comic* by Randy Stradley is published by Dark Horse Comics.

This manga-sized adaptation of *Empire* featured frames taken from the film and used as panels in a comic book style format.

November 4th, 2008

• Re-release of *The Empire Strikes Back* Special Edition and Unaltered Version on DVD.

A reissue of the 2006 release with new packaging.

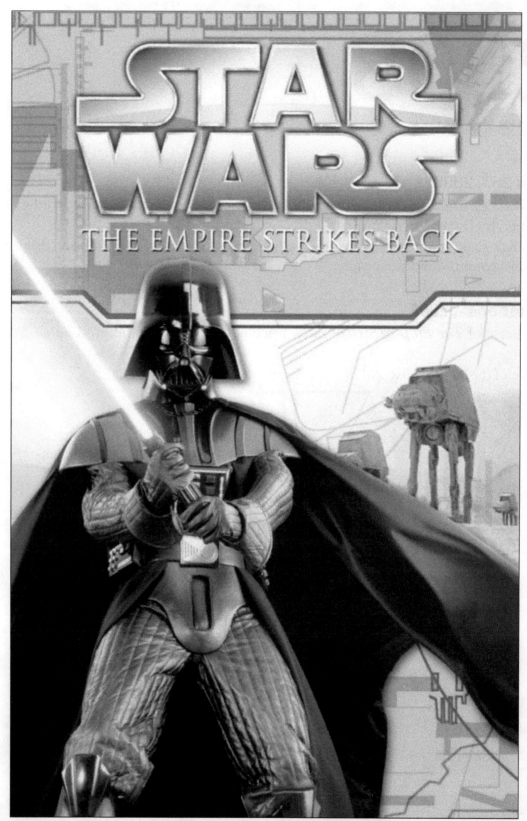

(TESB Photo Comic ©2008 Dark Horse Comics)

2009

━●━━━━●━━━━●━━━━●━━━━●━

August 24th, 2009

• Nintendo's *Super Star Wars: The Empire Strikes Back* is released in North America on the Virtual Console: a line of downloadable SNES games for Nintendo's Wii and Wii U home gaming consoles and the Nintendo 3DS portable gaming console.

October 2nd, 2009

• Nintendo's *Super Star Wars: The Empire Strikes Back* is released on the Virtual Console in PAL format.

December 22nd, 2009

• *Family Guy*'s *Empire* parody *Something, Something, Something, Dark Side* is released on DVD and Blu-Ray.

(DVD cover of the Family Guy EMPIRE parody ©2009 Twentieth Century Fox)

2010

May 7th-8th, 2010

• Chicago's Field Museum hosts special charity screenings of *The Empire Strikes Back* for the film's 30th Anniversary.

A reception at the museum featuring George Lucas took place on Saturday May 8th. The museum held a contest in which they asked fans to create their best one-minute reenactment video from the movie and post it to the museum's Facebook page. The video that received the most Facebook votes won six tickets, six gift bags, and two parking vouchers for the May 8th screening.

The film was shown once on Friday, May 7th and three times on Saturday, May 8th.

May 19th, 2010

• Charity screening of *The Empire Strikes Back* at the Arclight theater in Hollywood, CA featuring a Q&A with Harrison Ford.

Tickets for the screening were $100 each and proceeds from the screening benefitted St. Jude Children's Research Hospital. Other celebrity guests at the screening included Ewan McGregor, Jon Favreau, Peter Mayhew, Billy Dee Williams, Kevin Feige, and others.

May 23rd, 2010

• The *Family Guy* parody *Something, Something, Something Dark Side* airs on the Fox Channel.

It was the 20th episode of the show's eighth season.

August/September 2010

• *Star Wars Insider* magazine #119 features the 30th Anniversary of *The Empire Strikes Back*. This issue came in five different covers; Luke Skywalker, Han Solo, Princess Leia, Yoda, and Han in carbonite.

The issue featured interviews with Irvin Kershner, Billy Dee Williams, and author, J. W. Rinzler.

October 12th, 2010

• *The Making of The Empire Strikes Back* book by J. W. Rinzler is released.

It is one of the most comprehensive books about the making of the film ever published with many rare photos, production art and exclusive interviews with the cast and crew.

November 27th, 2010

• *Empire* Director Irvin Kershner dies at the age of 87 after a three year battle with cancer.

Kershner was most recognized for directing *Empire*, but also helmed other big budget films including the James Bond film, *Never Say Never Again*, and *Robocop 2*.

At the time of his death Kershner was working on a documentary about his good friend, author, Ray Bradbury, who said of the filmmaker upon his passing: *"Kersh was an amazing man, a good friend, and I loved him with all my heart."*

December 28th, 2010

• The Library of Congress announces that *Empire* is one of 25 films selected for preservation in the United States' National Film Registry for being "culturally, historically, and aesthetically significant."

Unfortunately the original 1980 version was never sent to the Library of Congress by Lucasfilm and the only version offered to the Library of Congress was the Special Edition version. The National Film Registry had refused it as the film that they had chosen for preservation was the original version which Lucasfilm still refuses to provide as of this writing.

(Irvin Kershner riding a Tauntaun on the set of EMPIRE in the Hoth Hangar ©1979 LFL)

2011

2011

• Re-release of *The Empire Strikes Back* Special Edition on Blu-Ray for the first time. Released as part of The Saga Collection box set and also as part of the Original Trilogy Collection box set these versions of the films were further altered by George Lucas, although *The Empire Strikes Back* was left unaltered.

January 1st, 2011

• *Star Wars Infinites: The Empire Strikes Back Volume 1* by Dave Land, Davide Fabbri, and Christian Dalla Vecchia is reprinted by Marvel Comics.

June 10th, 2011

• A screening of the Star Wars Trilogy occurs at the South Florida Museum in Bradenton, FL.

June 28th, 2011

• *Star Wars: Episode V: The Empire Strikes Back* eBook is published by Random House.

(The Saga Collection Blu Ray ©2011 Twentieth Century Fox Home Entertainment)

2012

January 1st, 2012

• *Empire* stunt trainer, sword master, and Darth Vader stunt stand-in Bob Anderson dies at the age of 90.
Anderson performed as Darth Vader for most of the Cloud City duel between Luke and Vader and also played Rebel Officer Trey Callum during the Battle of Hoth.

Anderson was an English Olympic fencer and regarded as the premier sword-fighting choreographer in Hollywood.

In addition to *Empire* he worked on such high profile films as *Highlander, The Princess Bride, The Lord of the Rings* trilogy, and many others. During his career he coached many famous actors including Errol Flynn, Sean Connery, Johnny Depp, Antonio Banderas, Viggo Mortensen, and Adrian Paul.

March 3rd, 2012

• Artist Ralph McQuarrie dies at his home in Berkeley, CA at the age of 83.
McQuarrie was most well-known for his science fiction and fantasy art and was actively sought after in Hollywood for his creative talent and visual storytelling abilities.

(Bob Anderson as Darth Vader on the Carbon Freezing Chamber set ©1979 LFL)

In addition to his contributions to the Star Wars trilogy McQuarrie worked on the original *Battlestar Galactica* series, *Star Trek,* and with Steven Spielberg on *Close Encounters of the Third Kind, E.T., Raiders of the Lost Ark,* and **batteries not included*. He also received an Academy Award for his work on the film, *Cocoon*.

McQuarrie appeared on screen in *The Empire Strikes Back* as General Pharl McQuarrie and was immortalized in plastic when an action figure of his character was produced by Hasbro in 2007 for the Star Wars 30th Anniversary line.

April 1st, 2012

• *The Empire Strikes Back* Junior Novelization by Ryder Windham Kindle edition and eBook is published by Scholastic.

(Ralph McQuarrie during EMPIRE preproduction ©1979 LFL)

2013

2013
• Re-release of *The Empire Strikes Back* Special Edition in the first ever Blu-Ray/DVD combo pack box set.

January 30th, 2013
• *Star Wars Omnibus: Infinities* is published by Dark Horse Comics.
A collection of comics previously released which tell the stories of *A New Hope*, *The Empire Strikes Back,* and *Return of the Jedi* with alternate storylines unfolding due to familiar events played out with different results.

(Star Wars Omnibus Infinities ©2013 Dark Horse Comics)

2014

2014
• Disney releases Disney Store exclusive trading cards of *The Empire Strikes Back*.

February 15th, 2014
• Actor Christopher Malcolm dies at the age of 68.
Malcolm portrayed Rebel Pilot Zev Senesca in *Empire*, the Snowspeeder pilot who locates Han and Luke on Hoth after they've gone missing and also participates in the Battle of Hoth as part of Luke's Rogue Squadron. The character is killed in the battle when an AT-AT destroys his ship.

March 18th, 2014
• *William Shakespeare's The Empire Striketh Back* by Ian Doescher is published by Quirk Books.

May 4th, 2014
• *Empire* junior novelization re-released as an eBook under the new Disney-Lucasfilm Press.

May 10th, 2014
• *Star Wars: Episode V: The Empire Strikes Back* eBook published by Lucas Books.

May 30th, 2014
• *Empire* magazine holds a fan-poll for the greatest movies of all time.
The Empire Strikes Back was voted #1, beating out *The Godfather* which was pushed to second place.

July 1st, 2014
• *LEGO Star Wars: The Empire Strikes Back* children's reading book is published by DK Publishing.

October 10th, 2014
• Release date of *The Empire Strikes Back: Uncut*, a Lucasfilm sponsored fan-film

project incorporating over 1,500 submissions of fan-made scenes from *Empire* compiled into the complete film made-up of various styles of animation, live-action and stop-motion.

December 27th, 2014

• Team Negative 1 (a group of dedicated fans preserving original versions of the Star Wars trilogy) release *The Empire Strikes Back* Grindhouse version – a scan of an original 35mm print of the film with all of the dirt, scratches, and discolorations that are synonymous with grindhouse movies.

The first release had issues being played back on some devices and so a second version was released the following month which was compatible with more players.

2015

2015
• The 35th Anniversary of *The Empire Strikes Back*.

• Re-release of *The Empire Strikes Back* Special Edition in Blu-Ray steelbooks.

• Topps releases a plethora of *The Empire Strikes Back* trading card sets including:
 - Star Wars Illustrated The Empire Strikes Back
 - Star Wars Illustrated The Empire Strikes Back – Artist Autographed Base
 - Star Wars Illustrated The Empire Strikes Back – Artist Signed Star Wars Celebration Promo
 - Star Wars Illustrated The Empire Strikes Back – Authentic Film Cel Relics
 - Star Wars Illustrated The Empire Strikes Back - Bronze
 - Star Wars Illustrated The Empire Strikes Back - Gold
 - Star Wars Illustrated The Empire Strikes Back – Movie Poster Artist Reinterpretations
 - Star Wars Illustrated The Empire Strikes Back – One Sheet Reimagined
 - Star Wars Illustrated The Empire Strikes Back – One Sheet Reimainged Printing Plate Black
 - Star Wars Illustrated The Empire Strikes Back – One Sheet Reimagined Printing Plate Cyan
 - Star Wars Illustrated The Empire Strikes Back – One Sheet Reimagine Printing Plate Magenta
 - Star Wars Illustrated The Empire Strikes Back – One Sheet Reimagined Printing Plate Yellow
 - Star Wars Illustrated The Empire Strikes Back – One Year Earlier

• Team Negative 1 releases the second version of *The Empire Strikes Back* Grindhouse release which is Blu-Ray compatible.

January 8th, 2015
• *Star Wars Manga: The Empire Strikes Back Volumes 1, 2, 3, and 4* Kindle editions are published by Marvel Comics.

March 10th, 2015
• *Star Wars: The Empire Strikes Back* Read-Along Storybook and CD is released by Disney-Lucasfilm Press and features artwork by Brian Rood.

April 10th, 2015
• Digital release of *The Empire Strikes Back* along with the other five Saga films for streaming and purchase on iTunes Store, Amazon Video, Vudu, Google Play, and Disney Movies Anywhere.

April 14th, 2015
• *Star Wars Epic Yarns: The Empire Strikes Back* children's book by Jack and Holman Wang is published by Chronicle Books.

June 4th, 2015
• Secret Cinema launches their *Empire Strikes Back* cinema experience of the film in England that lasts through August 2nd, 2015.

• *Star Wars The Empire Strikes Back Activity Book* by Lucasfilm is published by Egmont Books and features puzzles, mazes, activities, word hunts, stickers and more.

July 21st, 2015
• *Star Wars: The Empire Strikes Back: So You Want To Be a Jedi?* book by Adam Gidwitz is published by Disney-Lucasfilm Press.
This was a new version of the story written for a junior audience.

July 28th, 2015
• Little Golden Book version of *The Empire Strikes Back* is published by Golden Books, written by Geof Smith with illustrations by Chris Kennett.

December 25th, 2015
• Jason Wingreen, the original voice of Boba Fett in *The Empire Strikes Back* dies at the age of 95.
He was best known for his role as Harry Snowden in the TV series *All in the Family* and its spin-off, *Archie Bunker's Place*.

2016

January 8th, 2016

• Sony Classical releases a remastered version of the original 1980 *Empire* soundtrack as a two-disc LP, copying all aspects of the original RSO release, down to the labeling.

April 3rd, 2016

• Don Francks dies at the age of 84.
Francks voiced Boba Fett for the *Star Wars Holiday Special*.

April 6th, 2016

• *Star Wars: The Empire Strikes Back Junior Graphic Novel* by Alessandro Ferrari and Igor Chimisso is published by Edgemont.

April 19th, 2016

• *Star Wars: The Empire Strikes Back: The Original Topps Trading Card Series, Volume Two* by Gary Gerani is published by Abrams Books.
This hardcover book showcased the artwork of the *Star Wars: The Empire Strikes Back* Topps vintage trading card series.

July 13th, 2016

• *Al Williamson's Star Wars: The Empire Strikes Back Artist's Edition* by Al Williamson, Carlos Garzon, Archie Goodwin, Ed King, Jim Novak, Rick Veitch, Scott Dunbier, Ted Adams, Scott Tipton and Serban Cristescu is published by IDW Publishing.
The book featured the entire *Empire Strikes Back* Marvel Comics film adaptation comic series plus the complete Star Wars #98 and featured select pages from *Return of the Jedi* and other Star Wars pages and pin-ups by Williamson.

August 6th, 7th, 11th, 12th, 13th, 20th, 27th, 2016

• Alamo Drafthouse's 'Return of the Trilogy' roadshow screens *Star Wars*, *The Empire*

Strikes Back, and *Return of the Jedi* at various theaters in cities across the United States including Los Angeles, San Francisco, Washington D.C., New York, Miami, Boston, Denver, Philadelphia, and others.

(Kenny Baker on the Millennium Falcon hold set during the filming of THE EMPIRE STRIKES BACK ©1979 LFL)

August 13th, 2016

• Kenny Baker dies at the age of 81.

Mostly known for portraying R2-D2 in the Star Wars franchise, Kenny Baker's career is full of other notable films such as *The Dark Crystal, Labyrinth, Time Bandits, Willow, The Elephant Man,* and *Flash Gordon*. His early career included a successful comedy act called the Mini-Tones with fellow entertainer and Star Wars alumni Jack Purvis.

October 8th, 2016

• USA screening of *Empire* at the Mill Valley Film Festival.

December 27th, 2016

• Carrie Fisher dies at the age of 60.

Although she is most recognized as Princess Leia from the Star Wars franchise, Fisher has had a successful career as not only an actor, but as a prolific writer, script doctor and stage performer.

Always very vocal about her personal life, Fisher openly talked about her addiction to drugs as well as her mental health issues. She was also a strong advocate for animal's rights, women's rights, and the LGBT community.

Fisher shared the screen with her daughter, Billie Lourd, in the Star Wars sequel films *The Force Awakens* and *The Last Jedi* and appeared posthumously in the final film of the Skywalker Saga, *The Rise of Skywalker.*

(Carrie Fisher on the Cloud City set during the filming of EMPIRE ©1979 LFL)

2017

●━━━●━━━●━━━●━━━●

2017
• Re-release of *The Empire Strikes Back* Special Edition on Blu-Ray in a 6-film box set and Original Trilogy box set, both with new packaging art.

May 4th, 2017
• *Empire* Junior Novelization is edited and re-released by Egmont UK Ltd. to fit the current canon.

September 12th, 2017
• *Star Wars: The Empire Strikes Back Notebook Collection* by Lucasfilm is published by Chronicle Books.
The book featured posters, concept art, and promotional artwork.

December 8th, 2017
• Columbia Sportswear® releases three jackets inspired by *Empire*'s main characters; Luke Skywalker, Leia Organa, and Han Solo.
Called the Echo Base Collection, each jacket was designed to reflect the original wardrobe from the film in style, color, and aesthetic. The jackets were sold exclusively on Columbia's website and at Columbia retail stores. The window displays for the jackets featured them on giant action figure blister packs, mimicking the original Kenner line of toys. The jackets retailed for $400 each and quickly became highly sought after on the secondary market once they were sold out both online and in stores.

A special, limited edition brown version of Han Solo's jacket (called the Han Solo Echo Base Archive Edition) was sold only at select Columbia stores and were all personally autographed by Harrison Ford himself. All proceeds benefitted Conservation International; a global organization dedicated to protecting nature.

(Echo Base Collection jackets – (l) Leia (c) Han (r) Luke ©2017 Columbia Sportswear Company)

2018

●━━━● ●━━━● ● ●━━━● ●━━━● ●

May 4th, 2018

• *The Empire Strikes Back* soundtrack is re-released as a remastered version.

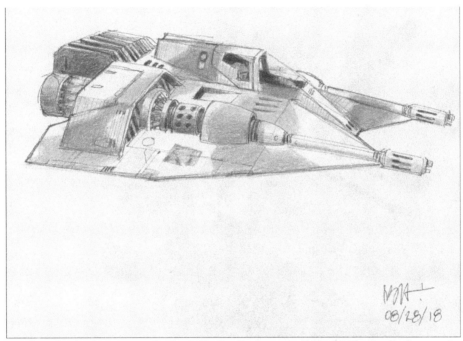

(sketch of a Snowspeeder by Nilo Rodis-Jamero ©2018 Nilo Rodis-Jamero)

August 28th & 30th, 2018

• Original Lucasfilm artist Nilo Rodis-Jamero finishes many concept sketches of familiar Star Wars vehicles, creatures, and characters including Boba Fett's Slave 1, AT-ST, Snowspeeder, Hoth tanks, Tauntaun, Luke Skywalker, and Boba Fett. The sketches were auctioned off in May of 2019.

September 19th & 30th, 2018

• Nilo Rodis-Jamero finishes more concept sketches of familiar Star Wars vehicles, creatures and characters including the Tauntaun, Luke Skywalker, the Imperial Probe Droid, and others.

(Gary Kurtz on location in Norway during the filming of EMPIRE ©2004 Kurtz/Joiner Archive)

September 23rd, 2018

• Producer Gary Kurtz dies from cancer in London at the age of 78.

Kurtz had worked with George Lucas on *American Graffiti, Star Wars,* and *The Empire Strikes Back*, but left Lucasfilm shortly after *Empire* completed filming due to conflicts between him and Lucas. He would go on to help produce the Jim Henson and Frank Oz film *The Dark Crystal* soon after.

Kurtz was a very hands-on producer and was loved by the cast and crew of every film he worked on. He was an integral part of every production and would often step in to do small jobs that needed to get done. He was a big influence on *The Empire Strikes Back* and not only produced the film, but also took on the role of 2nd Unit Director after the death of John Barry. His contributions to *Empire*'s story and dialogue are very prominent and the film greatly reflects him and Director Irvin Kershner's influences.

Kurtz was also an avid photographer and was always taking behind-the-scenes photos during every production he was a part of. His film career continued after Star Wars with not only *The Dark Crystal*, but also *Return to Oz* and *Slipstream* - which reunited him with Mark Hamill.

George Lucas: *"Gary's passing will be felt throughout the* Star Wars *family. Through what were sometimes challenging shooting difficulties and conditions, his contributions as a producer helped bring the stories to life onscreen. My heart goes out to his family."*

November 7th & 9th, 2018
• Nilo Rodis-Jamero finishes more concept sketches of familiar Star Wars vehicles, creatures and characters including the Tauntaun, Luke Skywalker, and the Imperial Probe Droid.

December 7th, 2018
• Columbia Sportswear and Lucasfilm release a limited edition reproduction Crew Jacket from *The Empire Strikes Back*.
The jacket was based on the original jackets worn by the cast and crew while filming on location in Norway. Available only online at Columbia's website and exclusively at Columbia retail stores, the jackets were sold for $500 and only 2000 were made available for retail.

A small number of the jackets were autographed by Mark Hamill and sold in select US stores for $1,980 with all proceeds benefitting charity.

(EMPIRE crew parka reproduction
©2018 Columbia Sportswear
Company)

2019

January, 2019

• Topps releases *The Empire Strikes Back* Black and White trading cards.
Black and white photos from the film presented on 150 base trading cards with a guaranteed sketch or autograph included in every box.

January 7th, 2019

• Nilo Rodis-Jamero finishes more concept sketches of familiar Star Wars vehicles, creatures and characters including the Tauntaun, Luke Skywalker, and AT-AT.

March 5th, 2019

• Disney releases a new *Empire* graphic novel adaptation written by Alessandro Ferrari and published by IDW.

• Hasbro launches their final fan vote for a new action figure in their six inch Black Series line to celebrate the 40th Anniversary of *Empire*.
Choices included: Lobot, 2-1B Droid, Hoth Rebel Soldier, Willrow Hood, Wedge Antilles, Princess Leia (Bespin Gown), Luke Skywalker (Dagobah), Ugnaught, Imperial Probe Droid, and FX-7 Medical Droid. The final round of selections were based on previous votes compiled by select Star Wars fan sites. The final voting was conducted via the HasbroPulse Instagram page.

The winning action figure was Luke Skywalker (Dagobah).

March 8th-10th, 2019

• Finse 1222 (the original hotel used by the cast and crew of *Empire* during production) commemorates the 40th Anniversary of the making of *The Empire Strikes Back* with a special 3-day event at the hotel including a special tour of the filming locations in Norway.

March 14ᵗʰ-17ᵗʰ, 2019

• The Indianapolis Symphony Orchestra presents special screenings of *Empire* while performing the film's score live.

March 16ᵗʰ, 2019

• Bunny Alsop dies.

Former assistant to Gary Kurtz (as well as his sister-in-law), Alsop was instrumental in the day-to-day operations of Lucasfilm during Kurtz's time there.

April 12ᵗʰ, 2019

• *The Empire Strikes Back* is screened at the Marriott in Chicago, IL for Star Wars Celebration.

• Hasbro reveals the first *Empire Strikes Back* 40ᵗʰ Anniversary Black Series six inch action figure: Boba Fett painted in the original Kenner color scheme.

The packaging had the Star Wars logo with a 40ᵗʰ Anniversary *Empire* emblem imprinted on the top left of the card back. It also came with both his standard blasters as well as a Stormtrooper E-11 blaster as homage to the original Kenner action figure which was packaged with an Imperial Stormtrooper blaster.

The figure debuted at Star Wars Celebration in Chicago, IL and was available at San Diego Comic-Con for $24.99 and later at other various conventions and online retailers including Hasbro's own online store. Hasbro Pulse members were able to purchase the figure in advance on September 9ᵗʰ while the general public was able to purchase it the following day.

(Boba Fett Black Series action figure prototype packaging ©2019 Hasbro)

April 30ᵗʰ, 2019

• Peter Mayhew passes away at his home in Texas at the age of 74.

Chosen by George Lucas and Gary Kurtz for his height Peter brought a warmth and endearing element to the character of Chewbacca that has made him one of the most beloved characters in the Star Wars universe. Mayhew was very active with various charity organizations through his own nonprofit, The Peter Mayhew Foundation.

He was an avid attendee of conventions up until his passing and will be remembered as a very generous, kind, and warm-hearted man who loved his fans. Mayhew's final portrayal of Chewbacca can be seen in *The Last Jedi*.

(Peter Mayhew on location in Norway during filming of EMPIRE ©1979 LFL)

May, 2019

• Online novelty store Merchoid releases an official replica of Han Solo's parka from *Empire* for $146 available exclusively on their website.

May 14th, 2019

• Bonham's auction house auctions off an official Darth Vader costume from *The Empire Strikes Back*.
The costume was suspected to be an inauthentic item never used in the film and was withdrawn from auction pending verification.

June 1st-2nd, 2019

• The Milwaukee Symphony Orchestra presents special screenings of *Empire* while performing the film's score live at the Riverside Theater.

June 8th, 2019

• The Star Wars Trilogy (including *Empire*) is screened in Syracuse, NY at the Palace Theater.

June 11th, 2019

• *Star Wars Insider* #190 focuses on *The Empire Strikes Back* with the newsstand cover featuring a black and white still photo of Han Solo, Chewbacca, C-3PO, and R2-D2 in the Hoth hangar set.
The issue also featured interviews with Jeremy Bulloch (Boba Fett) and Julian Glover (General Veers).

June 12th, 2019

• *Star Wars Insider* #190 Exclusive Edition features an alternate cover with a painting of *Empire* imagery including Darth Vader, the Millennium Falcon pursued by TIE Fighters, and Rebel soldiers on Hoth.

June 27th-29th, 2019

• Benaroya Hall in Seattle, WA presents special screenings of *Empire* with the score being performed live by the Seattle Symphony.

July 4th-6th, 2019

• The Vancouver Symphony Orchestra presents special screenings of *Empire* while performing the film's score live.

(Star Wars Insider magazine alternate cover for issue #190 ©2019 LFL)

July 5th–6th, 2019

• The Hong Kong Cultural Centre in Kowloon, Hong Kong presents special screenings of *The Empire Strikes Back* with the score being performed live by the Hong Kong Philharmonic Orchestra.

July 26th, 2019

• The Mann Center for the Performing Arts in Philadelphia, PA presents a special screening of *The Empire Strikes Back* with the score being performed live by the Philadelphia Orchestra.

• Limited Run Games re-releases *The Empire Strikes Back* video game cartridges for the NES and Nintendo Gameboy gaming systems on special blister packs reminiscent of Kenner's vintage toy line.
Premium Limited Edition versions of both games were released which came in foil-stamped boxes that were numbered and included exclusive items such as a collectible coin, collectible pin, and an 18x24 reversible poster.

August 1st-2nd, 2019

• The Embarcadero Marina Park South in San Diego, CA presents special screenings of *The Empire Strikes Back* with the score being performed live by the San Diego Symphony.

August 3rd–25th, 2019

• *The Empire Strikes Back in the Park* is presented by Hello Earth, a non-profit organization based in Seattle, WA who are most known for their live stage play performances of Star Trek and *Star Wars: A New Hope*.
Their performance of *Empire* ran through the month of August at Blanche Lavizzo Park in Seattle, WA. All shows were free to the public.

August 13th, 2019

• Lucasfilm holds a private screening of *The Empire Strikes Back* for employees only. The screening featured a display table full of rare and vintage *Empire* merchandise and memorabilia including carded C-3PO and IG-88 action figures, the Yoda board game, the *Empire* movie program, *The Empire Strikes Back* metal lunchbox, Boba Fett Halloween costume, press kit, magazines, RSO Records promotional jacket for *Empire*, *Empire* party supplies, an ILM crew shirt, and much more.

August 30th-September 1st, 2019

• The Dallas Symphony Orchestra in Dallas, TX presents special screenings of *The Empire Strikes Back* while performing the score live.

September 6th-7th, 2019

• Abravanel Hall in Salt Lake City, UT presents special screenings of *The Empire Strikes Back* with the score being performed live by the Utah Symphony.

• The Perth Convention and Exhibition Centre in Perth, Western Australia presents special screenings of *The Empire Strikes Back* with the score being performed live by the West Australian Symphony Orchestra.

September 13th-15th, 2019

• Arlene Schmitzer Concert Hall in Portland, OR presents special screenings of *The Empire Strikes Back* with the score being performed live by the Oregon Symphony.

September 21st-23rd, 2019

• The Royal Albert Hall in the UK screens *The Empire Strikes Back* along with the London Philharmonic Orchestra performing the score live – the first time this is ever done in the UK.

September 24th, 2019

• Release date of the Star Wars Trilogy Cinescape Comic Collection.
This 3-book box set featured the original Star Wars trilogy done in Fumetti style using high resolution images from the movies and word balloons like a comic book.

The standard version of the *Empire* book came with the Special Edition movie poster cover art while a hardcover collector's edition version came with the original 'Gone with the Wind' style movie poster cover art.

September 25th-26th, 2019

• An original screen-used Darth Vader helmet from *Empire* goes up for auction.
Profiles in History holds another one of their famous Icons & Legends of Hollywood auctions

and features a Vader helmet worn by David Prowse in *The Empire Strikes Back.*

September 27th, 2019

• Manchester Arena in Manchester, England presents a special screening of *The Empire Strikes Back* with the score being performed live by the Novello Orchestra.

September 27th– 28th, 2019

• Orchestra Hall in Detroit, MI presents special screenings of *The Empire Strikes Back* with the score being performed live by the Detroit Symphony Orchestra.

September 28th, 2019

• First Direct Arena in Leeds, Northern England presents a special screening of *The Empire Strikes Back* with the score being performed live by the Novello Orchestra.

September 29th, 2019

• The SEC Armadillo in Glasgow, Scotland on the Scottish Event Campus presents a special screening of *The Empire Strikes Back* with the score being performed live by the Novello Orchestra.

October 1st, 2019

• Arena Birmingham in Birmingham, UK presents a special screening of *The Empire Strikes Back* with the score being performed live by the Novello Orchestra.

October 2nd, 2019

• M&S Bank Arena in Liverpool, England presents a special screening of *The Empire Strikes Back* with the score being performed live by the Novello Orchestra.

October 2nd–6th, 2019

• The Minnesota Orchestra in Minneapolis, MN presents special screenings of *The Empire Strikes Back* while performing the score live.

October 5th, 2019

• The Morrison Center for the Performing Arts in Boise, ID presents a special screening of *The Empire Strikes Back* with the score being performed live by the Boise

Philharmonic.

October 26th, 2019

• The Belgian National Orchestra in Brussels, Belgium presents a special screening of *The Empire Strikes Back* at Palais 12 while performing the score live.

November 2nd, 2019

• The Silva Concert Hall in Eugene, OR presents a special screening of *The Empire Strikes Back* with the score being performed live by the Eugene Symphony.

November 7th–10th, 2019

• The Houston Symphony in Houston, TX presents special screenings of *The Empire Strikes Back* while performing the score live.

November 11th, 2019

• *The Empire Strikes Back Unauthorized Timeline* book by Justin Berger is published by Anchorhead Publishing.

2020

January 23rd–26th, 2020

• The St. Louis Symphony Orchestra in St. Louis, MO presents special screenings of *The Empire Strikes Back* at Powell Hall while performing the score live.

February 8th–9th, 2020

• The Jacksonville Symphony in Jacksonville, FL presents special screenings of *The Empire Strikes Back* while performing the score live.

February 29th–March 1st, 2020

• The Kentucky Center in Louisville, KY presents special screenings of *The Empire Strikes Back* at Whitney Hall with the score being performed live by the Louisville Orchestra.

March 6th-8th, 2020

• Finse 1222, the hotel where the original *Empire* cast and crew stayed while filming in Norway, holds its 4th Annual 'Visit Hoth' event where fans are invited to stay at the hotel and participate in tours of the filming locations from the movie.

March 8th, 2020

• The Adrienne Arsht Center for the Performing Arts in Miami, FL presents a special screening of *The Empire Strikes Back* with the score being performed live by a full Symphony Orchestra.

• The Hallenstadion Zürich in Zürich, Switzerland presents a special screening of *The Empire Strikes Back* with the score being performed live by the Czech National Symphony Orchestra.

April 25th, 2020

• The Altria Theater in Richmond, VA presents a special screening of *The Empire Strikes Back* with the score being performed live by the Richmond Symphony.

May 1st–2nd, 2020

• The Holland Center in Omaha, NE presents special screenings of *The Empire Strikes Back* with the score being performed live by the Omaha Symphony.

May 8th, 2020

• The Music Center at Strathmore in North Bethesda, MD presents a special screening of *The Empire Strikes Back* with the score being performed live by the Baltimore Symphony Orchestra.

May 16th, 2020

• The Bushnell in Hartford, CT presents a special screening of *The Empire Strikes Back* with the score being performed live by the Hartford Symphony Orchestra.

May 21st, 2020

• The 40th Anniversary of the theatrical release of *The Empire Strikes Back*.

May 30th, 2020

• The Adler Theatre in Davenport, IA presents a special screening of *The Empire Strikes Back* with the score being performed live by the Quad City Symphony Orchestra.

Written by
JUSTIN BERGER

Birthdays

Ivor Beddoes .... April 28, 1909
Sir Alec Guinness .... April 2, 1914
Leigh Brackett .... December 7, 1915
Jason Wingreen .... October 9, 1920
Bob Anderson .... September 15, 1922
Irvin Kershner .... April 29, 1923
John Hollis .... November 12, 1927
Ralph McQuarrie .... June 13, 1929
Peter Diamond .... August 10, 1929
Clive Revill .... April 18, 1930
Maurice Bush .... June 3, 1930
Bruce Boa .... July 10, 1930
David Tomblin .... October 18, 1930
James Earl Jones .... January 17, 1931
John Mollo .... March 18, 1931
John Williams .... February 8, 1932
Norman Reynolds .... March 26, 1934
Kenny Baker .... August 24, 1934
Julian Glover .... March 27, 1935
David Prowse .... July 1, 1935
Billy Dee Williams .... April 6, 1937
Jack Purvis .... July 13, 1937
Kenneth Colley .... December 7, 1937
Robert Watts .... May 23, 1938
Alan Harris .... May 28, 1938
Michael Culver .... June 16, 1938
Michael Sheard .... June 18, 1938
Brian Johnson .... June 29, 1939
Gary Kurtz .... July 27, 1940
Richard Edlund .... December 6, 1940
Peter Suschitzky .... July 25, 1941
Harrison Ford .... July 13, 1942
George Lucas .... May 14, 1944
Peter Mayhew .... May 19, 1944
Frank Oz .... May 25, 1944

Colin Skeaping .... June 18, 1944
Ian McDiarmid .... August 11, 1944
Harley Cokeliss .... February 11, 1945
Jeremy Bulloch .... February 16, 1945
Harrison Ellenshaw .... July 20, 1945
Marcia Lucas .... October 4, 1945
Paul Hirsch .... November 14, 1945
Anthony Daniels .... February 21, 1946
Christopher Malcolm .... August 19, 1946
Dennis Muren .... November 1, 1946
John Morton .... March 26, 1947
John Ratzenberger .... April 6, 1947
Denis Lawson .... September 27, 1947
Ben Burtt .... July 12, 1948
Lawrence Kasdan .... January 14, 1949
Joe Johnston .... May 13, 1950
Rick Baker .... December 8, 1950
Mark Hamill .... September 25, 1951
Phil Tippett .... September 27, 1951
Duwayne Dunham .... November 17, 1952
Craig Miller .... January 23, 1954
Carrie Fisher .... October 21, 1956
Deep Roy .... December 1, 1957
Cathy Munroe .... October 7, 1959

Bibliography

Arnold, Alan (1980) *Once Upon a Galaxy: A Journal of the Making of The Empire Strikes Back.* Ballantine Books. ISBN 0-345-29075-5

Call, Deborah (1980) *The Art of The Empire Strikes Back.* Ballantine Books ISBN 0345410882

Bouzereau, Laurent (1997) *Star Wars: The Annotated Screenplays* Del Rey ISBN 0-345-40981-7

Sansweet, Stephen J. (1998) *Star Wars Scrapbook: The Essential Collection* Chronicle Books ISBN 0811820602

Kaminski, Michael (2007) *The Secret History of Star Wars.* Legacy Books Press ISBN 978-0-9784652-3-0

Windham, Ryder (2010) *Star Wars Year by Year: A Visual Chronicle.* DK ISBN 0756657644

Rinzler, J.W. (2013) *The Making of Star Wars: The Empire Strikes Back.* Ballantine Group ISBN 9780345543363

Butler, Nathan P. (2017) *A Saga on Home Video.* Createspace Independent Publishing ISBN 1545550883

Stevens, Craig (2018) *The Star Wars Phenomenon in Britain.* McFarland ISBN: 1476628505

Official Star Wars Fan Club Bantha Tracks Newsletter
Star Wars Insider Magazine
Starlog Magazine
Starburst Magazine
Famous Monsters Magazine

www.starwars.com
www.wookieepedia.com
www.wikipedia.com
www.goodreads.com
www.propstore.com
www.nerf-herders-anonymous.com
www.theswca.com
www.giantbomb.com
www.originaltrilogy.com

https://www.retrojunk.com/article/show/283/boba-fett-on-ice
https://strangewars.livejournal.com/4552.html
https://www.hollywoodreporter.com/heat-vision/star-wars-flashback-no-theater-wanted-show-movie-1977-846864
http://fromscripttodvd.com/70mm_in_los_angeles_special_screenings_1987.htm

References

[1] https://weminoredinfilm.com/2016/05/30/box-office-history-how-star-wars-and-smokey-and-the-bandit-changed-memorial-day-forever/

[2] https://www.tested.com/starwars/460476-star-wars-and-explosion-dolby-stereo/

[3] https://www.telegraph.co.uk/culture/film/3600116/Film-makers-on-film-Irvin-Kershner.html

[4] Rinzler, J.W. (2013) *The Making of Star Wars: The Empire Strikes Back*

[5] http://digitalbits.com/columns/history-legacy--showmanship/force-defeated-empire-strikes-back-35th

[6] https://www.boxofficemojo.com

Index

Lando Calrissian
42, 45, 48, 55, 64, 89-91, 93-97, 109, 111, 112, 117-120, 122, 124, 125, 129, 132, 133, 135, 175, 176, 185, 190, 192, 197, 211, 255

Leia Organa
45, 48, 49, 55, 59, 73, 75, 76, 78, 81-84, 89-91, 94-97, 107, 109, 110-112, 115, 116, 118-120, 122, 124, 129, 132, 133, 137, 145, 173, 176, 184, 187, 190-192, 195, 199, 211, 264, 275, 289, 291, 292, 297

Lobot
132, 199, 249, 297

Luke Skywalker
31, 33, 44, 45, 47, 48, 54, 66, 70-73, 78, 81, 82, 86-88, 91, 92, 94-96, 100, 105, 108, 109, 112-114, 119, 123, 125-128, 130-133, 137-146, 148, 149, 151-159, 162-166, 168, 169, 171-177, 179, 180, 183-185, 190, 195-197, 200, 202, 211, 212, 215, 216, 221, 227, 251, 257, 264, 275, 279, 283, 291-293, 295, 297

See-Threepio (C-3PO)
55, 75, 76, 78, 81, 82, 84, 88-91, 94-96, 110-112, 115, 116, 118, 120, 122, 124, 125, 129, 133, 135, 146, 173, 175, 176, 179, 184, 195, 197, 211, 212, 300, 301

Stormtrooper
35, 37, 45, 91, 94-96, 109, 111, 119-121, 134, 135, 137, 139, 140, 155, 181, 184, 188, 196, 298

Ugnaught
41, 76, 146, 199, 211, 297

Yoda
38, 42, 53, 60, 142, 143, 147, 152-154, 156-159, 162, 163, 165, 166, 168, 171, 183, 185, 192, 193, 195, 197, 199, 201-204, 211, 216, 221, 222, 275, 301

PLANETS, CREATURES, SHIPS & VEHICLES

AT-AT/Imperial Walker
37, 41, 45, 60-63, 67, 83, 87, 102, 107, 113, 126, 143, 168, 172-174, 177, 179, 195, 197, 199, 202, 203, 208, 212, 213, 229, 283, 297

Asteroid / Giant Space Slug
53, 67, 74, 98, 99, 114, 121, 169, 173, 202

Bespin / Cloud City
29, 37, 38, 41, 42, 45, 48, 50, 54, 58, 77, 80, 84, 86, 87-90, 92-97, 109, 112, 117-119, 121, 125, 132, 148, 151-153, 155, 157, 161, 174-176, 183-185, 194, 195, 199, 212, 244, 247, 265, 279, 289, 297

Carbon Freezing Chamber
119, 120, 121, 126, 128, 130, 131, 133, 137, 139, 140, 151, 194, 244, 279

Dagobah
37, 45, 48, 66, 77, 143, 153, 156, 157, 159, 160, 167, 168, 175, 197, 199, 216, 221, 297

Hoth
37, 38, 45, 48-50, 52, 53, 55, 69, 70, 71, 74, 77, 79, 93, 101, 112, 113, 168, 172, 173, 175-178, 180, 184, 185, 192, 195, 197, 199, 202, 208, 212, 215, 229-231, 237, 261, 265, 276, 279, 283, 291, 293, 297, 300

Millennium Falcon
37, 47, 48, 52, 57, 58, 60, 62-65, 72-78, 93, 101, 106, 107, 109, 110, 112-115, 118, 119, 121, 123, 125, 127, 129, 133, 143, 173, 174, 191, 194, 195, 201, 243, 247, 265, 288, 300

Mynock
110, 145, 151, 155, 202, 247

Probe Droid
48, 54, 67, 72, 80, 83, 117, 144, 170, 216, 293, 295, 297

Rebel Base
79, 80, 83, 86, 87, 112, 212, 291, 292

Slave 1
47, 63, 153, 199, 216, 293

Snowspeeder
41, 42, 44, 48, 49, 56, 59, 72, 80, 105, 107, 108, 113, 117, 121, 126, 130, 143, 145, 152, 169, 172-174, 185, 194, 208, 212-214, 229, 243, 283, 293

Star Destroyer
53, 54, 59, 63, 73, 93, 97-99, 103, 104, 114, 117, 130, 132, 136, 152, 157, 170, 185, 192, 195, 196, 200, 213

Tauntaun
43, 48, 50, 53, 55, 66-68, 70-72, 84-86, 93, 168, 172, 177, 180, 183, 196, 197, 211, 214, 276, 293, 295, 297

TIE Fighter/Bomber
114, 132, 136, 174, 177, 196, 211, 212, 216, 243, 300

Wampa
33, 70-72, 78, 80, 82, 85-87, 93, 100, 102, 179, 197, 247, 249

Wampa's Cave
93, 102, 179, 197, 247

X-wing
51, 53, 66, 113, 114, 121, 123, 125, 145, 155, 158, 159, 162, 163, 165, 166, 177, 196, 208, 211, 243

<u>CAST</u>
Baker, Kenny
66, 76, 78, 81, 82, 84, 91, 94-96, 135, 145, 148, 154, 158, 162, 163, 165, 167, 187-189, 256, 288

Bulloch, Jeremy
80, 88, 91, 92, 94-97, 99, 101, 109, 120, 152, 159, 204, 255, 300

Daniels, Anthony
61, 74-76, 78, 81, 82, 84, 87, 89-91, 94-96, 110-112, 115, 116, 118, 120, 122, 124, 127, 129, 133-135, 172, 176, 186, 187, 189, 211, 226, 264

Fisher, Carrie
45, 50, 61, 67-69, 73-76, 78, 79, 81-84, 87, 89-92, 94-96, 106, 109, 110, 111, 115-120, 122, 124, 127, 129, 132-134, 136, 137, 172, 186-189, 191, 192, 195, 258, 289

Ford, Harrison
45, 50, 61, 67, 69, 71-76, 78, 81-85, 87, 89-93, 102, 109, 110, 111, 115-118, 120-122, 124, 127, 129, 130, 170, 172, 186-189, 191, 195, 203, 256, 275, 291

Guinness, Sir Alec
107, 159, 166, 167, 189, 255, 256

Hamill, Mark
33, 45, 50, 61, 67, 68-76, 78, 79, 81, 82, 84-87, 91-96, 100, 102, 103, 105, 106, 108, 109, 112, 117, 119, 121, 123, 125, 126-128, 130, 131, 133, 134, 136-144, 148, 151-156, 158, 161-168, 172, 176, 177, 179, 186-189, 191, 195-197, 201, 211, 217, 258, 263, 295

Jones, James Earl
65, 172, 201, 227, 255

Mayhew, Peter
60, 61, 69, 74-76, 78, 81, 82, 87, 89-92, 94-96, 109-111, 115, 116, 118-120, 122-125, 127, 129, 130, 133, 134, 135, 137, 147, 149, 176, 186, 187-189, 275, 298, 299

Oz, Frank
152-154, 158, 168, 171, 187, 193, 201, 294

GENERAL

Industrial Light and Magic/ILM
41, 44, 46, 47, 49, 52, 55-59, 61-68, 73, 74, 77, 79, 80, 83, 86, 88, 93, 102, 113, 114, 117, 121, 126, 130, 132, 136, 143, 144, 146, 149, 152, 153, 157, 160, 161, 166, 168, 169, 171-174, 177-180, 182, 187, 190, 193, 219, 302

Kenner
113, 114, 170, 176, 179, 181, 184, 185, 187, 191, 192, 194, 196, 198-200, 202, 203, 207, 208, 210-216, 243, 291, 298, 301

Kyber (Kaiburr/Kiber) Crystal
43

Lucasfilm
35, 37, 41, 42, 44, 45, 47, 49, 51-57, 63-66, 72, 87, 126, 143, 153, 159, 160, 167, 169-173, 177, 178, 181, 182, 185, 186, 191, 192, 195, 200-204, 208, 211, 216, 219, 240, 245, 249, 276, 283, 286, 291, 293-295, 298, 301

Norway/Finse
48, 49, 60, 66-69, 72, 73, 77, 79, 80, 86-88, 97, 121, 196, 249, 294, 295, 297, 299

Twentieth Century Fox
34, 35, 46, 52, 65, 143, 181, 182, 186, 201, 202, 207, 219, 222, 226, 227, 240, 274, 278

About the Author

Justin Berger is a Jedi, like his father before him.

He currently resides in the Pacific Northwest with his wife, Michelle, their dog, Ruby, cat, Sophie, and bearded dragon, Ozzy.

When he's not locked in his office furiously typing away at a keyboard you can usually find Justin watching movies, playing video games, listening to music, or hitting thrift stores for hidden treasures.

CPSIA information can be obtained
at www.ICGtesting.com
Printed in the USA
BVHW010423060420
576961BV00008B/469